MW01618211

# Pop Surrealism

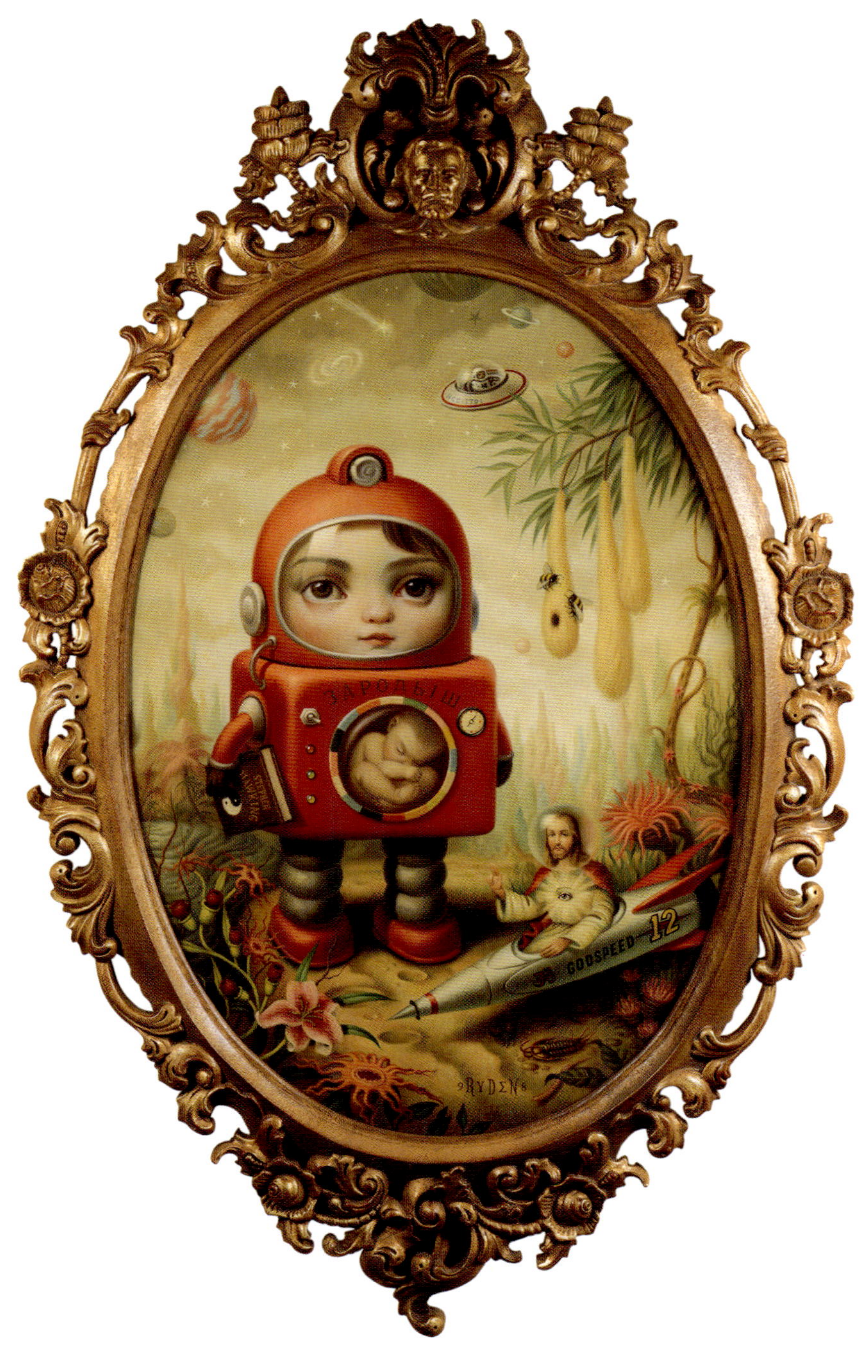


MARK RYDEN PRINCESS SPUTNIK 1998, oil on canvas, 32" x 22"

# Pop Surrealism

## THE RISE OF UNDERGROUND ART

Essays by
ROBERT WILLIAMS, CARLO MCCORMICK
and LARRY REID

Edited by
KIRSTEN ANDERSON

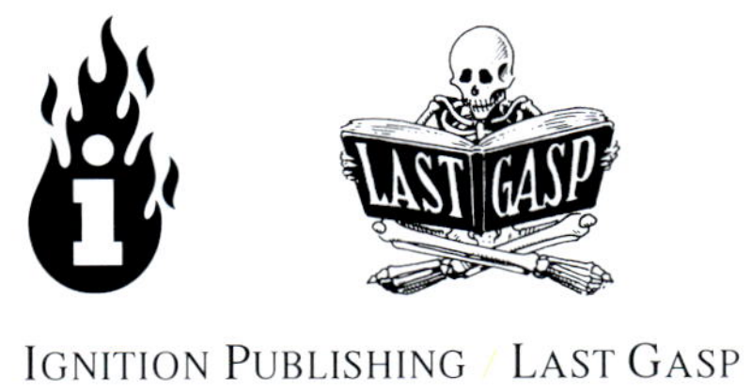


IGNITION PUBLISHING / LAST GASP

Book design by Mark Cox
and Amy Stella

We wish to thank the following for their generous input and support:

ALL the artists who graciously participated in the book, Robert and Suzanne Williams, Carlo McCormick, Greg Escalante, Billy Shire, Michel Chanel, Merry Karnowsky, Mary Harrison, Gary Pressman, Alyson Ryan, Queeve, Long Gone John, Martin McIntosh, Doug Nason, Mark Hanington, Elizabeth Lindquist, Amy Stella, Kenny Montana, Joe Newton, Tammy Watson, Mark Frauenfelder, Katie Kurtz, Jill Hanington and Bob Korpi, Kerry Ryan Simmons, Mark Long, Sarah Novotny and John Kintz, Juliette Torrez, Eric Reynolds, Joe Coleman and Whitney Ward, Mark Ryden and Marion Peck, Colin and Bucky at Last Gasp, Kenny Yu, Jamie O'Shea, Annie Tucker, Pete Brown, Tim Brown, Manuel Auad, Cindy Marks, Michael Martens, Jamey Calhoun, Christopher Beeson, Erica Carder, Michelle Lyons, Joyce and Don Stella, Bob Kelly, Chris Horn, Keith Wood, everyone at Juxtapoz magazine, and everyone at Last Gasp.

Very Special Thanks to Larry Reid, Alix Sloan, and Ron Turner.

*For Kenny and Amy*

POP SURREALISM: THE RISE OF UNDERGROUND ART



Published by
Ignition Publishing
www.ignitionpublishing.com

and

Last Gasp of San Francisco
777 Florida Street
San Francisco CA 94110
www.lastgasp.com

ISBN-13: 978-086719-618-4 ISBN-10: 0-86719-618-1 (hardbound)



10 9 8 7

Printed in China by Prolong Press Limited.

# Viva La Resistance

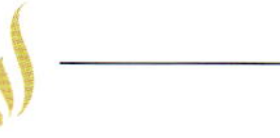

## A brief word from the Editor

**When discussing this art movement, and especially when compiling this book, one of the greatest challenges was figuring out what the hell to call it.** "*Lowbrow*" — the default term, and maybe the term that actually will end up sticking — left a bad taste in the mouth of some artists and dealers (even the esteemed Mr. McCormick finds the name problematic), yet there seems to be no all-encompassing term to fit. Well, not one that all of us would agree to. Some of the artists profiled here are slightly surprised to be even tied in with this loose-knit group of artists — each artist works in a world and vision of his own, speaks for himself and is answerable to no one.

But conversely, perversely, that's almost the very thing that keeps the dynamic of this movement moving, branching off into assorted hybrids while still retaining the elements that keep it separate from the mainstream and so appealing to those who love it. You can't pin it down, you can't cage it. There's room for rowdy young upstarts to slip in and warp it further. The artists thrill each other, annoy each other, engage in rivalry, and support each other.

And that's what keeps it so vibrantly alive.

I discovered this new art in 1996 while absent-mindedly flipping through a friend's magazines. I had picked up a copy of *Juxtapoz* magazine and was instantly riveted. I had an art background but had never seen *this* — an amalgamation of so many things: tattoo, graffiti, retro culture, cartoons, etc., all mashed up and used to create something that transcended its mere visual appeal, something that spoke profoundly to me (and untold others, as it turns out) about using pop culture's castoff detritus to create something meaningful and beautiful. And if it wasn't beautiful, well, it was exciting. It delighted the eye and shocked the sensibilities, and was a welcome change from the increasing boorishness of the recycled ideas and stale conceptualism found in most contemporary art. This art also gave a respectful nod to the Great Masters, Surrealism, Symbolism, the Pre-Raphaelites, Futurism, and vintage graphic design — then turned around and gave them all a hefty kick in the ass.

I began to seek out the artists I read about (in galleries such as La Luz De Jesus, Copro Nason, and Merry Karnowsky in Los Angeles), and rabidly devoured each issue of *Juxtapoz* as it came out — my pulse would quicken whenever I got a hold of a new copy. I could see that something really *important* was happening here, and a few years later I opened a gallery devoted to the new art, and then several years after that decided to do a book, this book, to chronicle some of what has been happening and to try to offer the beginnings of a comprehensive survey. This is, of course, but a taste of the talent in this movement. Regrettably, time and space keep me from covering every important artist, and there are many, and for that I must apologize to both artists and readers. My consolation is that I know that many more books will emerge, by writers who will dare to undertake the huge and hugely rewarding effort of further mining this rich field. To the artists who graciously agreed to appear in this book, and to the distinguished contributors, my most profound thanks.

— Kirsten Anderson, May 2004

# MID-CENTURY DEMENTIA AND BAD ASS LOW BROW

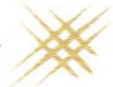

LARRY REID

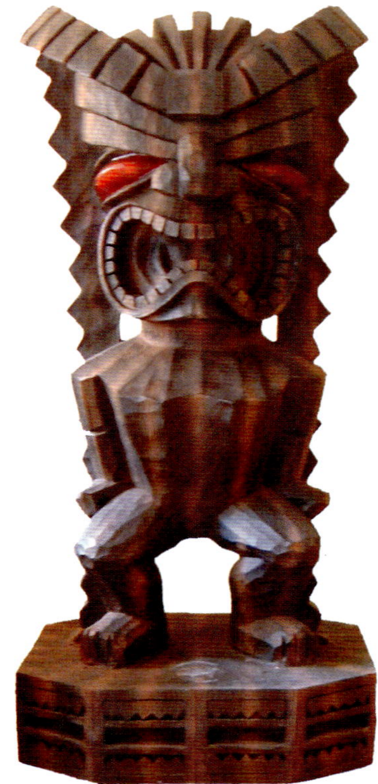

**Beneath the thin crust of conformity that characterized mid-century America lay a bubbling cauldron of** weirdness. Out of this primordial ooze emerged an assortment of primitive creatures that would enormously influence subsequent generations of American artists, and spawn a cultural movement that would indelibly alter the course of fine art. Rooted in the pop-culture iconography of 1950s and '60s Americana, a diverse group of iconoclasts is engaged in a re-examination of this anachronistic aesthetic in the context of contemporary society. The resultant movement is perhaps the most accessible and relevant development in art since the Pop Art movement.

America in the 1950s was a study in contradictions. The fabled societal conformity of that era gave rise to a spirited and exotic kitsch counterculture that soon penetrated the cultural lexicon. The Cold War assault on pop culture — fed by ravenous political ideologues and religious demagogues - produced a discreet rebellion against genteel convention. Hot rods, surfing, rock 'n' roll, monster movies and comic books were generally associated with juvenile delinquency, yet middle-class America soon embraced the aesthetics, if not the ideals, of this disposable ethos. As the decade of the 1960s dawned, hot-rod hero Ed "Big Daddy" Roth's disheveled Rat Fink caricature achieved the stature of a religious icon in the minds of American youth, and a generation of artists learned to draw imitating the style of Roth and his contemporaries.

An increasingly mobile society engendered a youthful passion for automobiles and their endless creative possibilities. As the prosperity of the post-war years created an emerging middle class, early model Fords of the '20s and '30s were discarded in favor of status-symbol sedans. The abundance of abandoned jalopies drove their prices down to the point that young drivers didn't hesitate to torture the original styles and running gear beyond recognition — adding high-performance motors, racing wheels and suspensions while stripping down excess weight to accommodate the need for speed. To accentuate reckless intentions, these vehicles were often decorated with flames, skulls and menacing accessories. Even those too young to drive spent wistful hours leafing through the latest issue of the J. C. Whitney custom parts catalogue.

Furtive imaginations were further fueled by a steady diet of drive-in monster movies that spawned a passion for plastic model kits featuring the grotesque stars of these films, often at the wheel of a fanciful hot rod. Ghoulish horror comics of the E.C. imprint introduced the stunning artwork and stories of writers who would later be considered literary legends. These comics enjoyed circulation in the millions, but soon fell victim to the hysterical cultural crusading of Dr. Frederick Wertham, whose influential book *Seduction of the Innocent* blamed these comics for causing deviant antisocial behavior and juvenile delinquency. Public outrage led to the establishment of the Comics Code, effectively banning comics of the horror genre. E.C. comics influenced MAD Magazine, which indoctrinated an entire generation in the fundamental principle of art in the service of degenerate discourse.

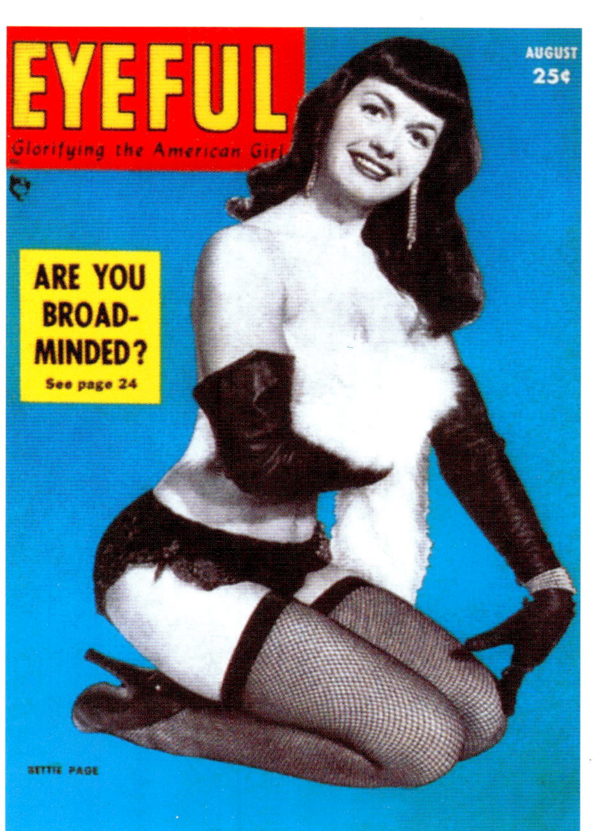


As television began to permeate America's consciousness, images of a mythic nuclear family were offset by Rat Pack playboys, Maynard G. Krebbs' beatnik persona, the prehistoric fantasy of "The Flintstones," and the futurism of "The Jetsons" – which more than any cathode characters defined our expectations for the new millennium. The customary family unit was satirized by the Gothic ghoulishness of "The Munsters" and "The Addams Family." Impressionable children were subjected to a daily dose of demented clowns and disembodied puppets as hosts of after-school entertainment programs. Fifties families routinely dined in exotic Tiki restaurants, replete with tawdry velvet paintings and extravagant Polynesian pageantry. A sexually repressed society nevertheless tolerated lurid pin-up imagery and racy pulp magazines. Gaudy roadside attractions enticed weary travelers, and family vacations were spent in ostentatious resort destinations featuring alluring carnival attractions and rowdy rock 'n' roll dances. During this decade of conformity, weirdness had indelibly stained the collective unconscious of America's youth.

The foundation for the current movement was laid in the late '50s and early '60s at the late Ed Roth's storied Maywood hot-rod emporium in Los Angeles. Employing the services of artists Rick Griffin, Robert Williams, and legendary pinstriper Von Dutch, Roth's studio became a gathering place for the misfits, miscreants and counterculture cognoscenti of the era. "Every day something amazing would happen," Williams recalls. "In the morning Sam the Sham and the Pharaohs could walk in, and a few minutes behind them would be Sonny Barger and some Angels. Erich Maria Remarque, the author of *All Quiet on the Western Front*, might arrive for lunch, and the afternoon would bring Tom Wolfe or Mickey Thompson, the land-speed record holder. Sometimes all these different personalities would all be there at the same time, and that was a giant scene." Wolfe would later document Roth's seminal influence in his now classic first book, *Kandy-Kolored Tangerine-Flake Streamline Baby*, which was published in 1965, and describe Roth as "the most colorful, the most intellectual, and the most capricious" artist of the period. Williams would later become a founding contributor to the '60s underground comix anthology *ZAP!*, which together with Griffin's psychedelic posters and album covers helped define the aesthetics of the Hippie era. Roth and Von Dutch became reclusive loners, only to be rediscovered decades later.

The enormous influence of these renegade artists was largely

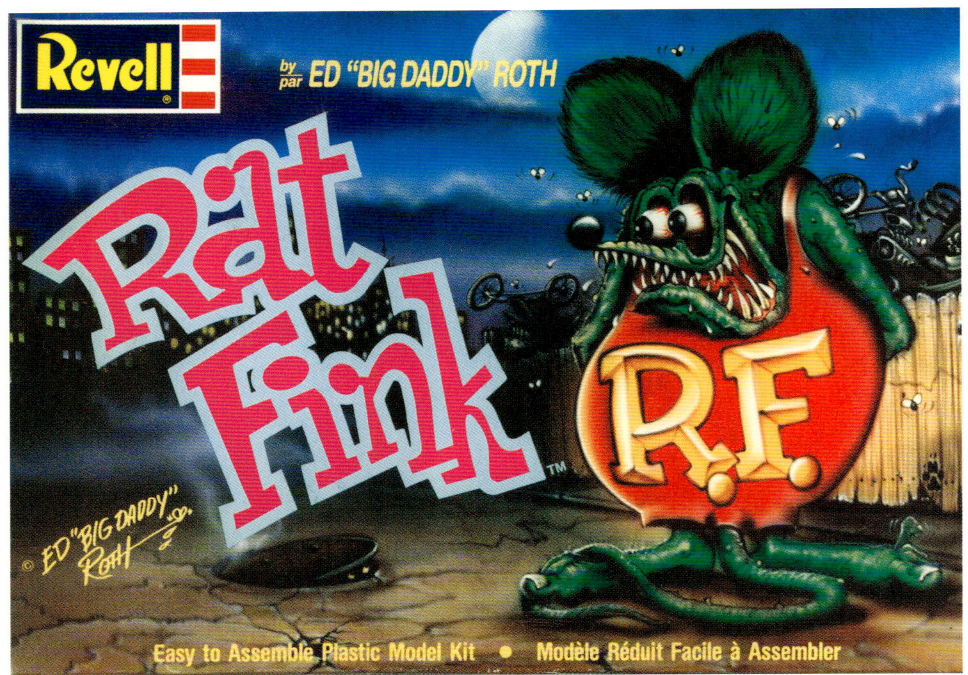
Revell
by
par ED "BIG DADDY" ROTH
Rat Fink
R.F.
© ED "BIG DADDY" ROTH
Easy to Assemble Plastic Model Kit • Modèle Réduit Facile à Assembler

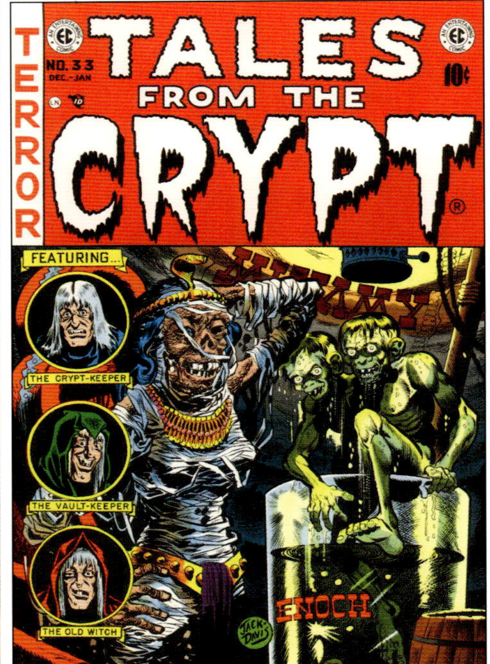
TERROR
TALES FROM THE CRYPT
NO. 33
DEC.-JAN
10¢
FEATURING...
THE CRYPT-KEEPER
THE VAULT-KEEPER
THE OLD WITCH
ENOCH

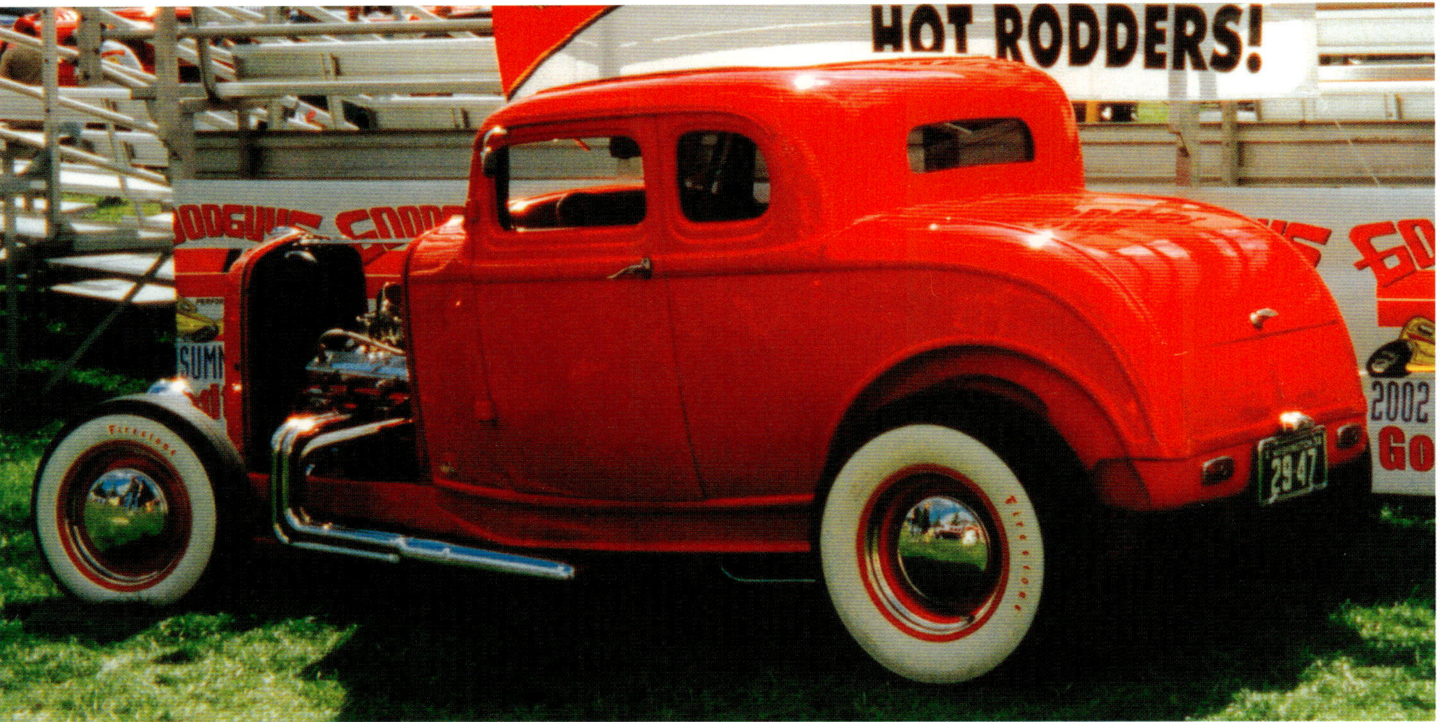
HOT RODDERS!
2002
2947

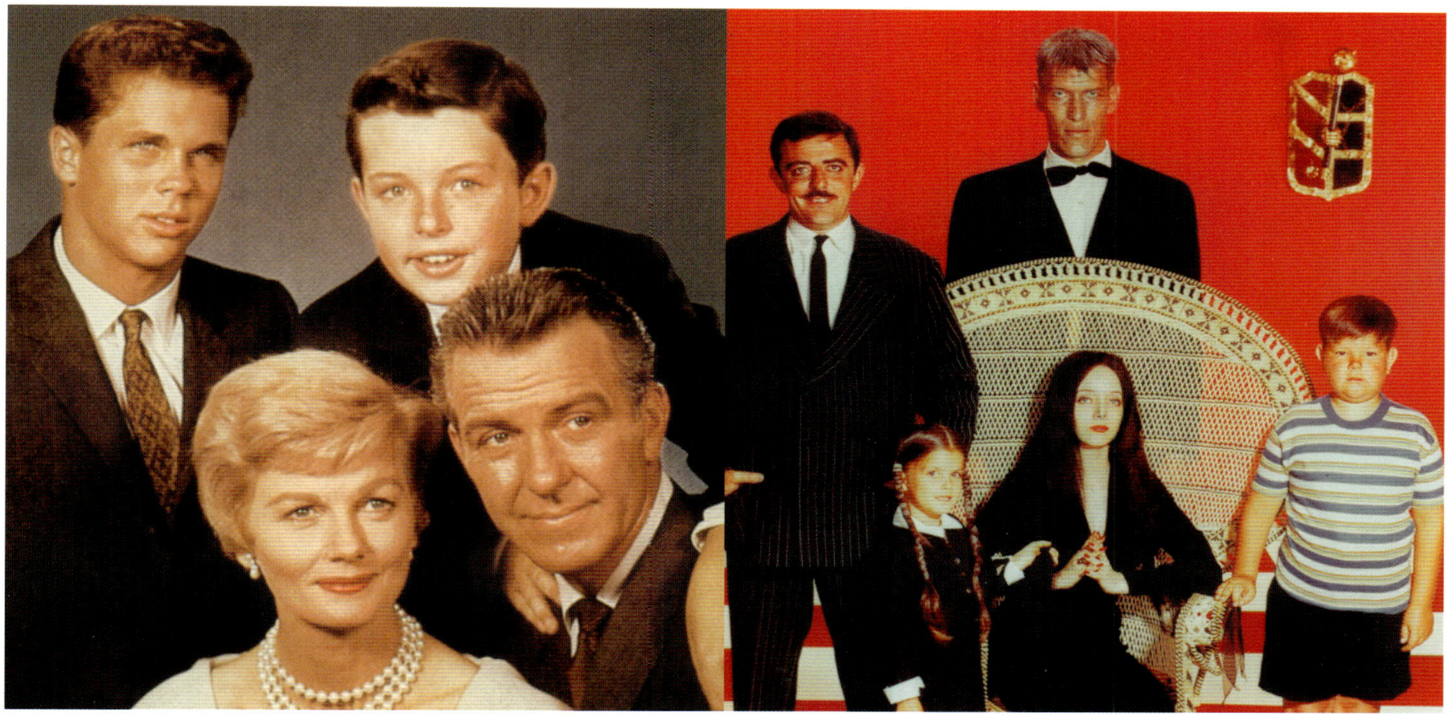

forgotten or ignored until the 1990s, when a confluence of events renewed public interest in the legacy of America's unheralded masters. "I was at the L.A. Art Fair in 1990," explains influential art collector Greg Escalante, "and I came across Ed Roth's name in the catalogue. An electricity shot through me. Maybe against my will I immediately recognized that he was the guy that got all these people started on their art careers." Robert Williams' paintings created a sensation at the historic "Helter Skelter" exhibit at MoCA's Temporary Contemporary in 1992. The landmark "Kustom Kulture" exhibition celebrated the work of Roth, Williams and Von Dutch, as well as introducing the work of a host of their progeny. The show opened at the Laguna Art Museum in 1993 before traveling to Baltimore and Seattle. The exhibit resonated with baby boomers as well as with a younger generation of artists and collectors inspired by the colorful exuberance and rebellious nature of the work. "Kustom Kulture" was greeted with superlative reviews and record-setting attendance at each stop. The show became the catalyst for a seismic shift in America's aesthetics at the dawn of the new millennium. It spawned a loose network of new galleries and enticed many established galleries to shift their focus, invigorated by the energetic work of inventive young artists. A bimonthly arts journal, *Juxtapoz*, soon appeared, which spread the style across the country and around the globe. Robert Williams emerged as the erudite spokesman and titular head of the movement.

Explanations for the revival of interest in this aesthetic are difficult and varied. Certainly, parallels can be drawn between contemporary society and the dominant social environment of the late '50s and early '60s. As was the case then, we live in an era of prosperity in which conservative politicians extol the virtues of nebulous "family values" while demonizing the influence of popular culture and foreign ideas. Following decades of inaccessible conceptual art and the opaque dialogue that accompanied it, a disconnected public was eager to embrace a movement that left behind the condescension and pretension of previous developments in the arena of fine art. While the art world has for the most part responded with typical truculence to this movement, the established order is in imminent danger of becoming irrelevant as this new art style experiences exponential growth and unprecedented popularity.

— Larry Reid, January 2004

# Notes On The Underground

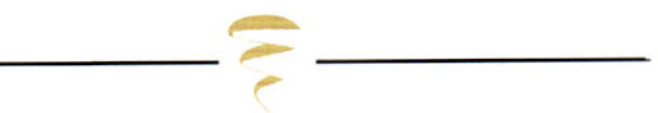

Carlo McCormick

## SEMANTICS (ASIDE)

Given the cumulative evidence here of so many visionary, iconoclastic, subversive and pictorially perverse artists mining a similar topography of popular cultural detritus, why is it that, after so many years, we still lack a definitive rubric for this genre? In the evolution of this book, perhaps an even trickier conundrum than the choice of artists has been its title. For the many artists who no doubt had great trouble with the mantle of Lowbrow, by which so much of this art has been categorized, I would gently remind them of the substantive difference in meaning between the adjective and the noun that these inverse qualifiers of highbrow connote. That is, lowbrow is inherently an oppositional confrontation with the dominant discourse of fine art — it is everything that highbrow is not. Now, when you think of highbrow as an adjective, signifying the highly cultured and intellectual, you can understand why some might respond to the lowbrow nomenclature with, "What — you callin' me dumb?" If, however, we can accept it as a noun, whereby we are talking rather of one who affects this pretense of learning and cultural sophistication, we have in fact something much closer to the veritable enemy of our shared aesthetic margins.

But so be it, we'll forego the Lowbrow label. After all, when what you are doing is not acknowledged by the status quo, it is indeed hard to exercise much irony in terms of self-definition. There are, however, myriad forms by which the dispossessed, alienated and ghettoized have adopted and reconfigured the signs and strategies of the prevailing culture to their own ends. From Jewish humor to African-American argot, it's often simply a practice of ironic appropriation and inversion. Come on, if punks could figure it out with the swastika, and twenty years later lesbian style can bring the wife-beater shirt back in fashion, it shouldn't be that hard for the art world to figure out. Perhaps if we were really smart we'd call the whole thing Stoopid Art. It certainly didn't hurt anyone's career to be in Marcia Tucker's 1978 landmark New Museum exhibition "Bad Painting." The problem unfortunately goes deeper than any verbal attitude, style or cleverness of coinage can address — it is endemic to a greater linguistic malaise where we actually seem to have run out of new ways to denote novelty.

Our terminology here, or rather its apparent absence, goes to the heart of our incessant cultural co-option. We have pillaged subcultures and plundered the avant-garde for so long, at issue is neither their continued existence nor relevance (for they are by nature self-perpetuating and metamorphic in relation to the mainstream), but the dear and fragile fact that we have come to a dead-end in the nomenclature of dissent. Edgy, trendy, hip, street, cool or hot, the lexicon is bankrupt. With due deference to the quality of this particular book, I cannot abide by the conjunction of those most overly (ab)used words Pop Surrealism. It's just so pop it's, like, surreal. Yet nothing could be more empty today than "underground," a space and place long ago colonized and commodified beyond recognition, or more malevolently corrupt than the facile convergence of self-taught, insane, criminal, spiritual and folk arts under the single market mantle of "Outsider Art."

No, no, ye are still a nameless lot. I think what you actually need is someone who really hates this art to name it. You might just be surprised how cluttered art history is with isms that were coined by the wicked pens of their harshest critics. Until such a time, however, let us very briefly entertain some ill-fitting frames by which this unruly mass of visual marginalia might be considered.

## MUTANTS & HYBRIDS

Once upon a time, there was this crazy artist named Nicolas Moufarrege who wrote amazingly strange and compelling essays on contemporary art. He's been dead decades now, and the once prestigious magazine that published much of his work, *Arts Magazine*, is long gone too. Perhaps he just sticks in my memory now because a lot of the stuff he championed, from Kenny Scharf to Jack Kirby, is relevant to us still, but a lot of his best texts were collectively called "The Mutant International" and serially numbered (V, VI, VII) until I lost count. The seduction of mutants, at a time before the mass-merchandizing and movie-making of X-Men turned it all into some Gen X surrogate, was the same metaphor for adolescent alienation and social disconnect then as might still appeal to us today, but could just as well be those kind of comic pulp references that bind us back to the post-World War II emergence of youth culture and its lineage of high/low convergences, from the proto-Beatles Liverpudlian Batman poems of the Scaffold to the Pop of Roy Lichtenstein et al.

For better or worse, such simple and direct pop citations do not work for us anymore. Born outside the naïve age of generational discovery into a more complex dynamic of immediate and utter immersion, we are media-damaged beyond recognition and have taken rampant appropriation to a frenzied level of mashed-up multitasking. The icon no longer stands alone: it is overlayered and warped along the fractured schematics of all others in an all-brand atrocity of manifold desire. This then is an era of hybridity, an infotainment age in which individuated meaning itself is lost to the all-subsuming spectacle of multiplicity. We may treasure the iconography of monster art and the nostalgias of children's illustration and retrographics, but we know that the truly grotesque, most reactionary and radically distorted fictions are a contemporary commonplace of our quotidian mainstream. The project is no longer to simply reclaim our disposable daily vernacular like some found object and call it art, nor even can we hope to make sense of it; the best we can aspire to is a point of identification within the incessant visual maelstrom so that somehow the generic and lowest common denominator can become a personal language. And the only way to speak that tongue is in polyglot rhyme.

## THE SALOON OF REFUGEES

Here's what I like: you basically have here a bunch of artists who exist in tangential relation to both the art world status quo and the mainstream of commerce, but who have chosen to occupy a common space for their own idiosyncratic and diverse ways of seeing things. Whatever they share in terms of style and content is hardly that significant and is certainly not the basis for their commonality. If Modernism got its legs via a big collective challenge to the Academy through the confrontational opposition posed by its "Salon des Refusés" exhibitions, these artists willingly co-exist with one another in a similarly nebulous space just beyond the cultural frame. Is it exile, expatriation or self-empowerment? Perhaps the reason there hasn't been a manifesto is precisely because they are autochthonous to no one manifestation. This is populism in its most pluralist form. It's not a discourse — it's a riot. And no matter how polite we may keep things in the halls of culture, let's at least admit that we like our art to be uncivil, irascible, voyeuristic and narcissistic.

How do you make a club out of people who simply are allergic to belonging? How for that matter do you make a party out of a bunch of misfits? They're fun company to be sure, but they hardly are what one would call a congregation. I'd rather think of them as belonging in some hypothetical bar room – a querulous, drunken, misanthropic lot, busy drawing on their stained napkins, demanding that someone change the TV station, feeding slugs into the juke box, making shamefully frequent trips to the loo and doing their very best to ignore one another. This too is a fiction, one more lie in the many that we practice whenever it comes time to make sense of individuals as group. Herein these pages are the statistics of anomaly in contemporary art: it's really up to each of us to draw our own radically inaccurate conclusions. Perhaps in the end it is an underground, squirreled away in back alleys and drainage ditches, chop shops and bordellos, a secret society that dares not speak its name. To see it all at once, you would have to step back, but there is no room, or to rise above it, if only any of us could really fly. But I like it down in the trenches, where understanding matters less than action and knowing history means nothing if you don't have fast reflexes. If you're looking for the definitive, it's not to be found in the words that academics string together, but more in the jigsaw puzzle of infinite contradiction and confrontation built by the deviant pictures in this book — something to hold and look at which might never fit on any wall but is, quite simply, the best group show that has yet to open.

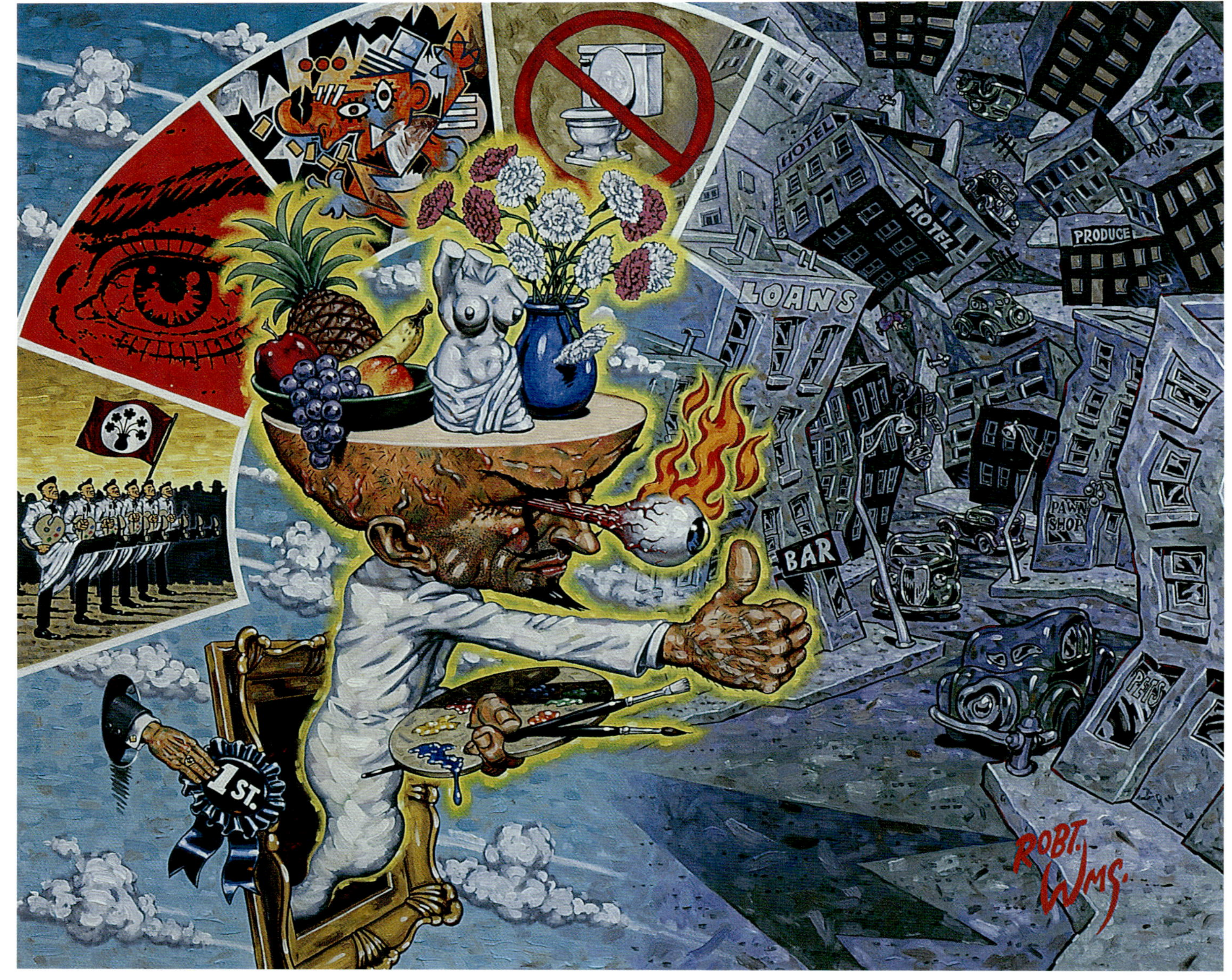


ROBERT WILLIAMS THE DECORATOR GENERAL 1987, oil on canvas, 30" x 36"

# Dumbing Down To DaVinci

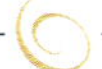

Robert Williams

In the spring of 1997 I received a phone call from a very knowledgeable art history writer named Nancy Dustin Wall Moure. This highly educated and soft-spoken woman explained to me that she had been working for some years on a serious art reference book about the complete history of California art. She then went on to say she had received assistance and suggestions from the well known Los Angeles art dealer, James Corcoran. Corcoran recommended to her, to make this large collection complete, that she might want to talk to me to round up any loose ends in the esoteric West Coast art underground. Nancy Moure had seemingly left no stone unturned in compiling a massive 560-page tome covering 450 years of California art. In my mind this book would go down in the annals of art education like Helen Gardner's *Art Through the Ages*, or John Canaday's *Mainstreams of Modern Art*. History books that were important textbooks.

The question was: How do you inform an extremely well-versed and perceptive art historian that, despite her extensive academic background, unbeknownst to her, lying coiled like a cobra at her feet is one of the most aggressive, vital, and overlooked art movements since Pop Art? How do you simply paraphrase fifty years of undocumented art evolution into a concise explainable statement, while keeping a straight face, to an expert who might be a little suspicious?

This is what I told her: "I belong to a rather loose-knit group of artists that, because of a fifty-year dominance of abstract and conceptual art, have been left isolated from the more conventional academic mainstream. All of us, with few exceptions, function in the craftsmanship-based realm of representational art. To better understand this, you have to realize that we gain our source material and inspiration from some of the most illustrious, colorful and controversial influences and graphic traditions that one could possibly emerge from."

"We spawn from story illustration, comic book art, science fiction, movie poster art, motion picture production and effects, animation, music art and posters, psychedelic and punk rock art, hot rod and biker art, surfer, beach bum and skateboard graphics, graffiti art, tattoo art, pin-up art, pornography and myriad other commonplace egalitarian art forms. And all are simply dismissed and treated with condescension by the formal art authorities."

I ended by saying: "I am not alone. I stand with hundreds, if not thousands, of like-minded artists. And enough of us exist to justify our own personal periodical (*Juxtapoz* magazine), which stands third in all art magazine sales."

Nancy Moure treated my concerns with respect and added a thoughtful and seriously considered passage that took up more than a page and a half in her book. For her patience with my claims I can only offer her my utmost gratitude.

For a more in-depth look at this array of non-ratified and somewhat profane arts we have to understand a few facts. I'm not issuing blame and retribution, but, starting at the end of the Second World War, the international and American fine arts communities have intentionally striven to move the graphic and sculptural arts into the province of total non-objective abstraction and semi-abstract expression – and this backed up years later with minimalism and conceptual theory. This means essentially that for fifty years the world's de facto fine art power brokers have completely eliminated representational painting, drawing, and sculpture from the whole fine arts sphere, with a few rare exceptions such as kitsch pop art.

This is all well and good for the high society cognoscenti, except for two problems. To begin with, representational art as a voice and language dates back to early Paleolithic Europe, and has evolved intelligently at a consistently rapid pace, developing a more involved and intricate vernacular of visual communications right up to the middle of the twentieth century when, for some unknown reason, it was curtailed. This crucial form of graphic expression will inevitably find other forms of social contact, and will probably eventually eclipse any art mode that suppresses it.

The second problem stems from the fact that possibly seven or eight individuals in any group of a hundred have the capacity, dexterity and will to express themselves in a pictorial syntax. But simply relegating these few artists to the status of facile drones and sub-intellectuals with quaint drawing skills is not preparing oneself for the eventual jolt of having to deal with brilliant draftsmen who are gifted with the additional cerebral skills of abstract thought. It is good to keep in mind that "abstract" does not always mean sloppy.

For some time now, many talented and imaginative artists have had to make do with participating in the near arts — art without sanction. This might change. These denigrated forms of expression do have the seminal characteristic of becoming the primary arts. The modern use of cartoon imagery is a good example. Always encumbered with the stigma of humor, the abstract use of the cartoon in the future might not leave anybody laughing.

There are some interesting aspects to this lowbrow or sub-sacrosanct art. But one of the major drawbacks is the difficulty these forms of art encounter as sophisticated decorative appointments that harmoniously integrate into modern environments and architecture. The rich subject matter, however, with its endless forms of mental engagement, easily makes up for this art's distracting and intrusive character.

Here are a couple of examples of art beyond decoration. At first glance, carnival and sideshow banners from the 1880s through the 1950s appear to be nothing more than tawdry collectables. You can consider freak banners done in lurid bad taste as intending to entice simple people into giving up their hard-earned money to ogle at pathetically deformed souls who've been put on public display. But, if the onlooker has advanced observational skills, the span between the fraudulent sideshow advertisement and the actual subject makes any abstract art pale by comparison. "The Octopus Man" portrayed on spectacular outside banners was represented as a large green cephalopod. This figure is seen jumping on the beach accosting a beautiful maiden, while sailors who have come to save her are being strangled in its tentacles. After paying fifty cents the curiosity seeker can go inside the tent and discover that this fierce creature is, in reality, a 45-year-old shirtless man completely covered with horrible skin growths, something like a knobby rind on a squash. The payoff here is the enormous gap between fact and fiction — this is where the rapacious imagination resides.

Another case would be for science fiction. This genre starts off as a pastime for gullible people with beliefs in the future. Let's compare the 1939 Buck Rogers movie star, Buster Crabbe, to the more modern astronaut, John Glenn. They are the same person. Bad comic books, lurid pulp magazines and trashy B-movies of the '30s, '40s and '50s made space travel a desired reality. The realistic difference between Buster Crabbe and John Glenn is a much shorter jump of imagination than "The Octopus Man" and the image on his promotional banner.

This brings me to the conclusion that lowbrow art is, if nothing else, an honest celebration of runaway human thought processes.

— Robt. Williams, January 2004

# Pop Surrealism

THE RISE OF UNDERGROUND ART

# Anthony AUSGANG

(Los Angeles, California)

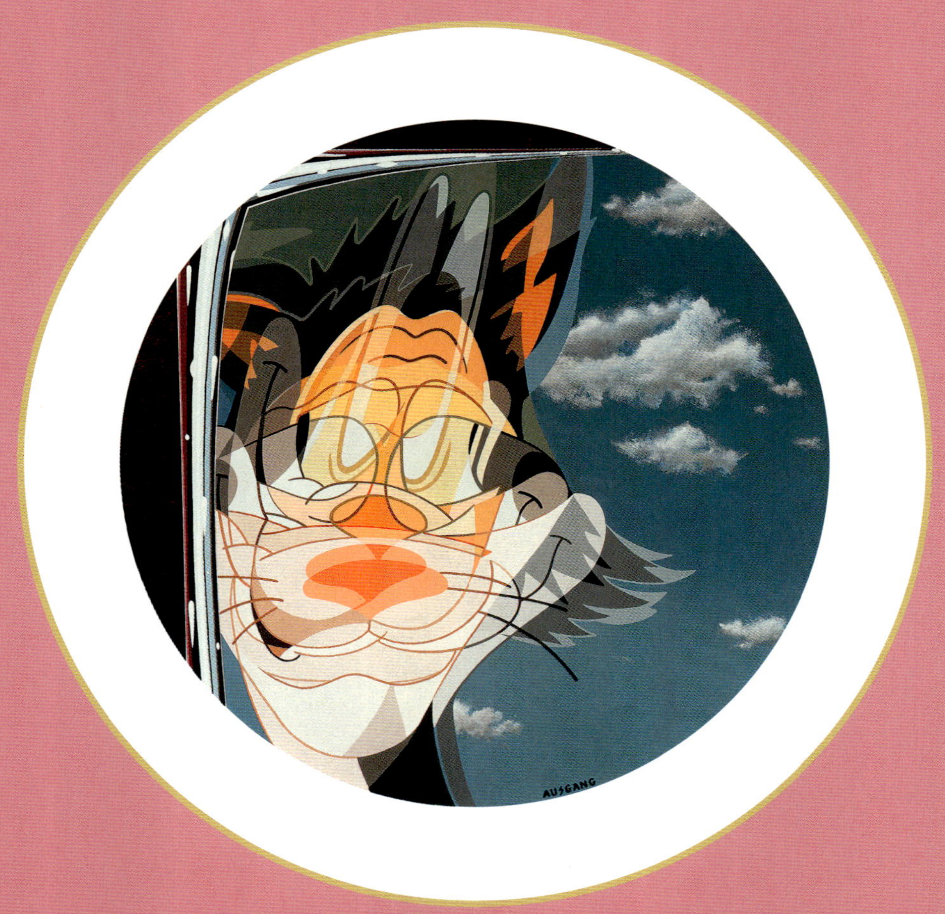


THE WINDOW WASHER 1998, acrylic on canvas, 30" diameter

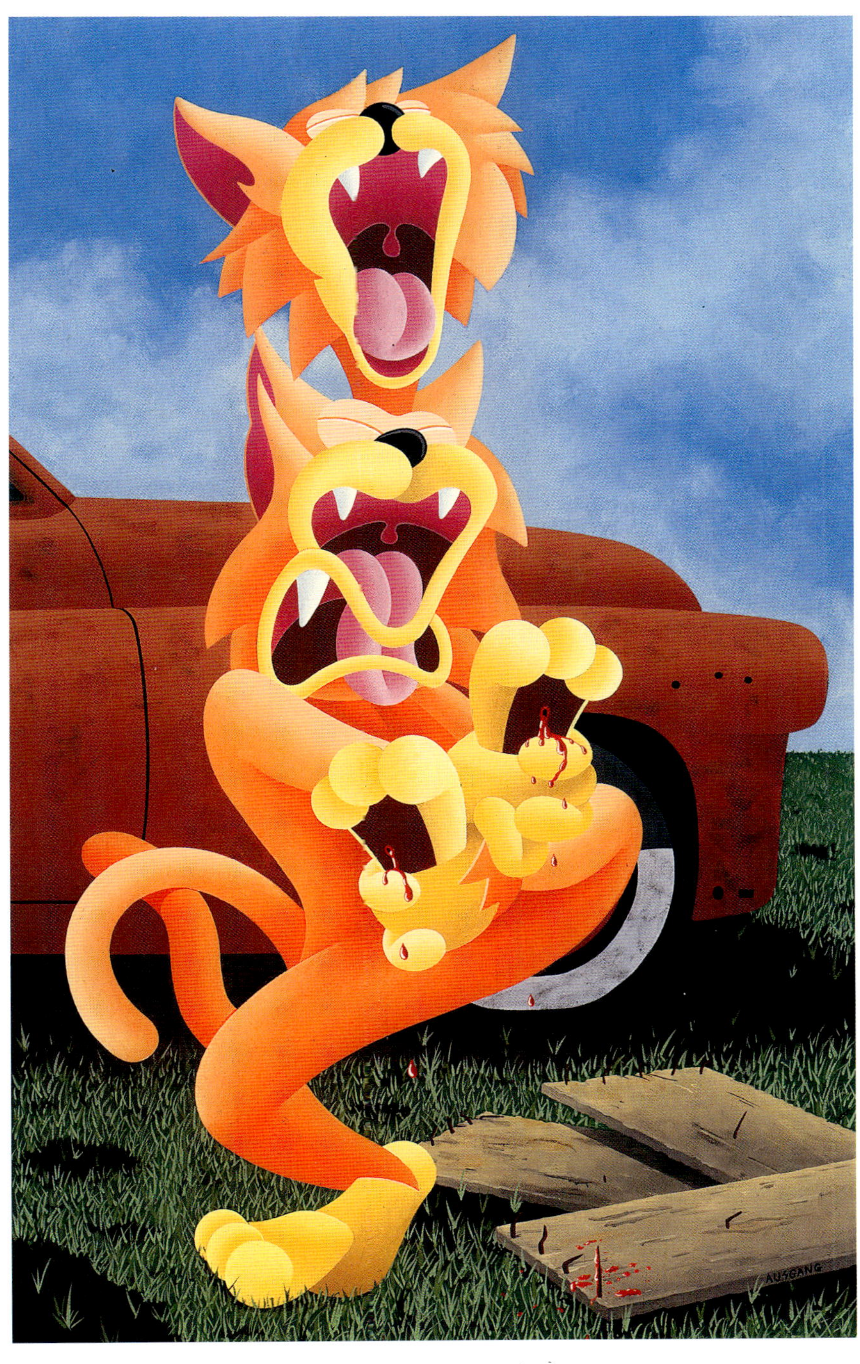


1995, acrylic on canvas, 40" x 50"

THE SCREECH

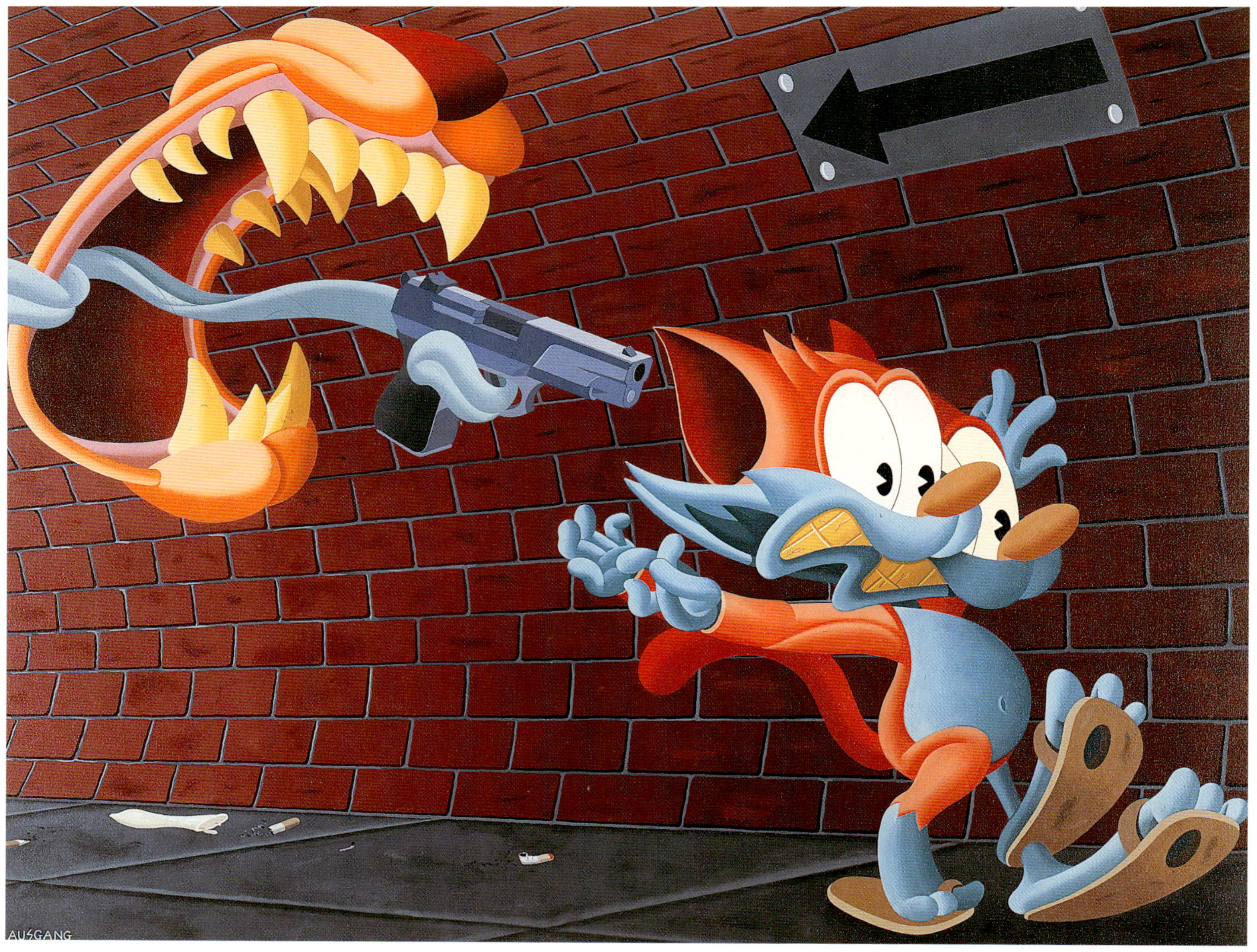


THE PURSUIT OF HAPPINESS

1993, acrylic on canvas, 48" x 60"

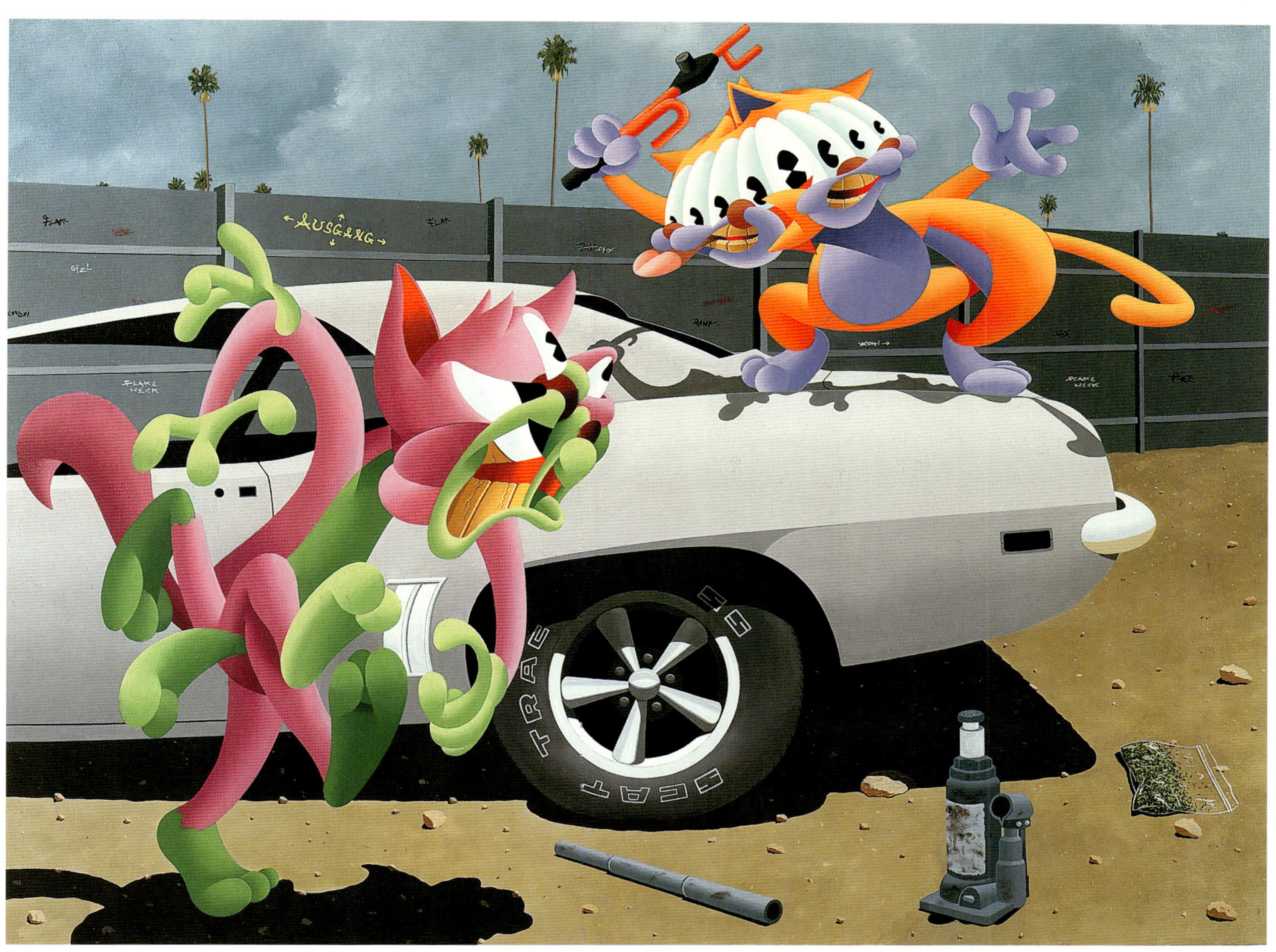


1994, acrylic on canvas, 40" x 50"

THE GREAT CATNIP DROUGHT

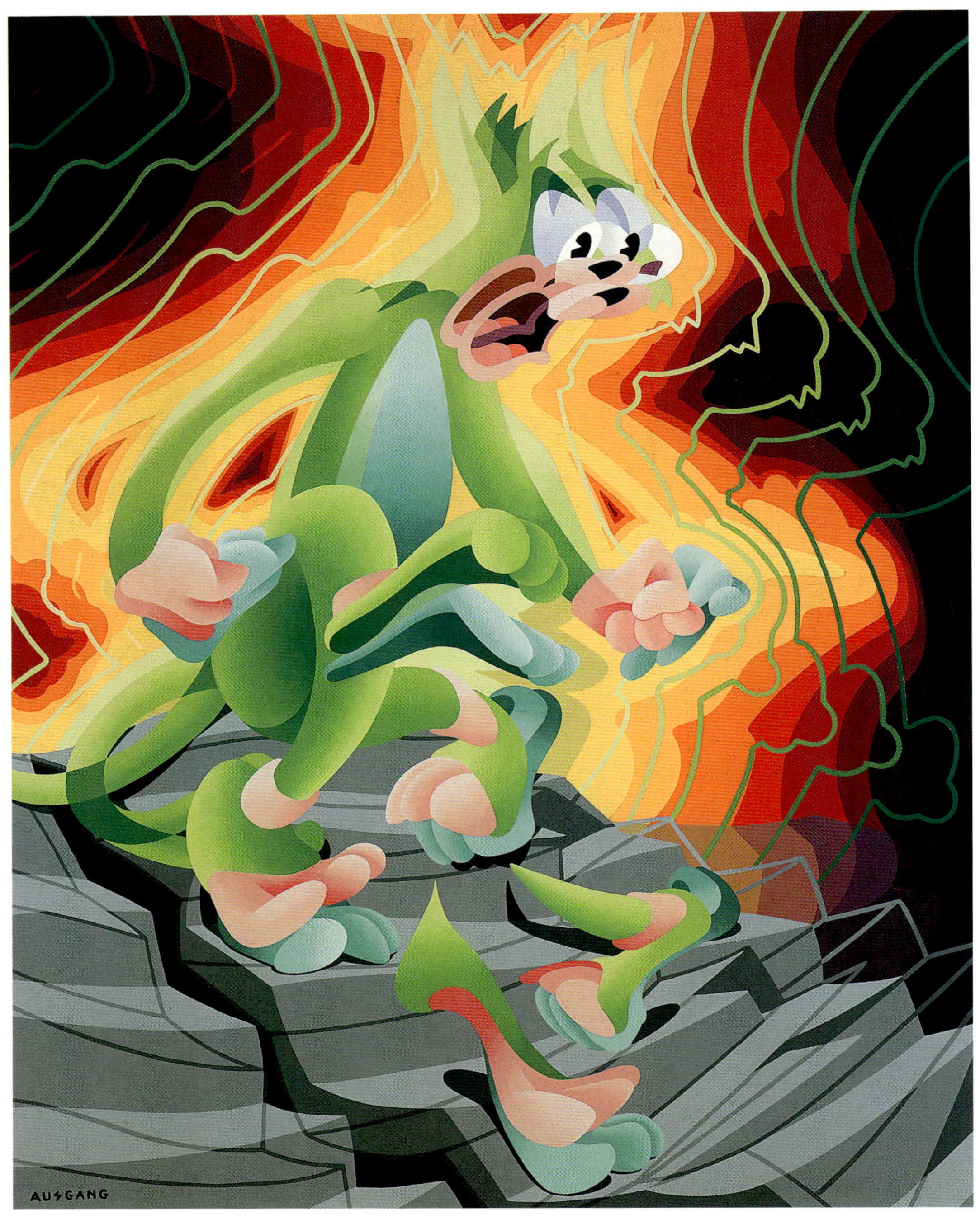


DUDE DESCENDING A STAIRCASE 1999, acrylic on canvas, 28" x 36"

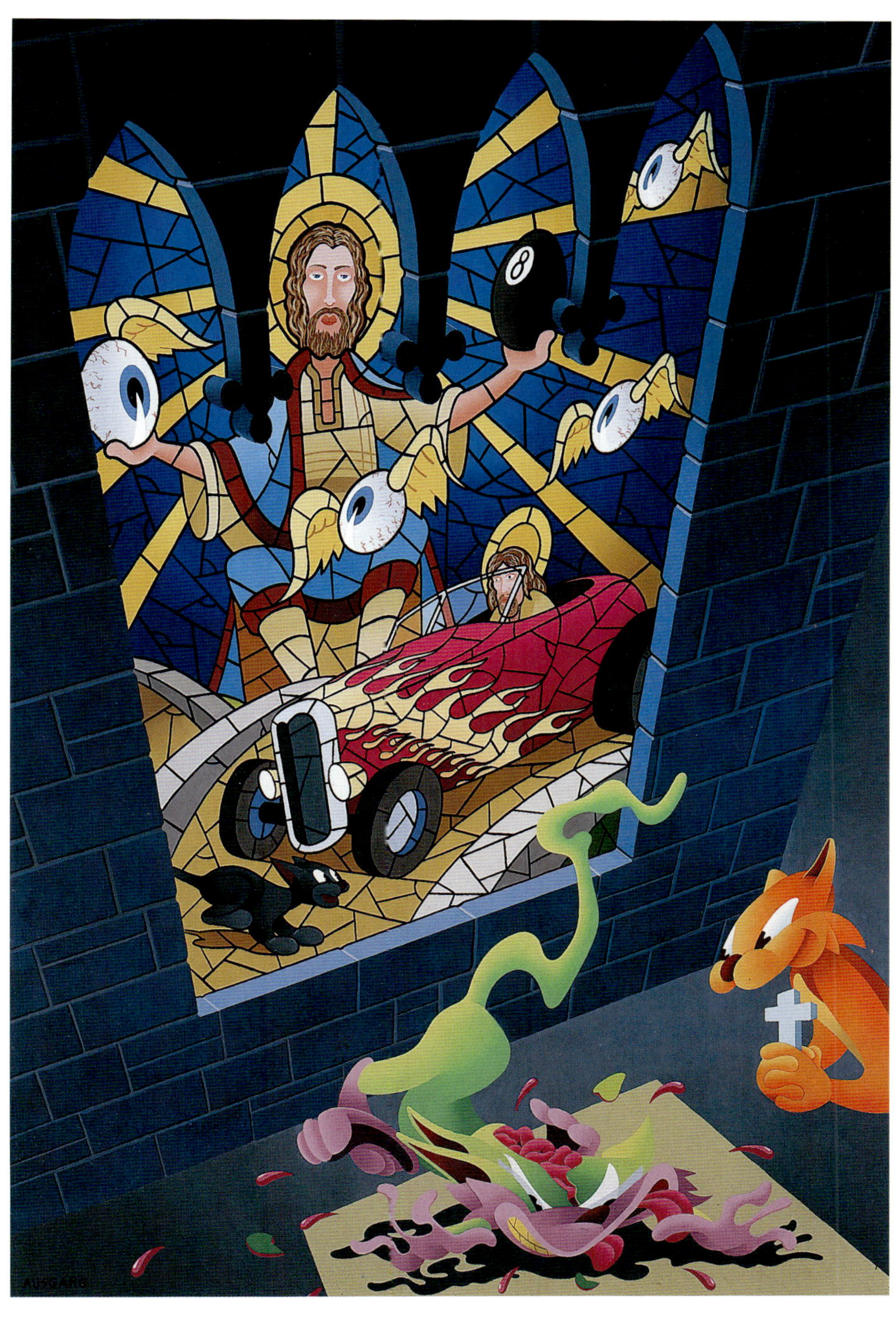

2000, acrylic on canvas, 30" x 45"

THE STIGMATA

# Glenn
# BARR

(Detroit, Michigan)

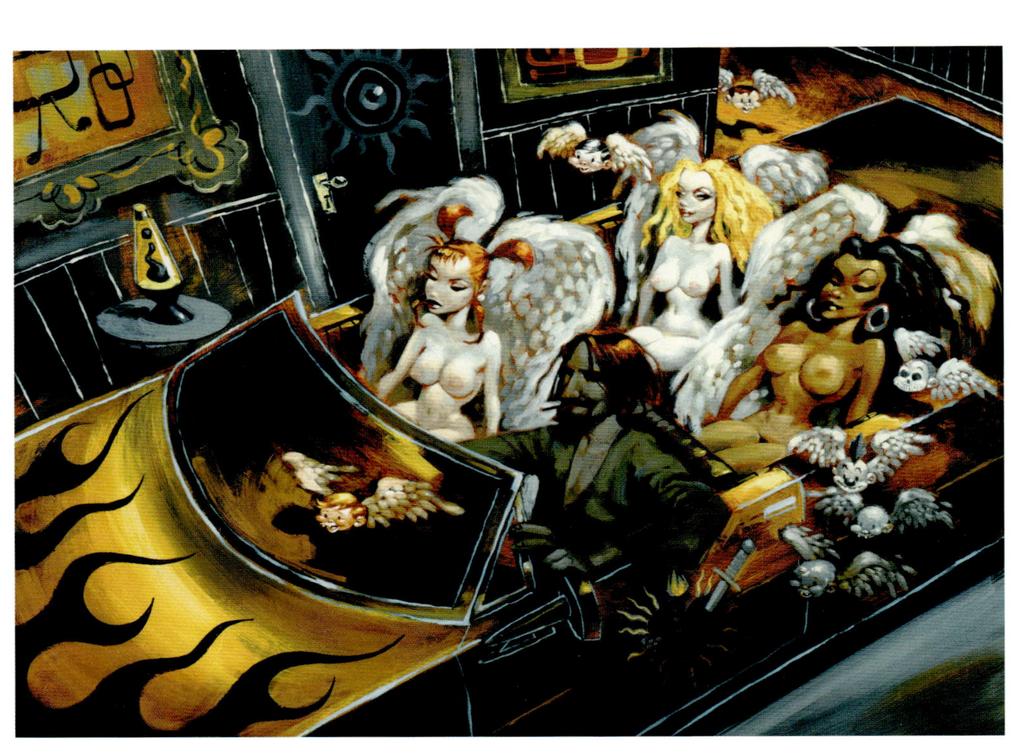

JESUS TOUR

2001, acrylic on masonite, 24" x 30"

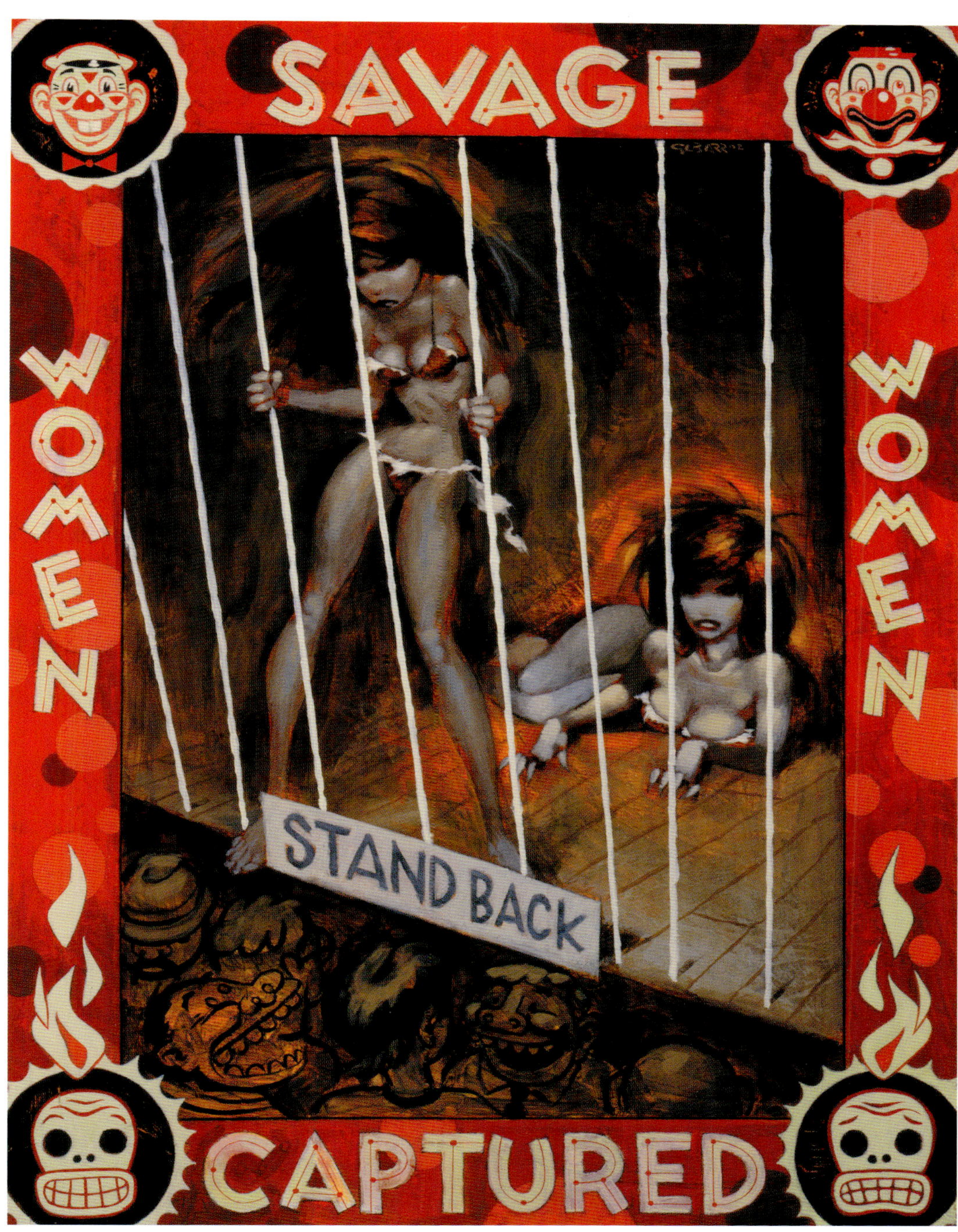


2003, acrylic on masonite, 16" x 20"

Savage

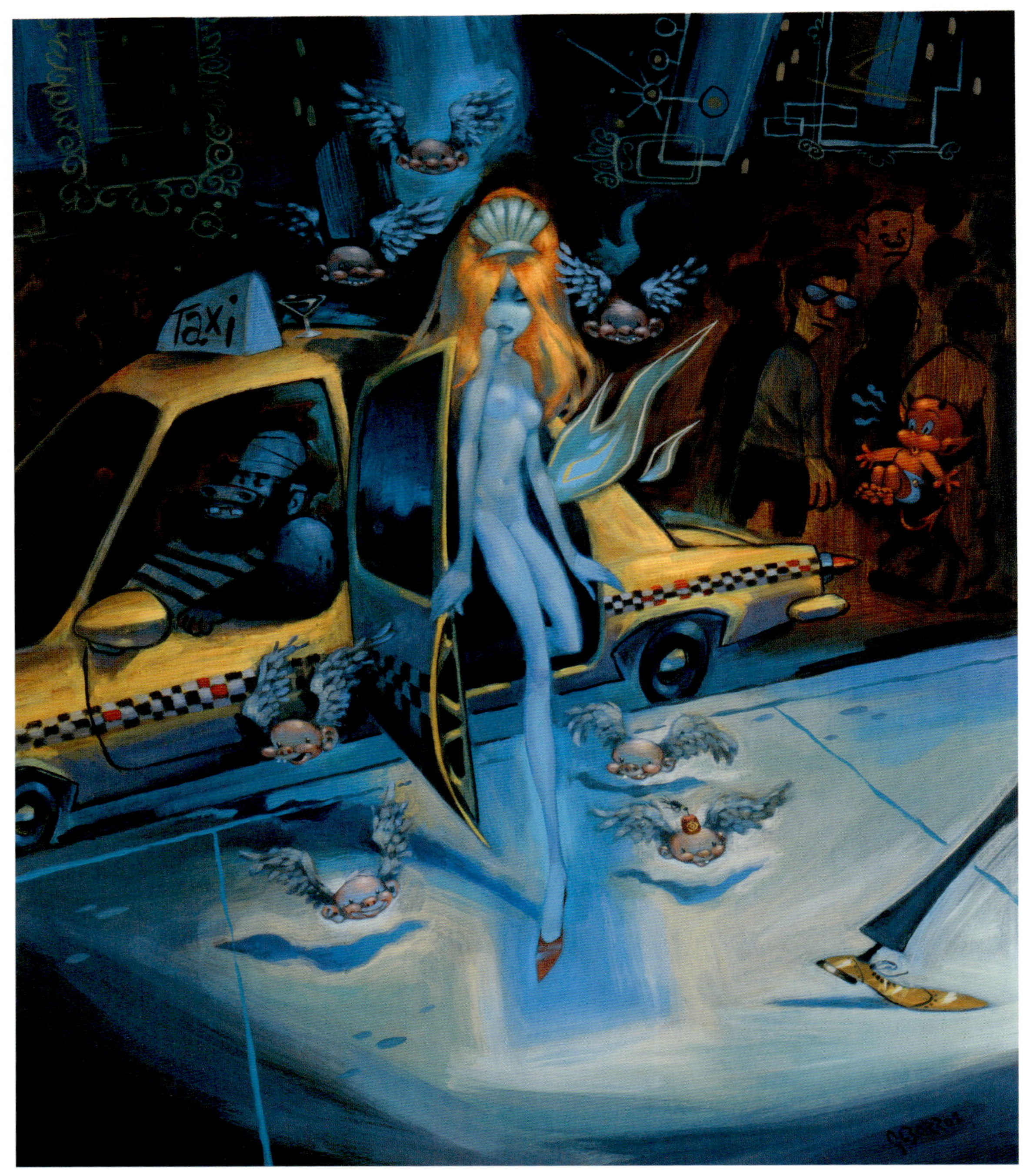


THE BIRTH OF VENUS ON AVENUE B

2002, acrylic on masonite, 25" x 30"

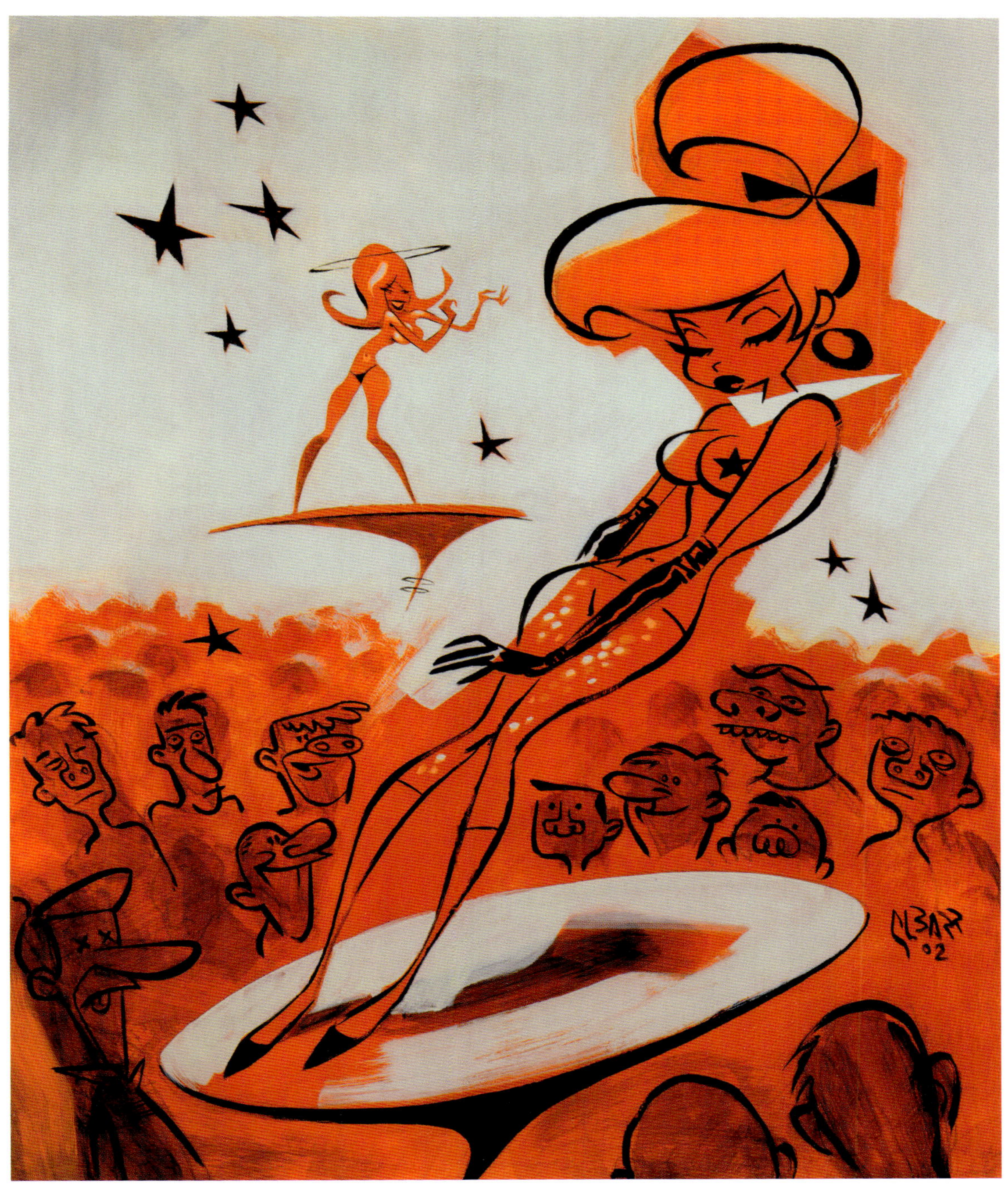

2002, acrylic on masonite, 16" x 20"

Trouble in Mind

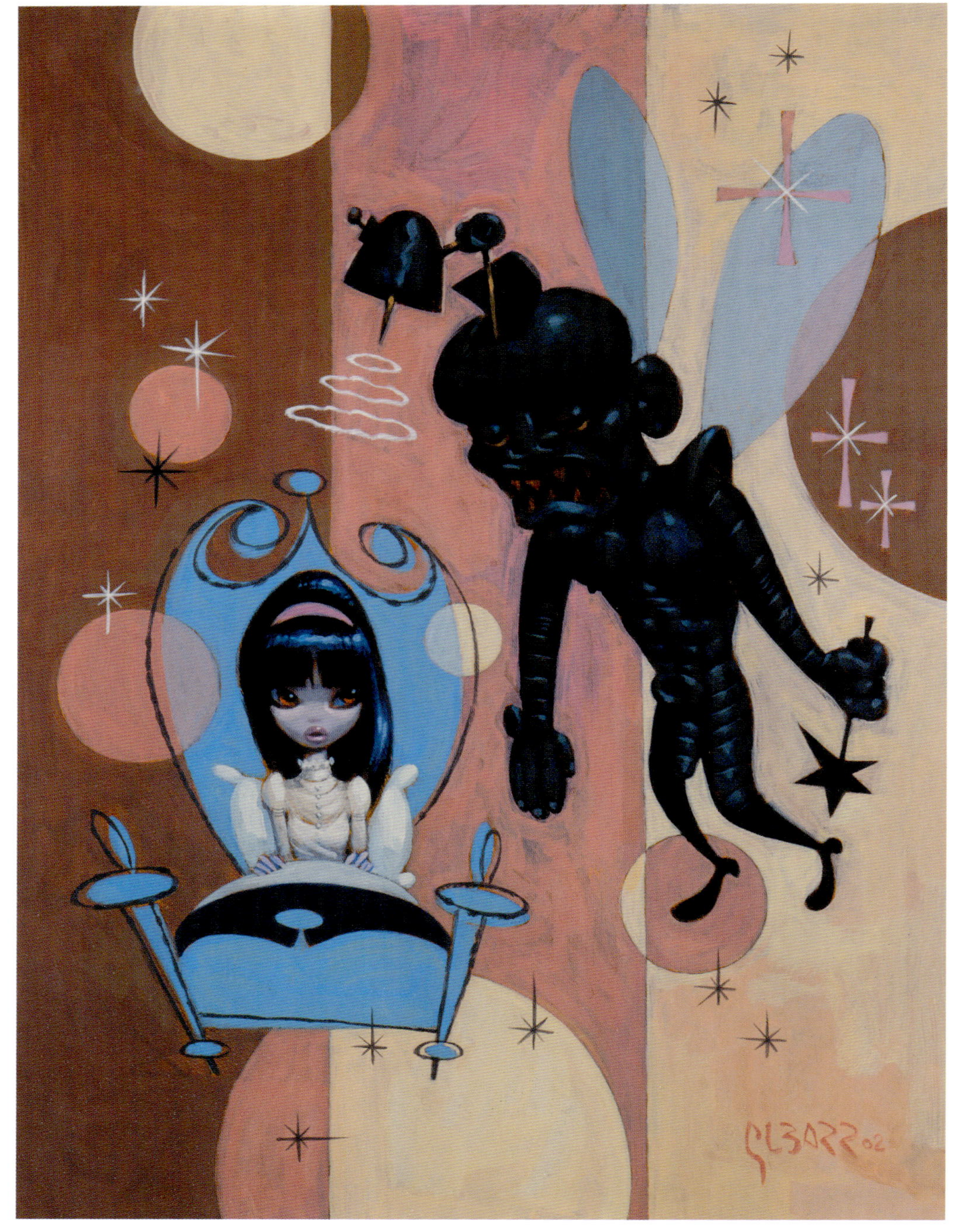

ENCRYPTED

2002, acrylic on masonite, 11" x 16"

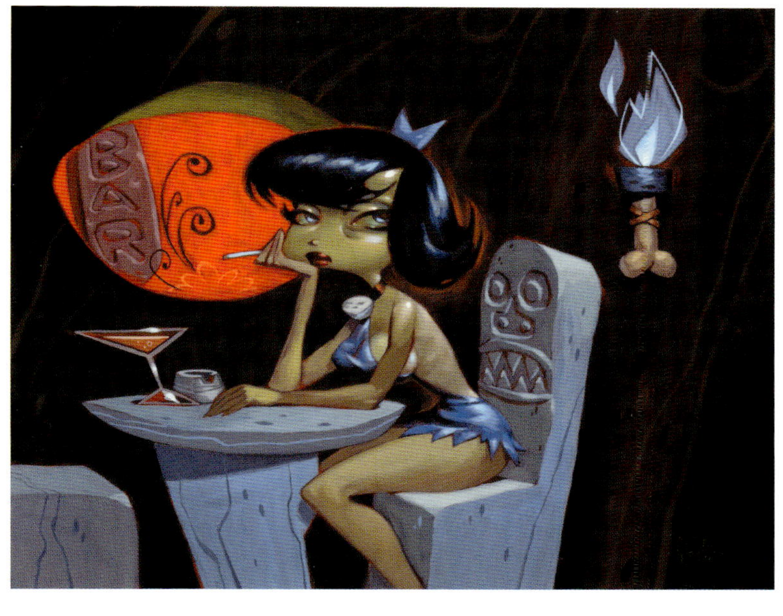


2002, acrylic on masonite, 11" x 14" BORED AND HORNY

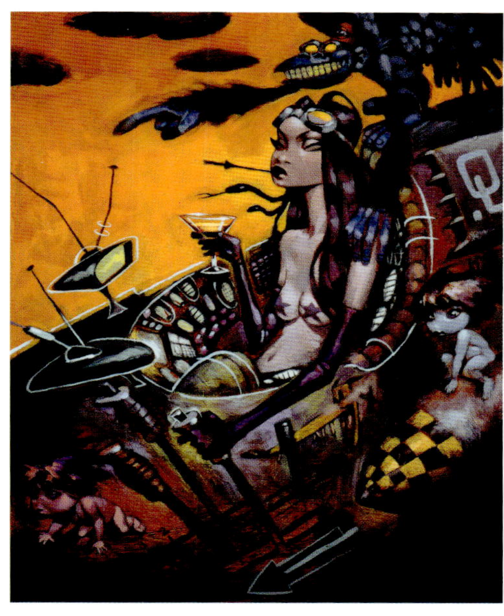

BENEATH THE VALLEY OF THE BRAIN
2002, acrylic on masonite, 16" x 20"

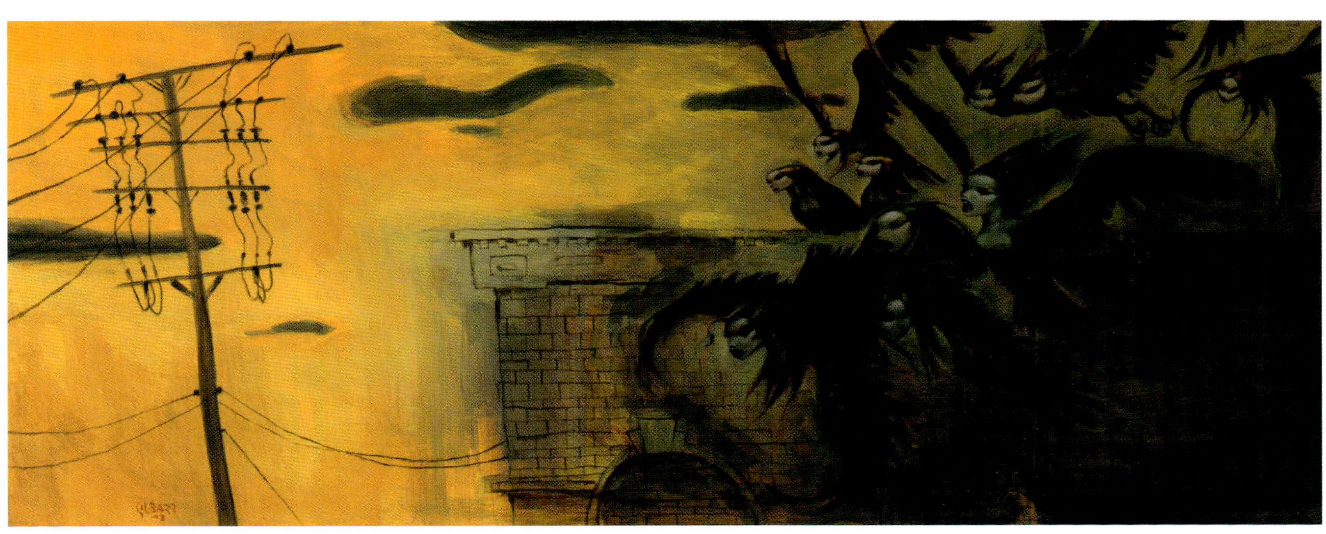

2003, acrylic on masonite, 12" x 30" CORRIDOR OF LUST

# Tim BISKUP

(Los Angeles, California)

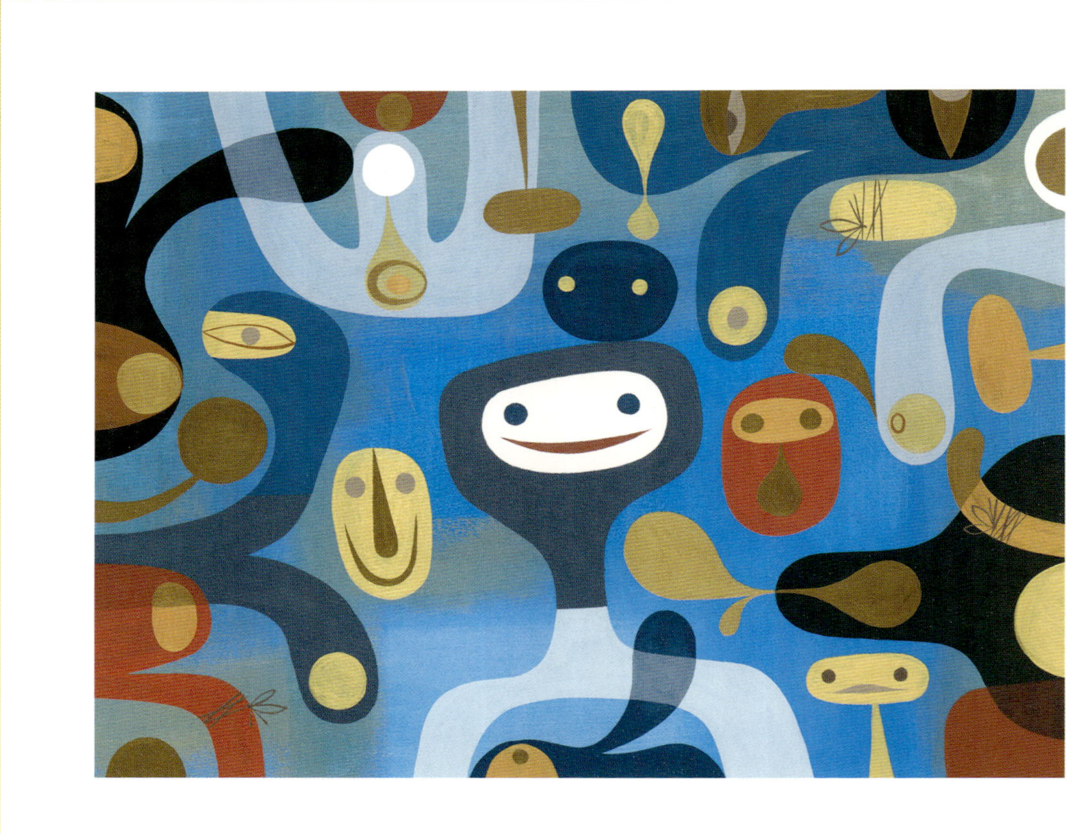

BUBBLEBATH 2002, gouache on wooden panel, 7" x 9"

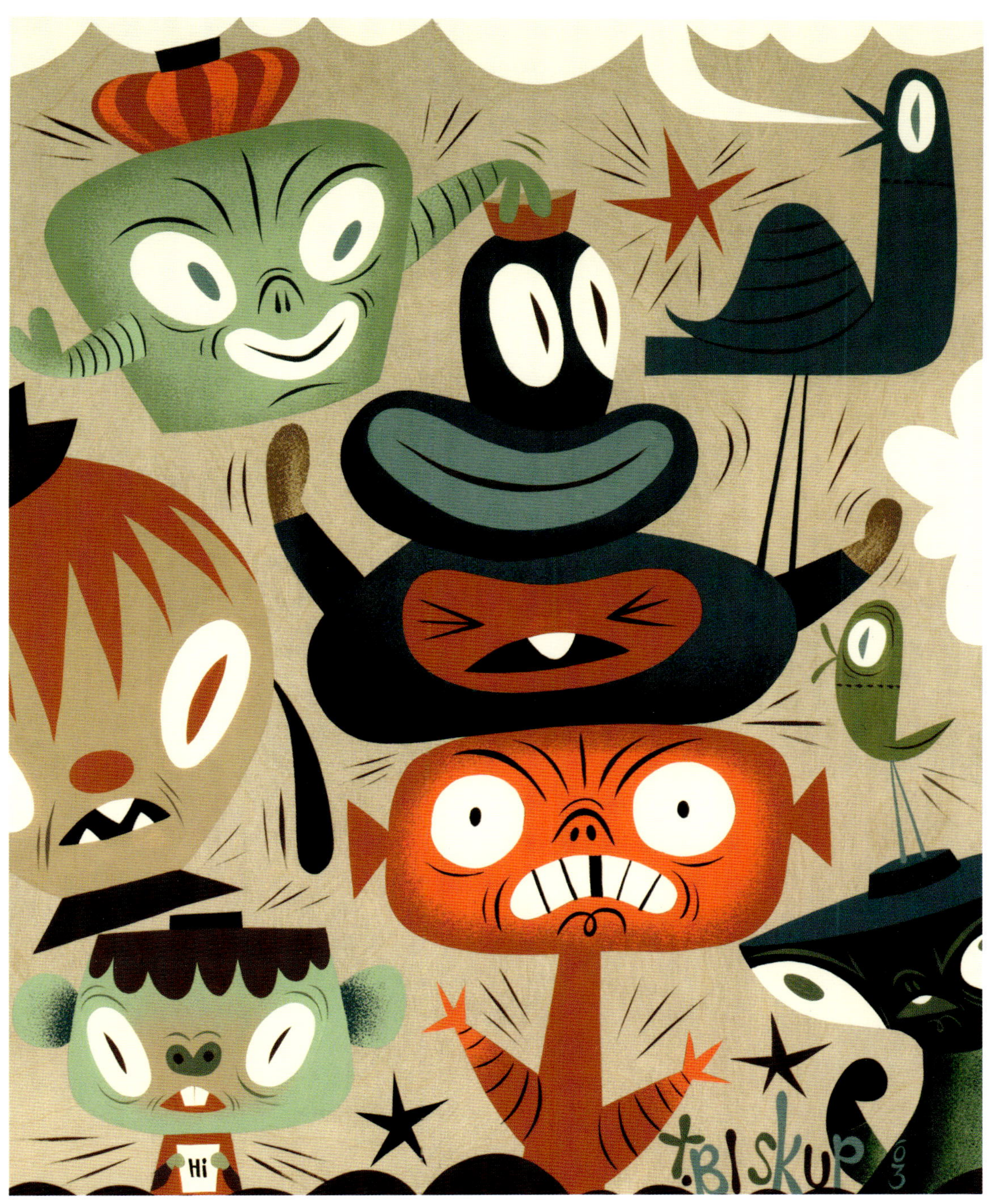


2003, acrylic on wooden panel, 16" x 20"

STACK PACK poster

(opposite page) DARKRIDE - HOT 2003, acrylic on wooden panel, 24" x 24"

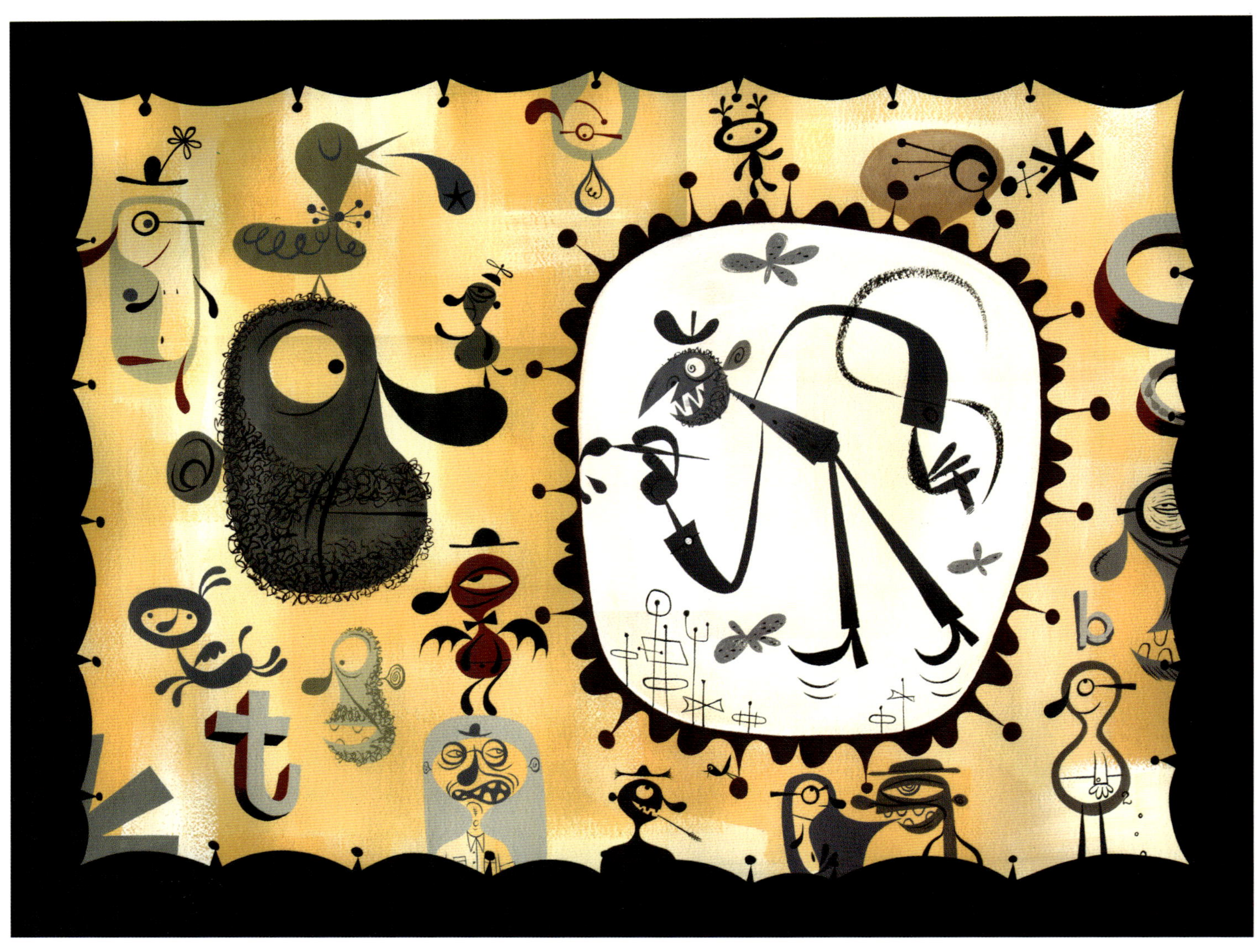


THE DEMON PAINTER 2001, gouache on paper, 24" x 18"

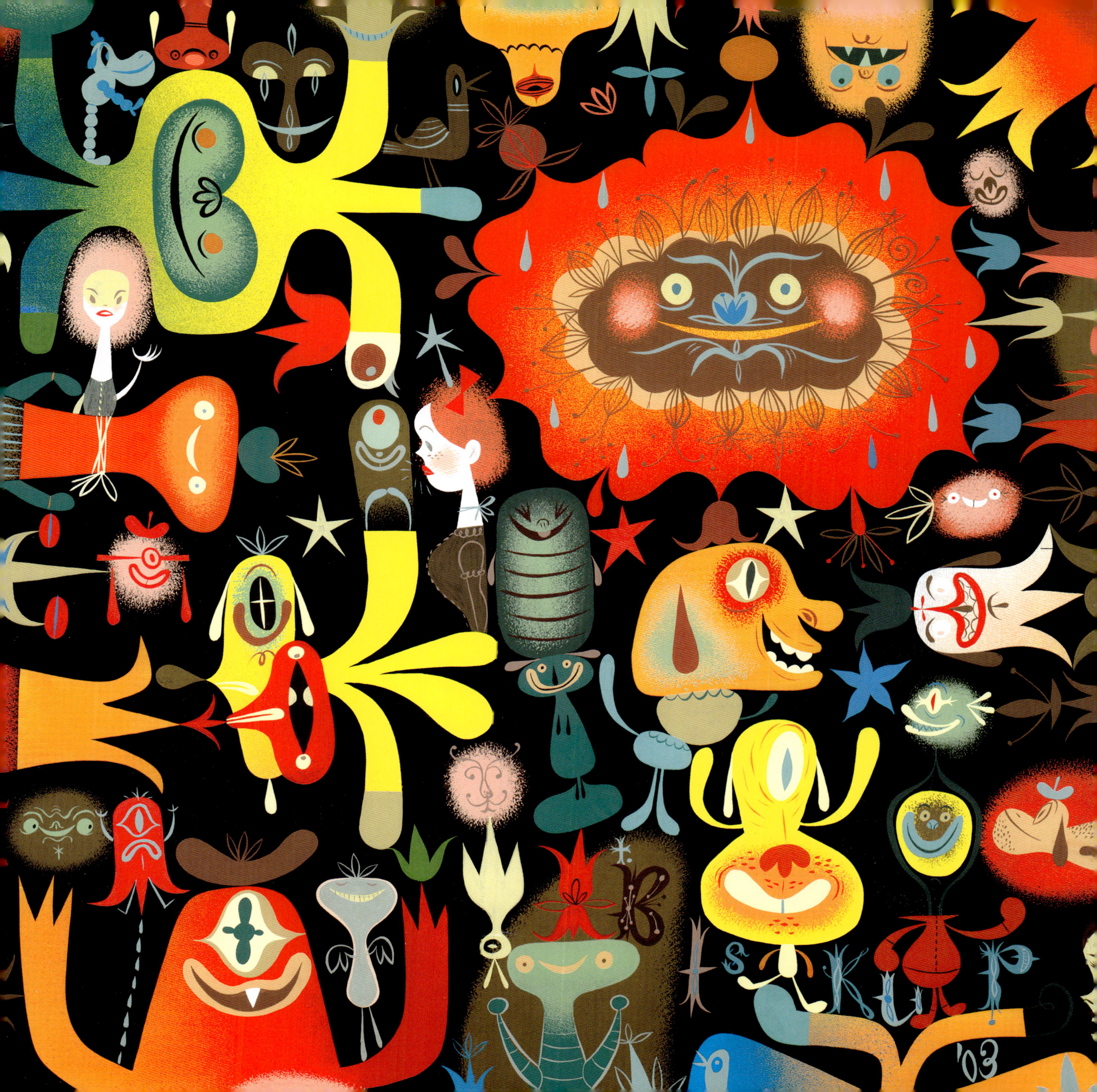
'03

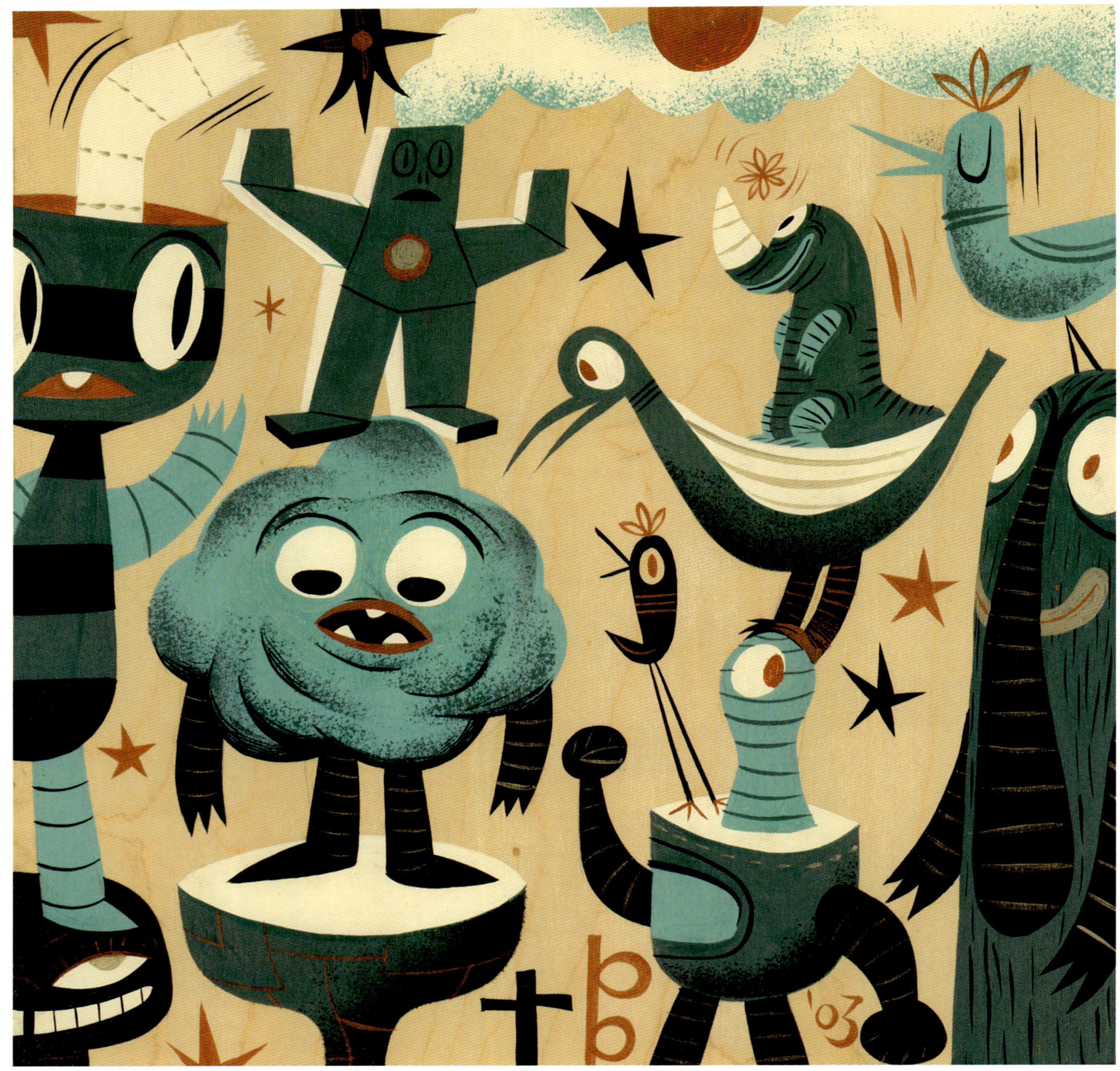


ALPHABESTIARY

2003, acrylic on wooden panel, 8" x 8"

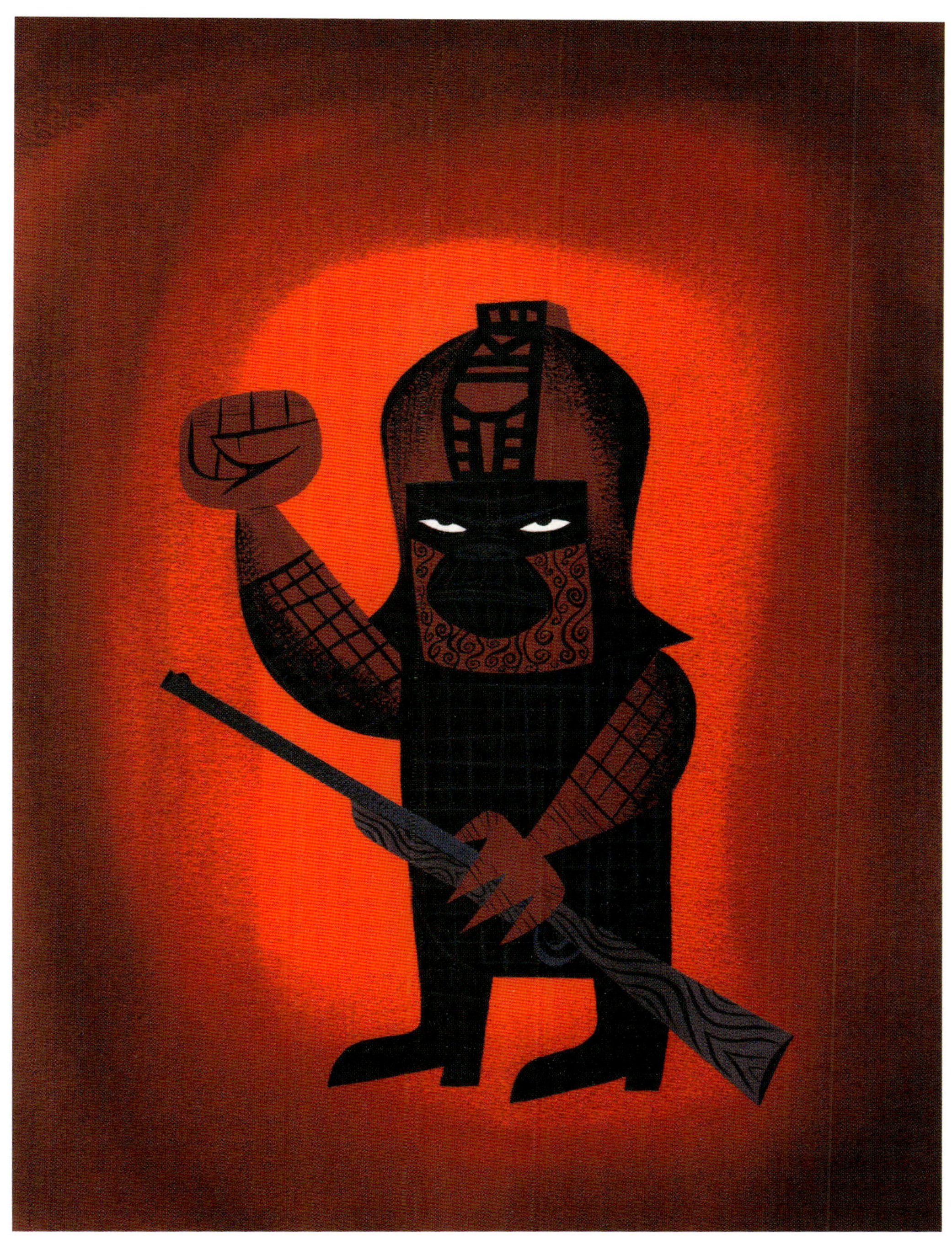

2001, gouache on paper, 14" x 11"

Ape Power

# Kalynn CAMPBELL

(Los Angeles, California)

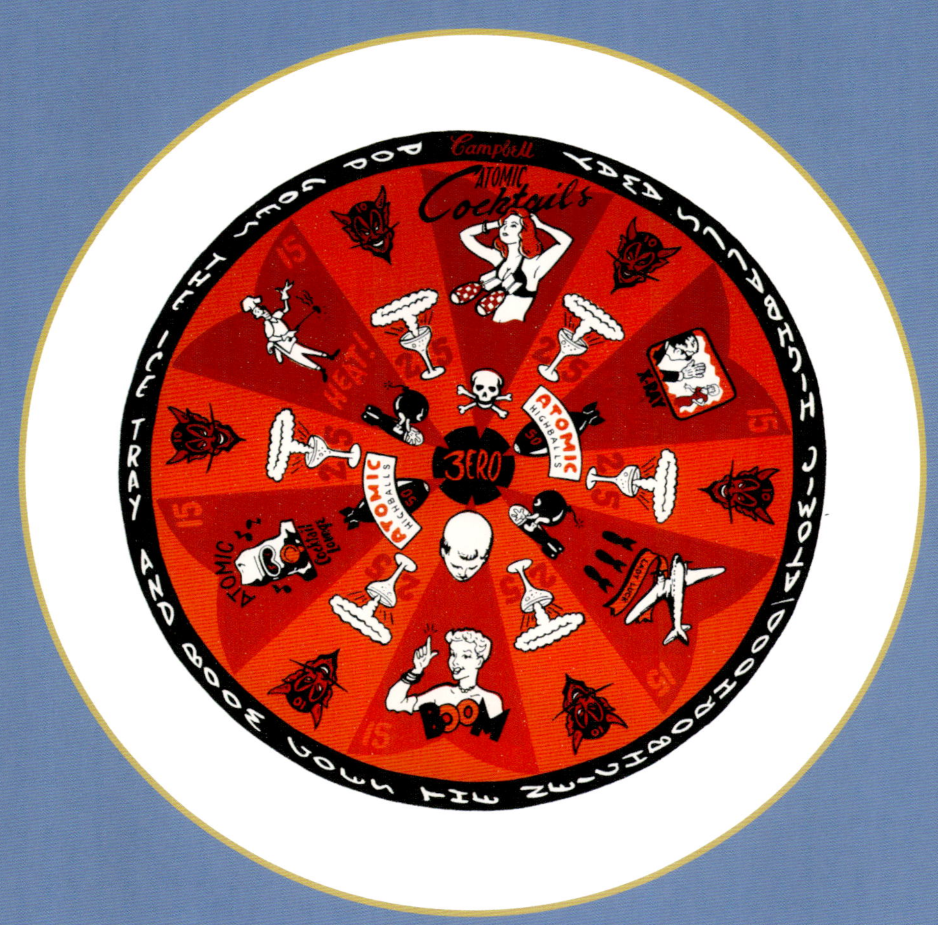


ATOMIC COCKTAILS

1991, serigraph, 20" round

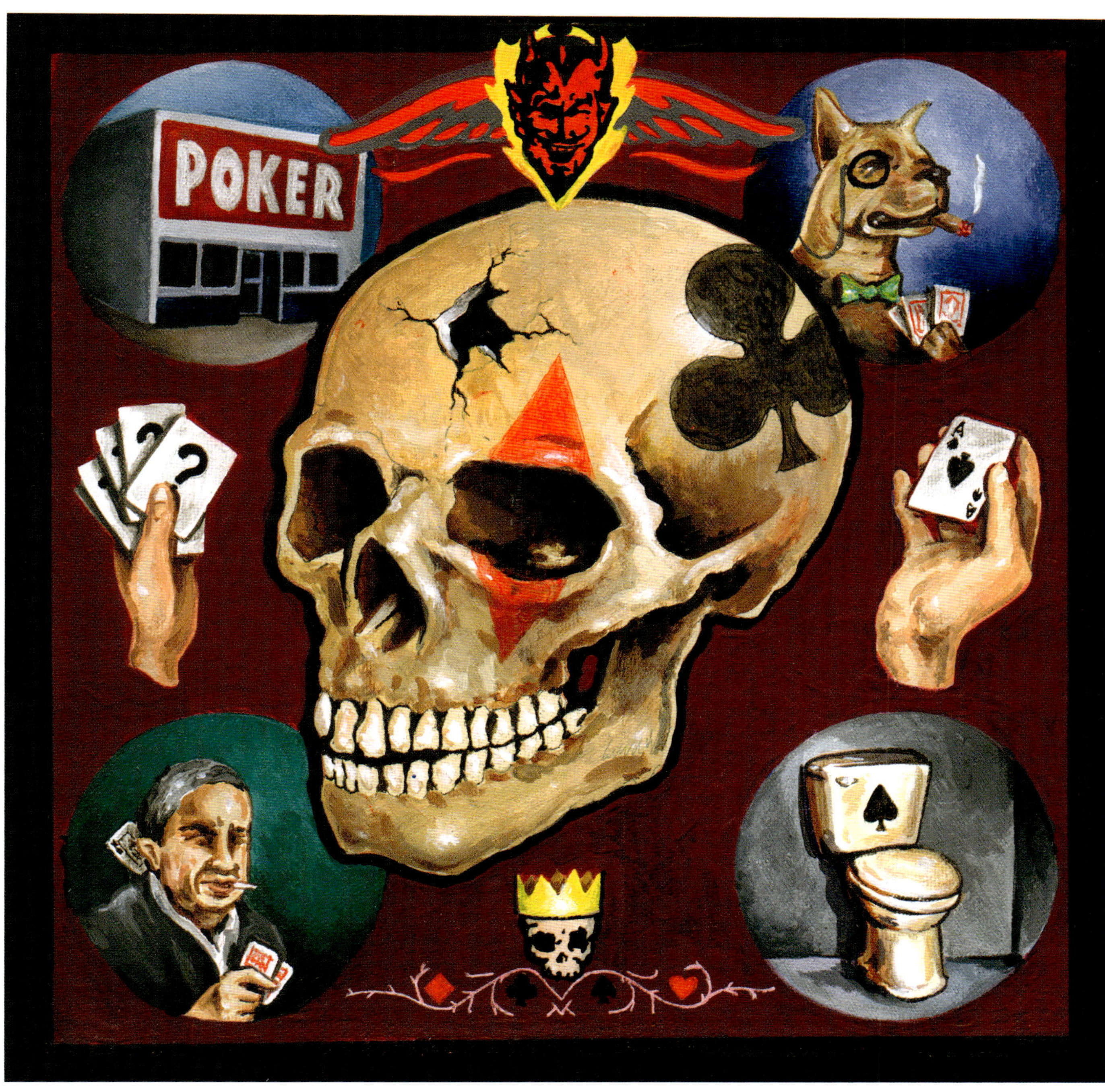


2000, acrylic on canvas, 12" x 12"

ROYAL FLUSH

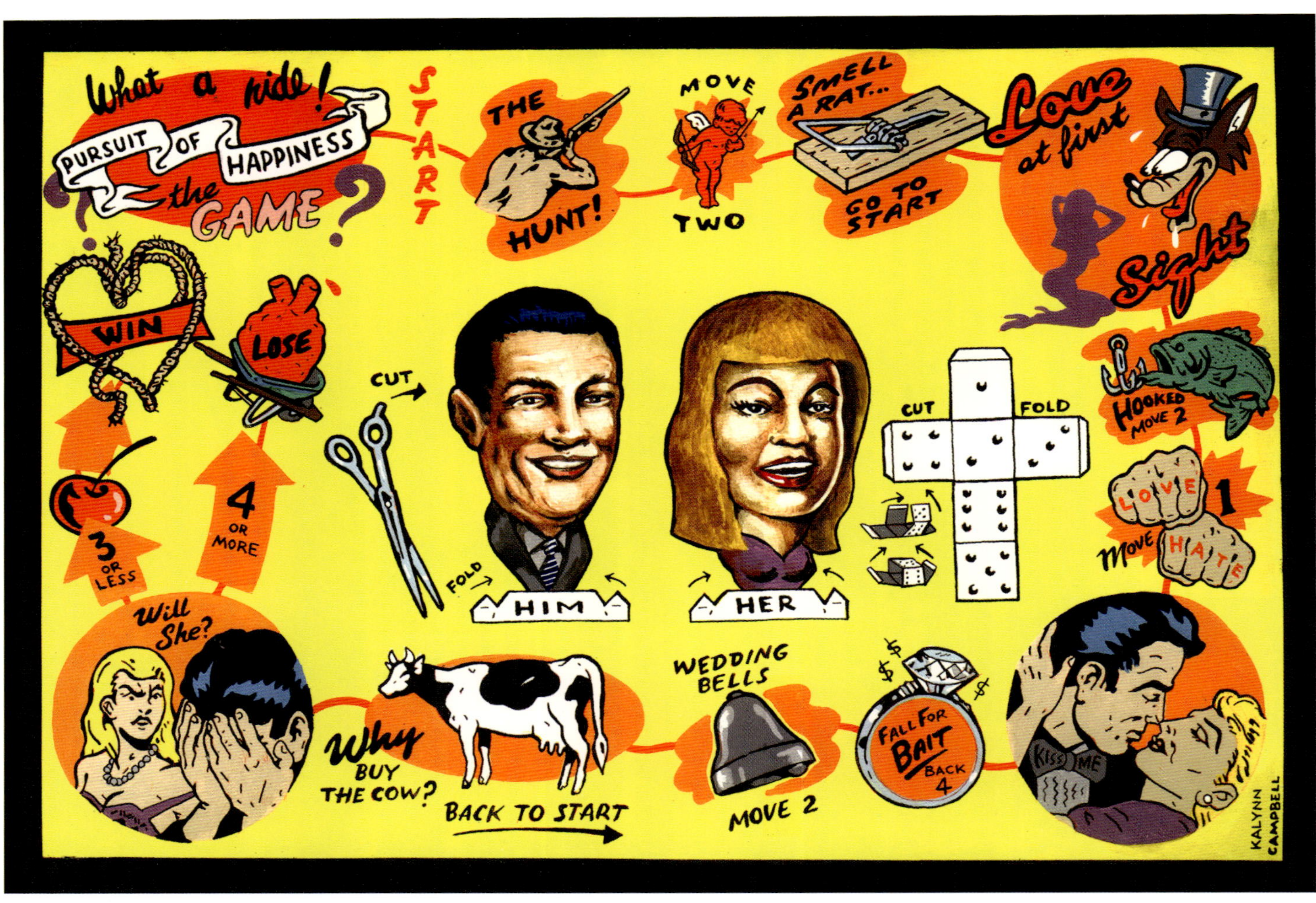


Happiness Game 2001, gouache and ink on board, 12" x 17"

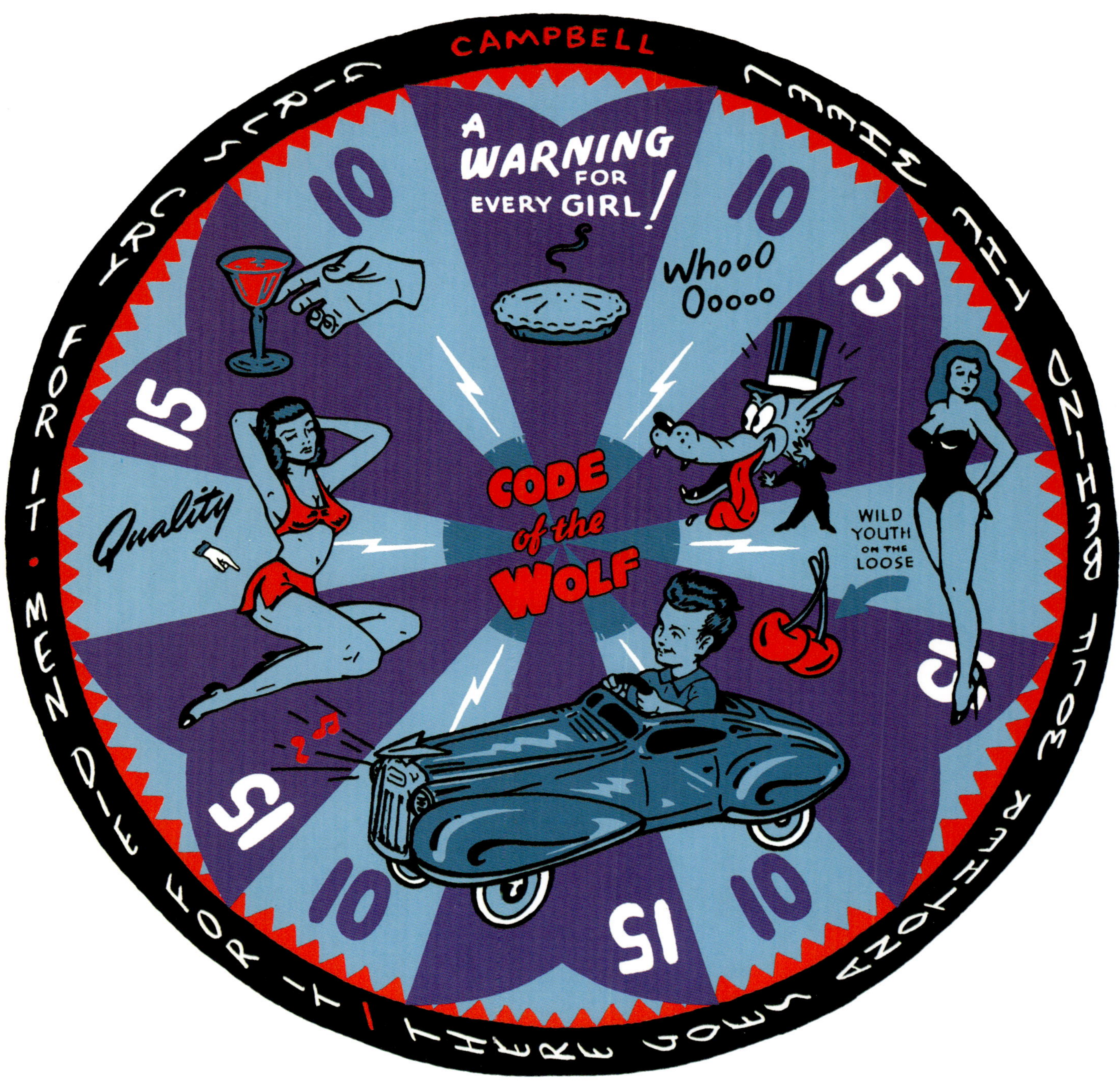


2003, serigraph, 20" round

LURE OF THE WOLF MOBILE

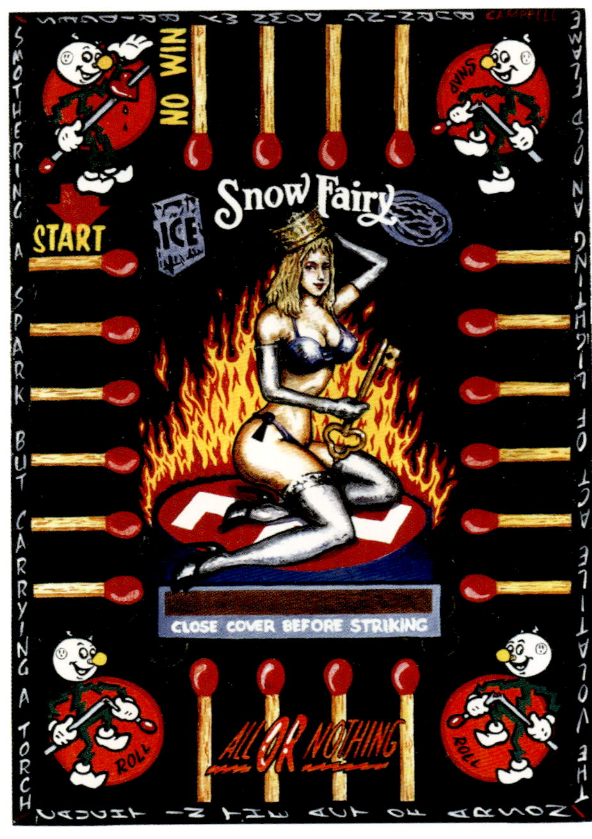


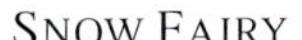
SNOW FAIRY 1994, oil on wood, 24" x 16"

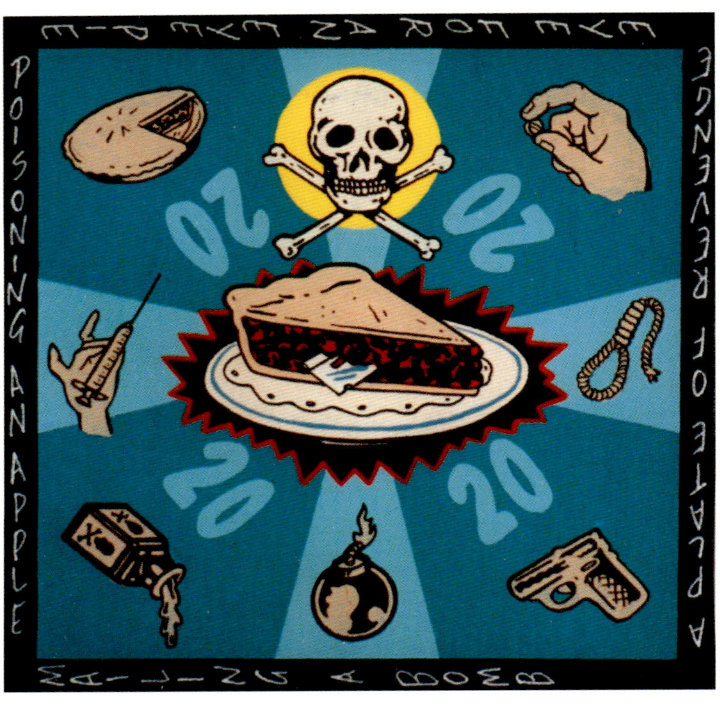


EYE 4 AN EYE PIE 2000, acrylic on canvas, 12" x 12"

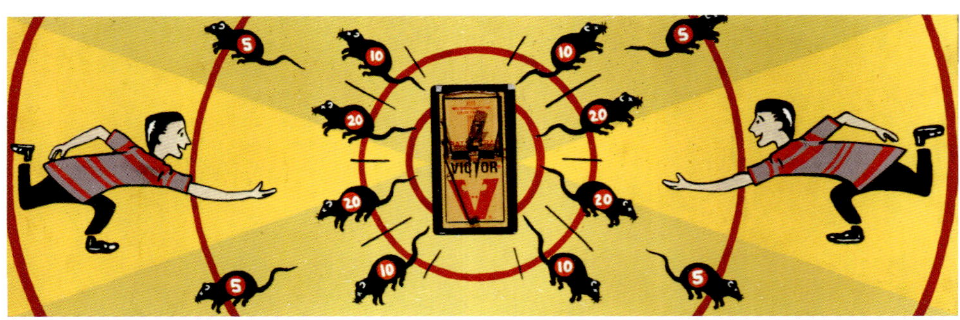


BOWLING FOR RODENTS 1993, acrylic on wood, found rat trap, 16" x 48"

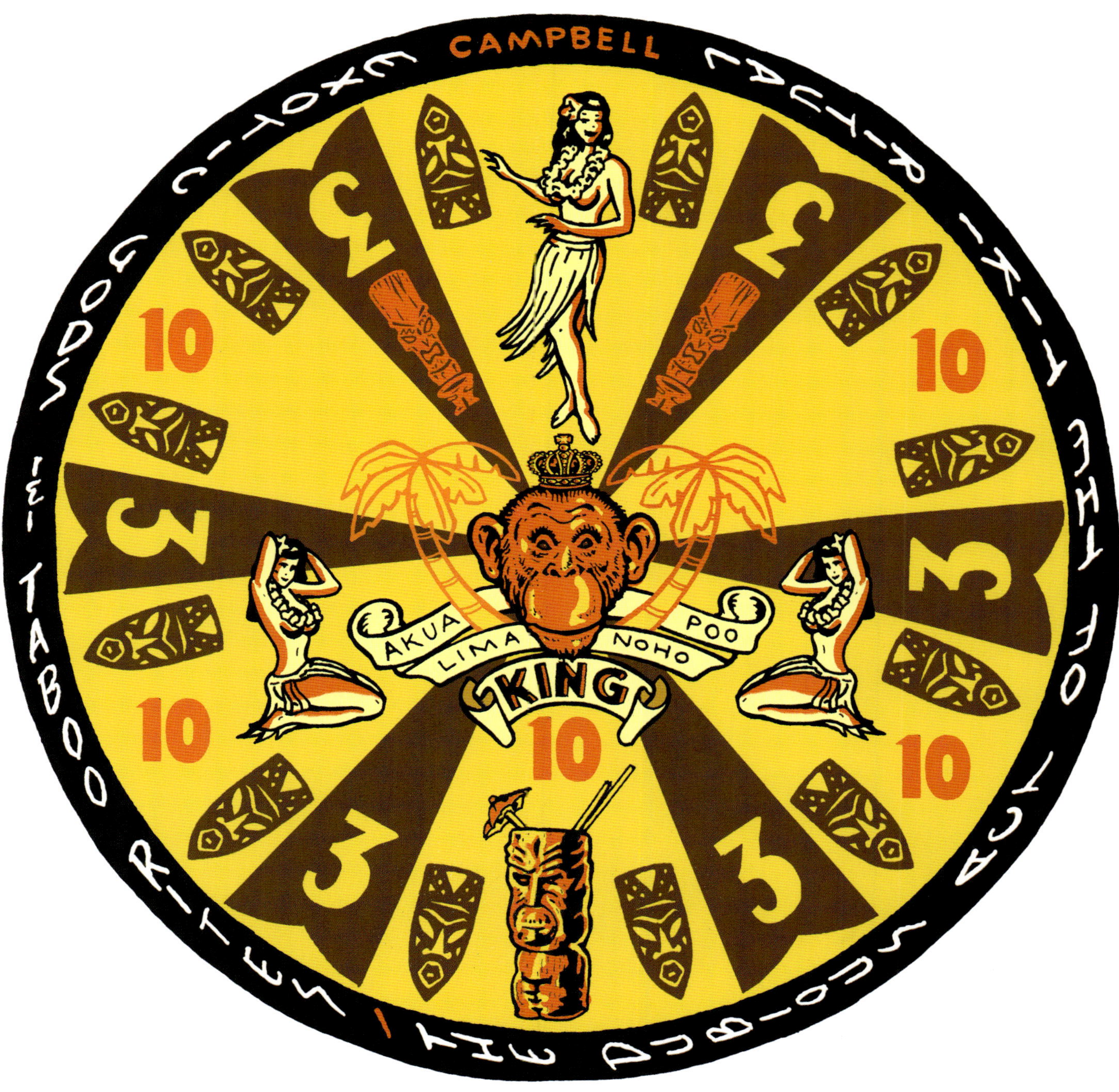


2000, serigraph, 20" round

# THE CLAYTON Brothers

(Los Angeles, California)

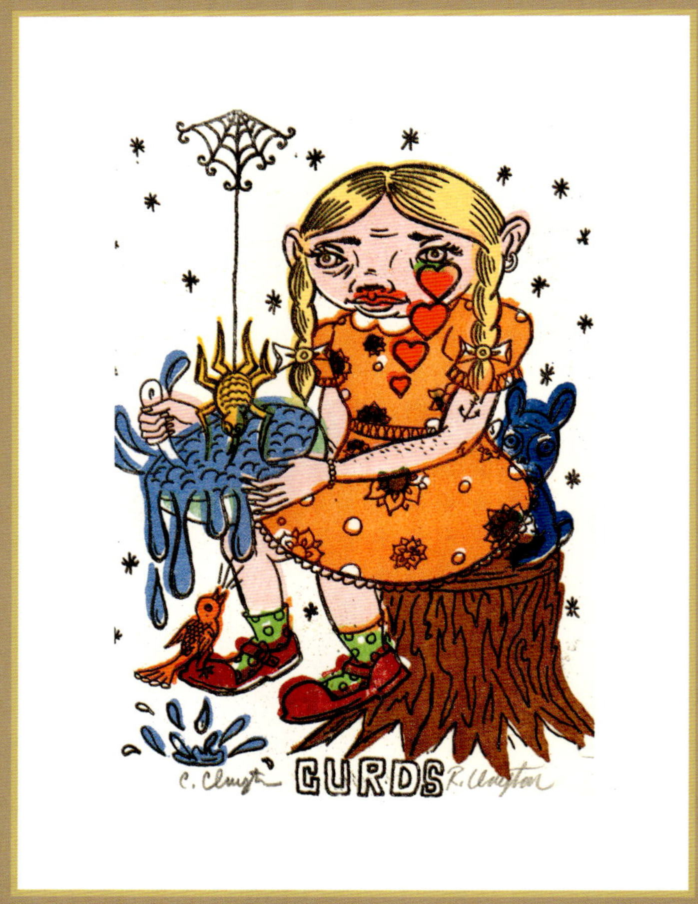


CURDS 2003, silkscreen (edition of 40), 4" x 6"

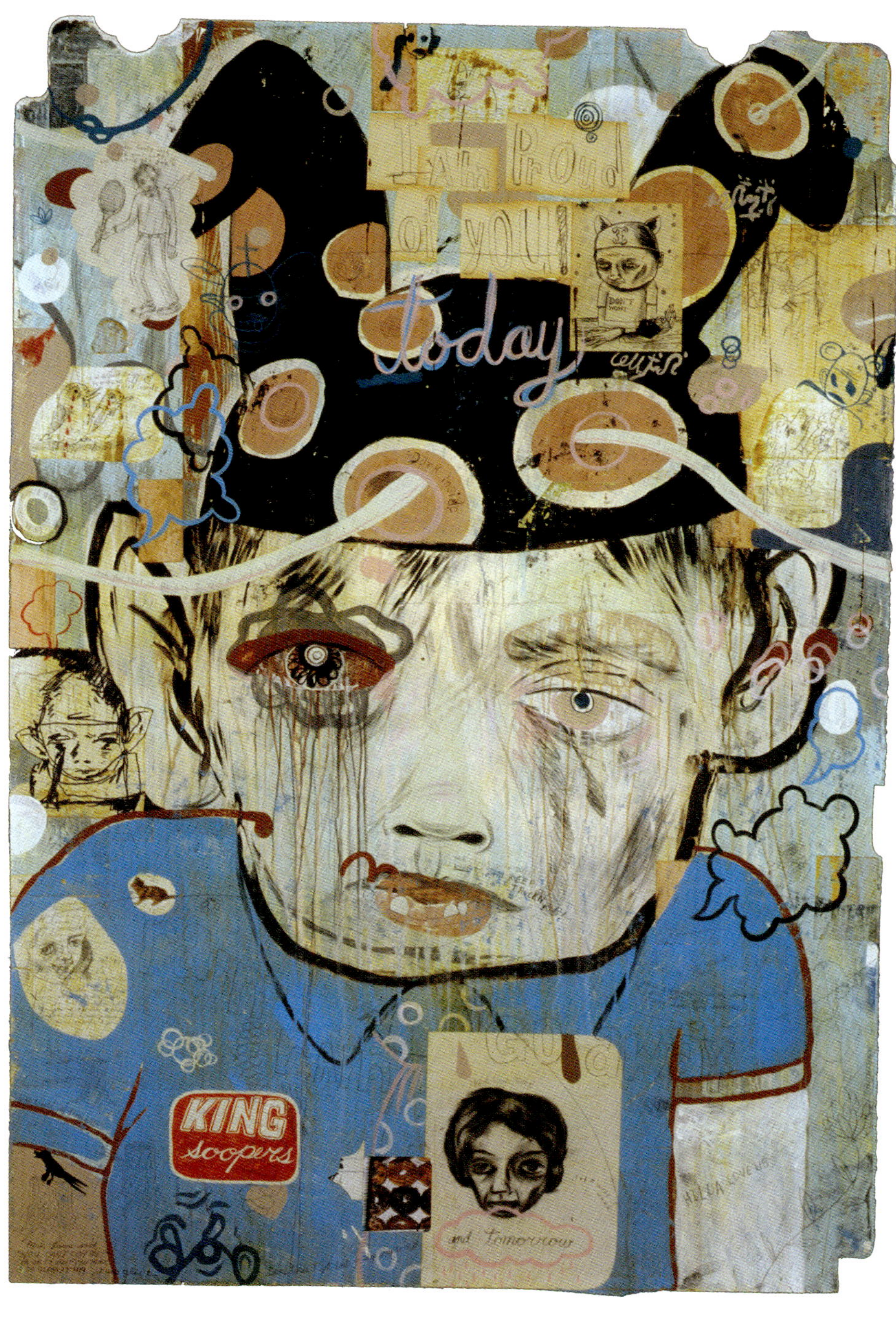




2003, mixed media on paper, 46.5" x 66"

I AM PROUD OF YOU TODAY

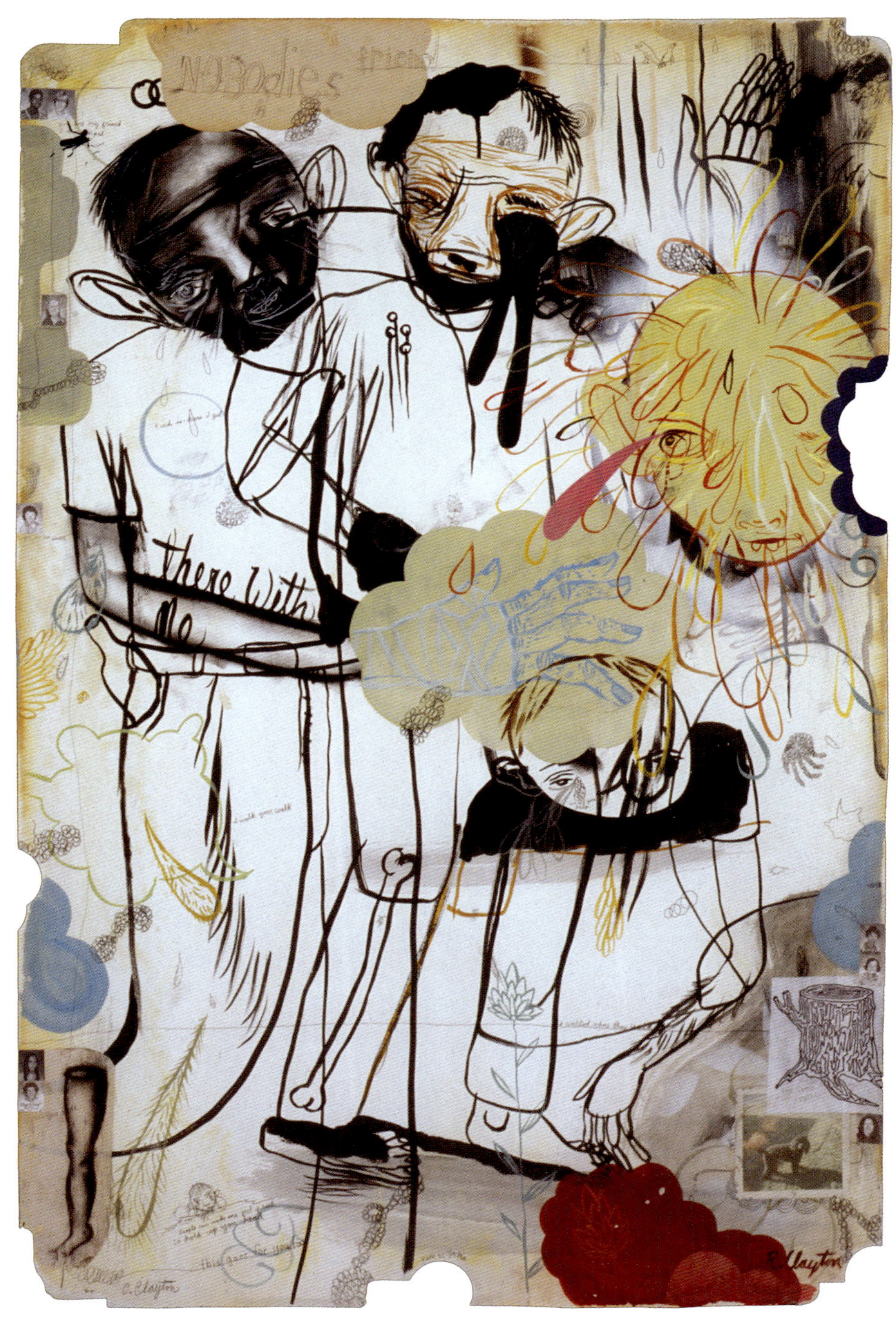


NOBODY'S FRIEND 2003, mixed media on paper, 27.75" x 39.75"

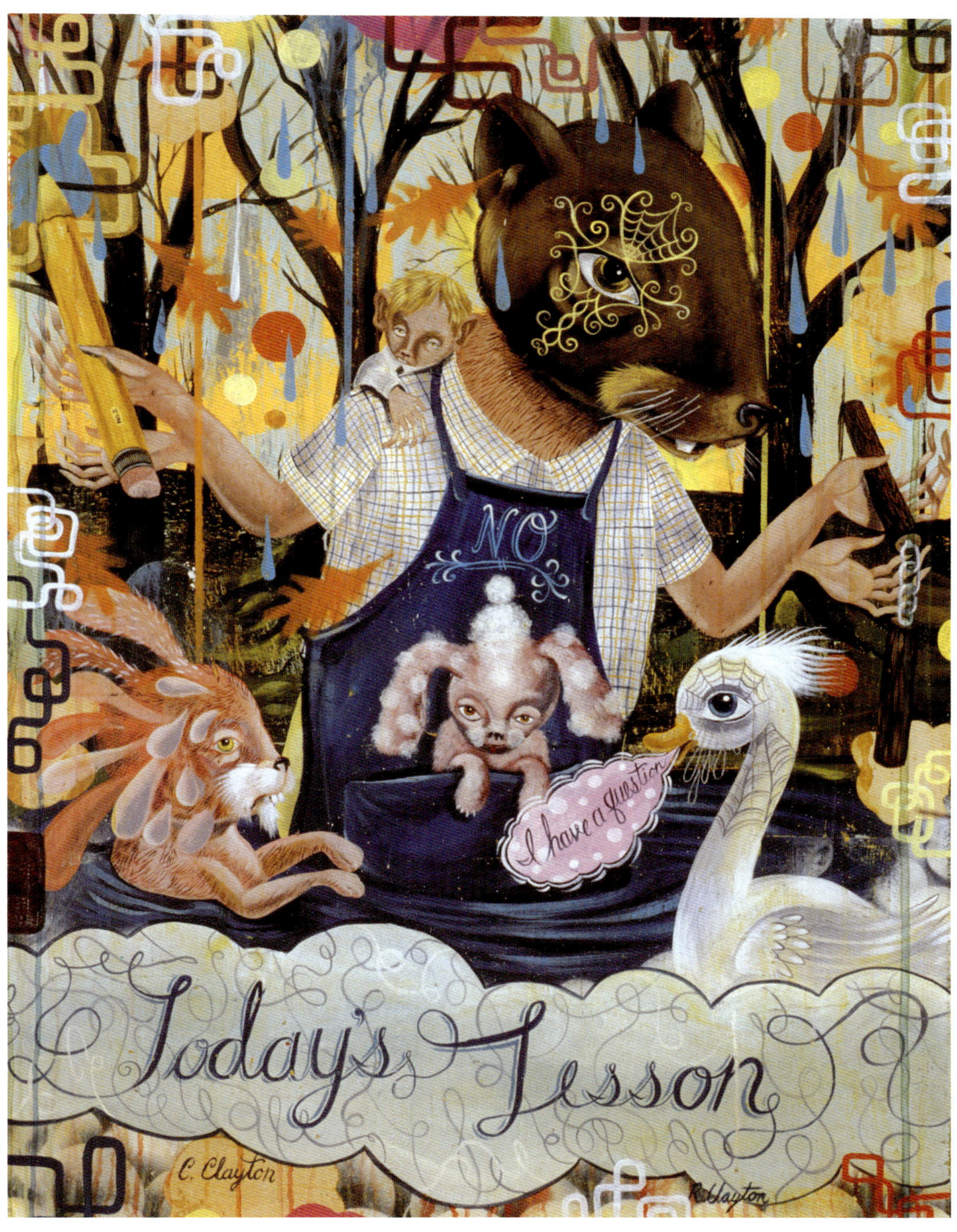


2003, mixed media on canvas, 30" x 40"

TODAY'S LESSON

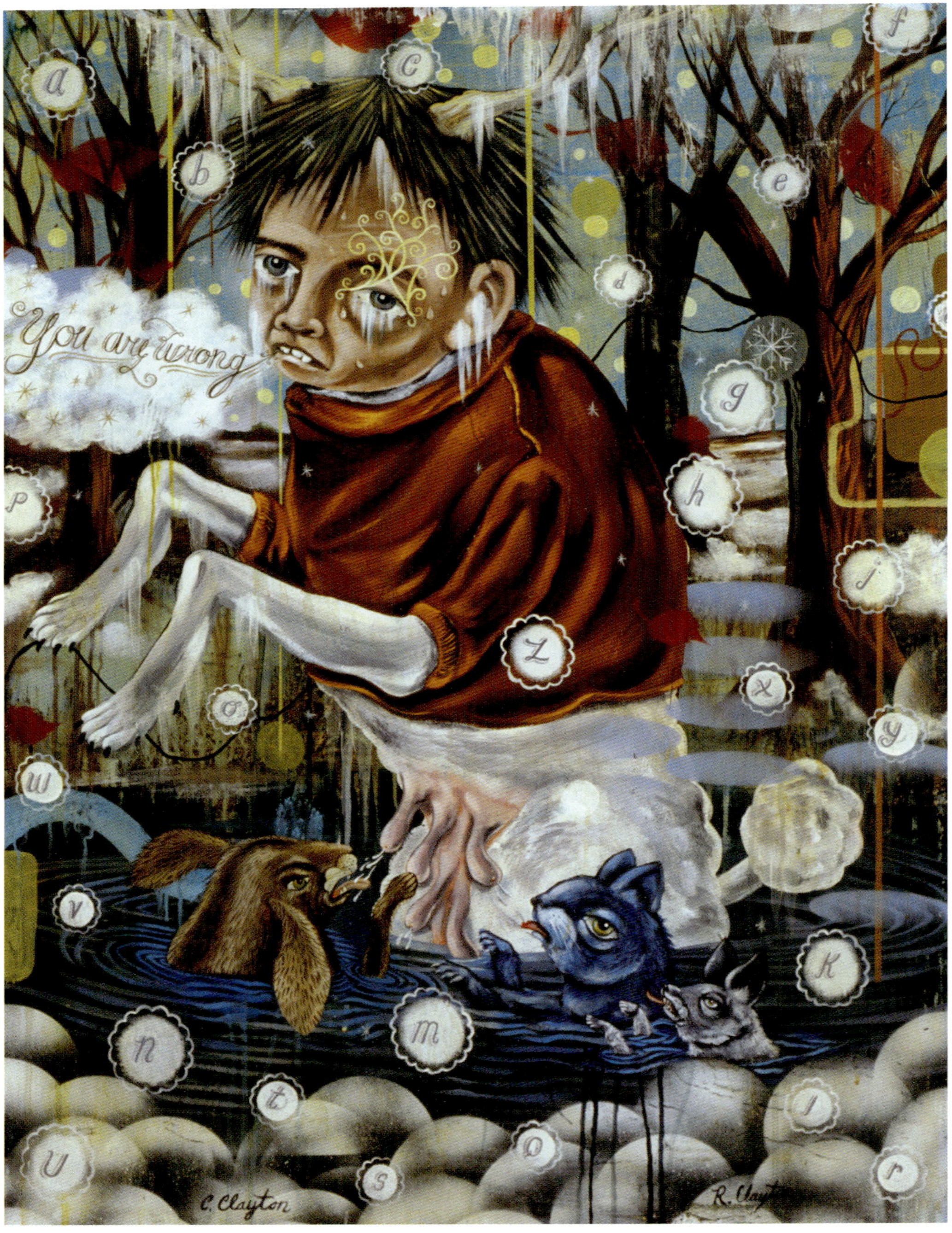


YOU ARE WRONG 2003, mixed media on canvas, 30" x 40"

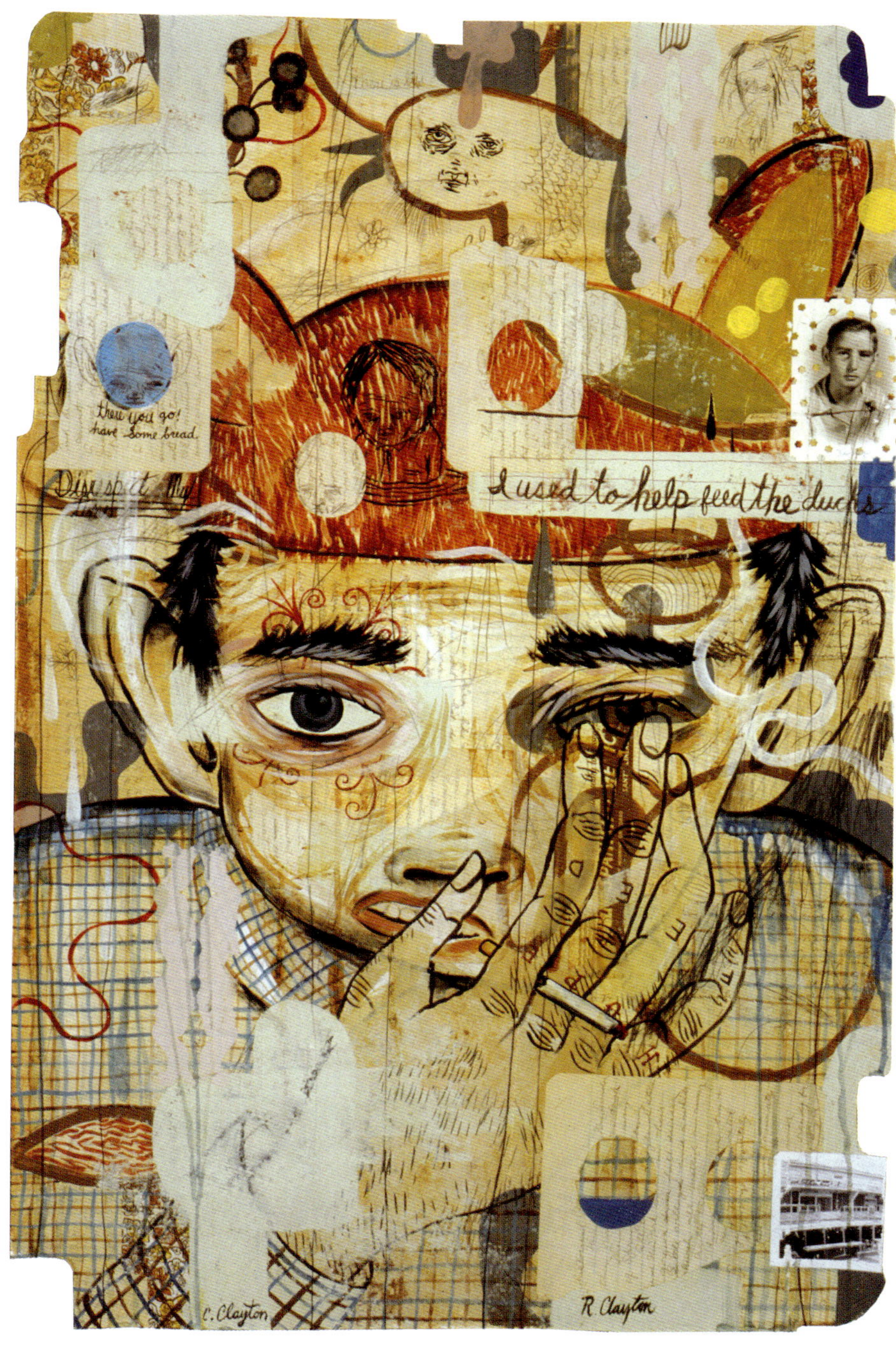


2003, mixed media on paper, 27.75" x 39.75" I USED TO HELP FEED THE DUCKS

Joe

# COLEMAN

(New York City, New York)

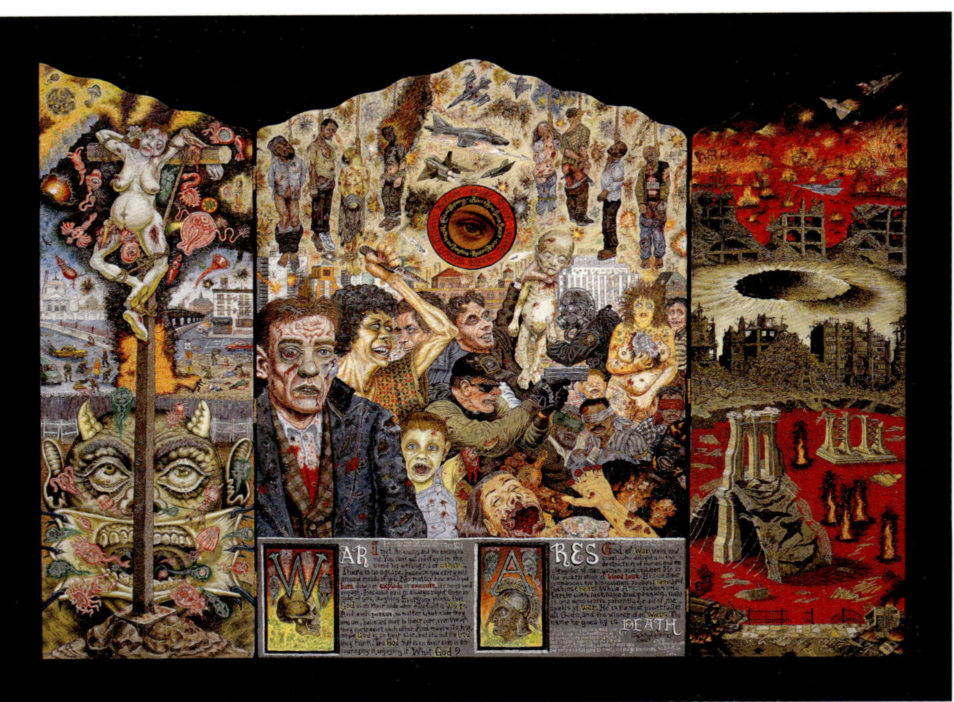


WAR TRIPTYCH

2003, acrylic on panel, 28" x 20"

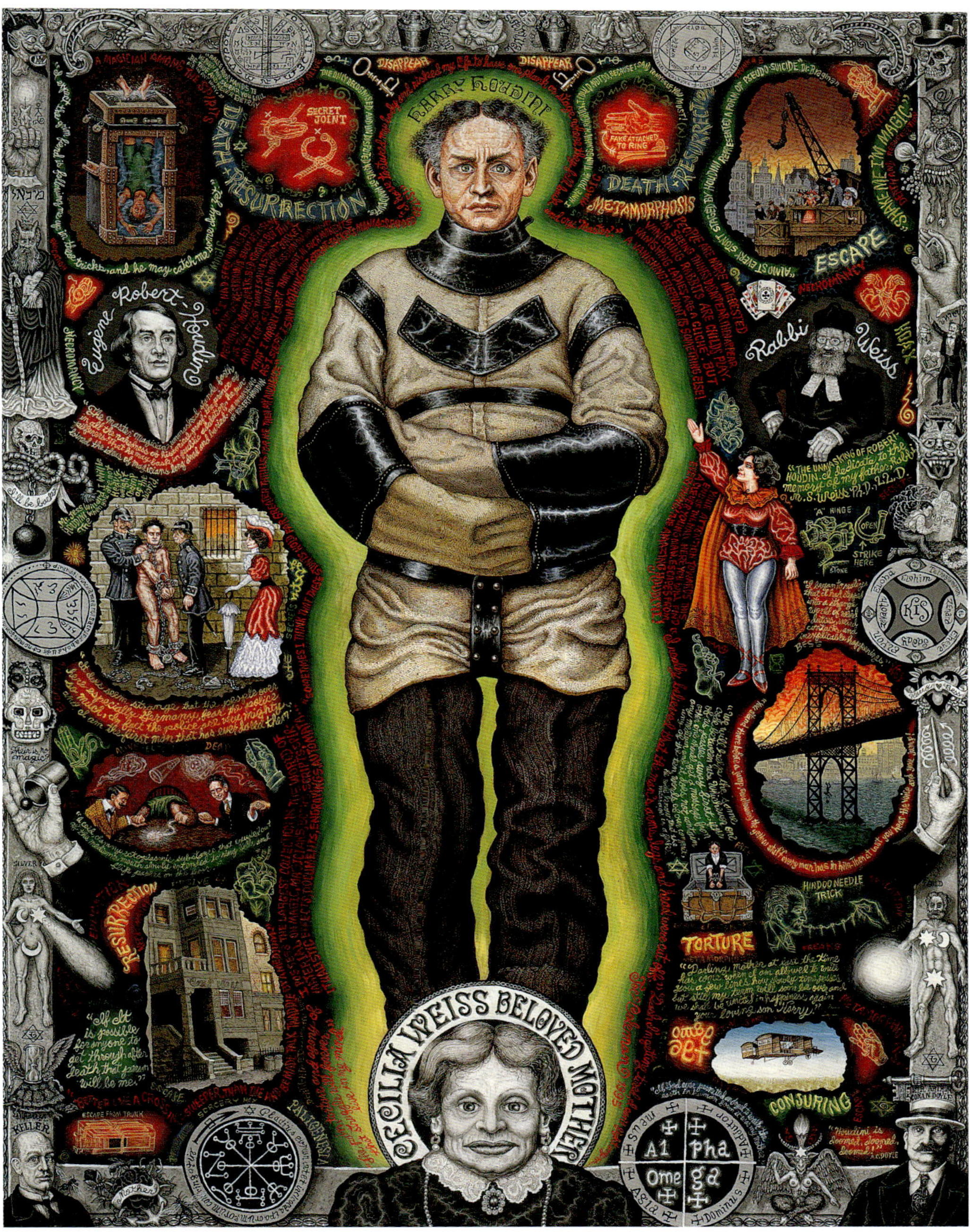


THE MAN WHO WALKED THROUGH WALLS

1995, acrylic on panel, mounted on priest's robe worn by Coleman during a live performance, 28" x 22"

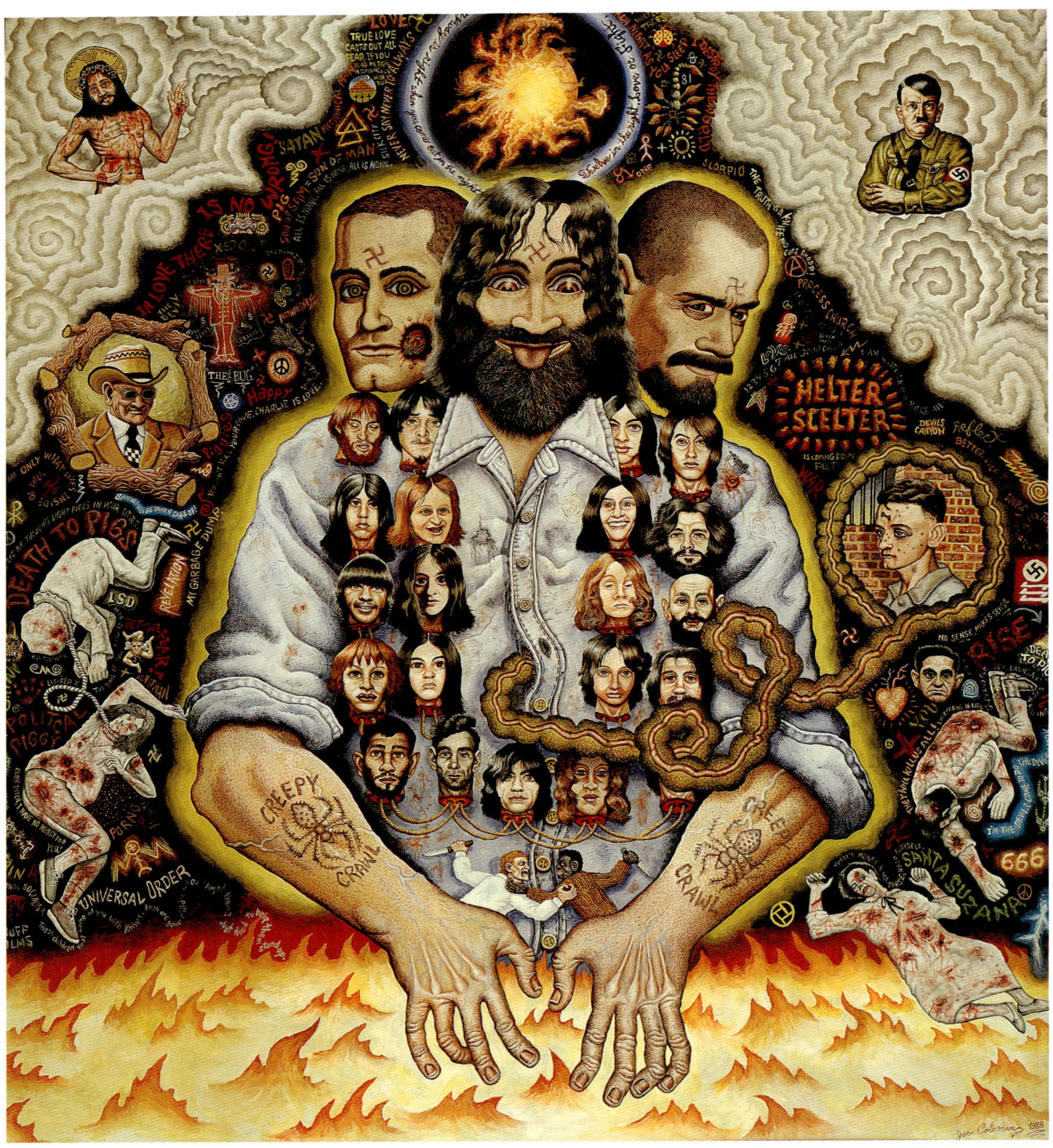


PORTRAIT OF CHARLES MANSON

1988, acrylic on wood, 50" x 44"

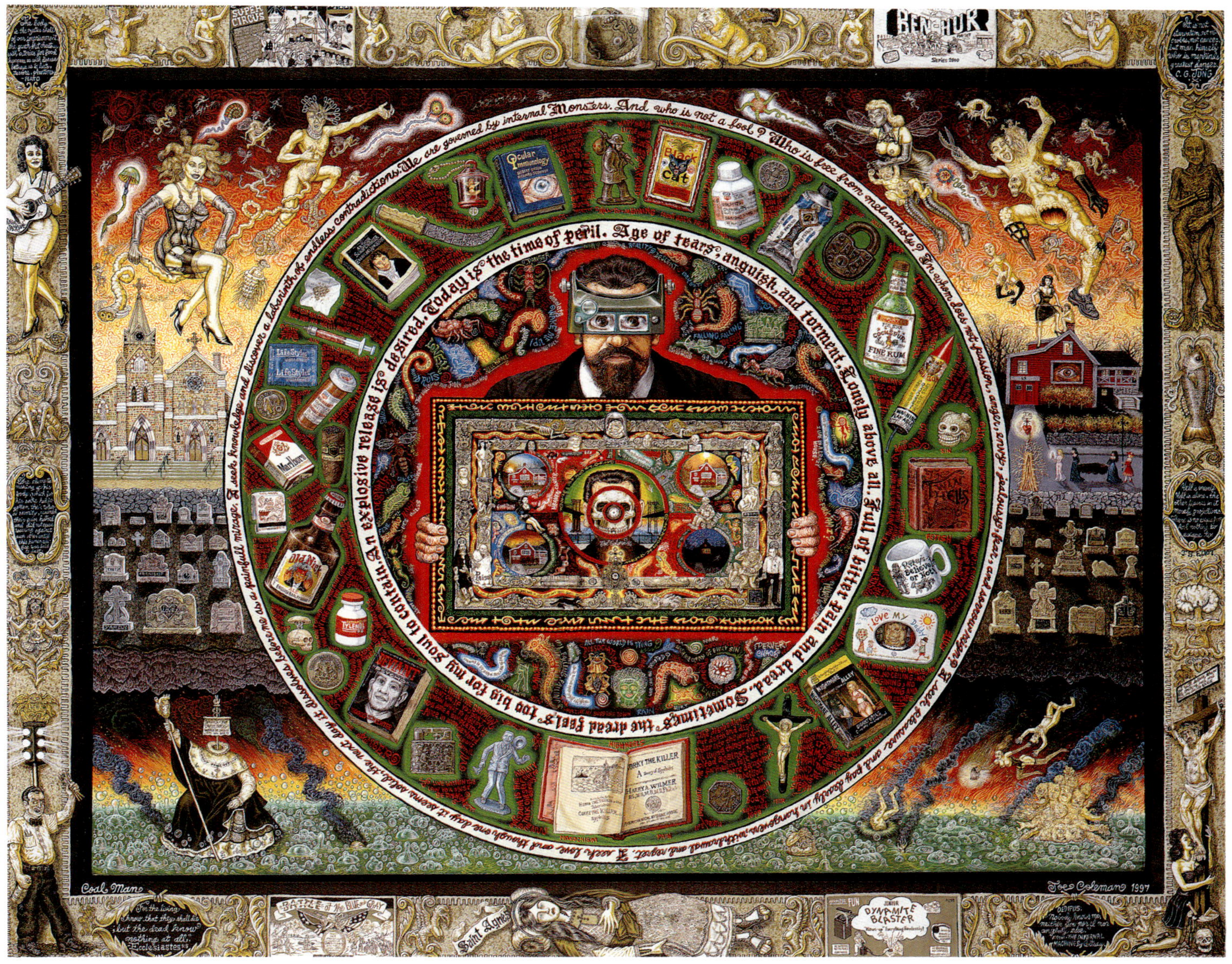


1997, acrylic on panel, 28" x 34"

COAL MAN

In the Realm of the Unreal
1998, acrylic on panel, mounted on a child's pajamas,
28" x 34"

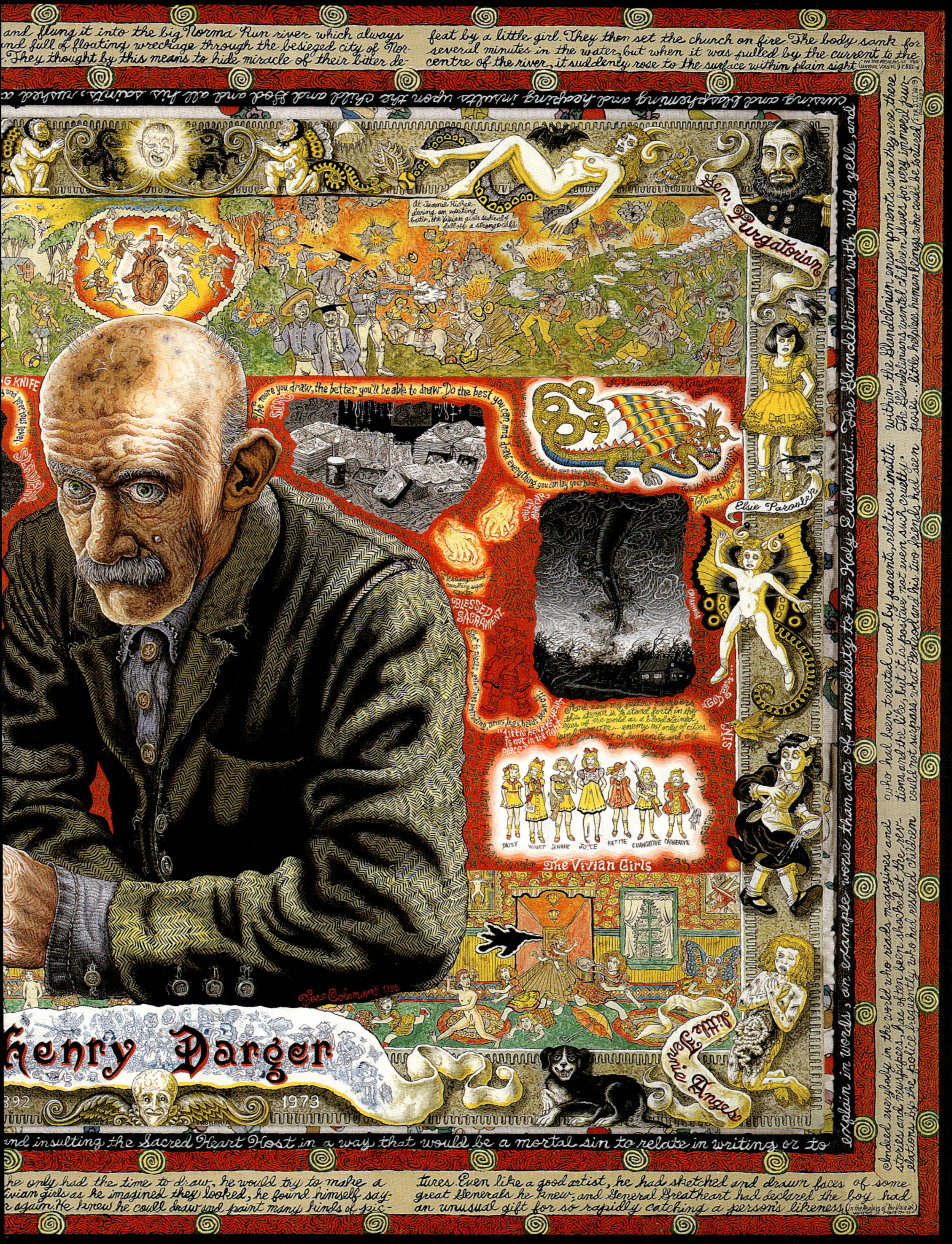

and flung it into the big Norma Run river which always
and full of floating wreckage through the besieged city of Nor-
They thought by this means to hide miracle of their bitter de-
feat by a little girl. They then set the church on fire. The body sank for
several minutes in the water, but when it was pulled by the current to the
centre of the river, it suddenly rose to the surface within plain sight

Gen. Purgatorian

The more you draw, the better you'll be able to draw. Do the best you can and draw everything you can lay your hands on

Elsie Paroubek

DAISY VIOLET JENNIE JOYCE HETTIE EVANGELINE CATHERINE

The Vivian Girls

Henry Darger

1973

and insulting the Sacred Heart Host in a way that would be a mortal sin to relate in writing or to

he only had the time to draw, he would try to make a
Vivian girls as he imagined they looked, he found himself say-
again. He knew he could draw and paint many kinds of pictures. Even like a good artist, he had sketched and drawn faces of some
great Generals he knew, and General Greatheart had declared the boy had
an unusual gift for so rapidly catching a person's likeness.

# Camille Rose
# GARCIA

(Los Angeles, California)

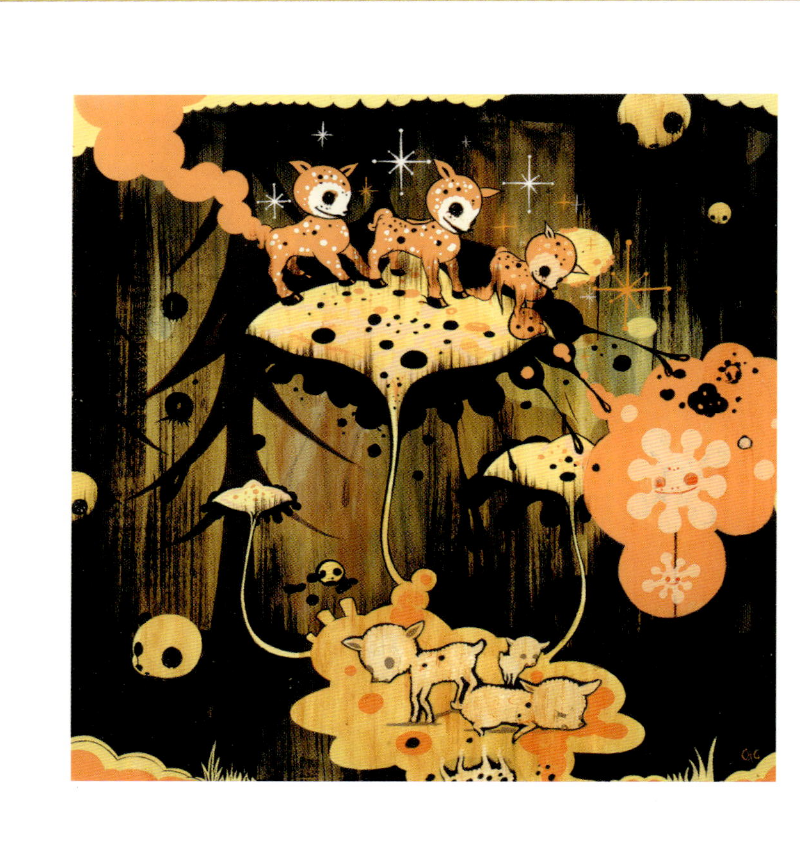

BUTTERCUP FARM BLOWUP 2001, acrylic and glitter on wood, 48" x 48"

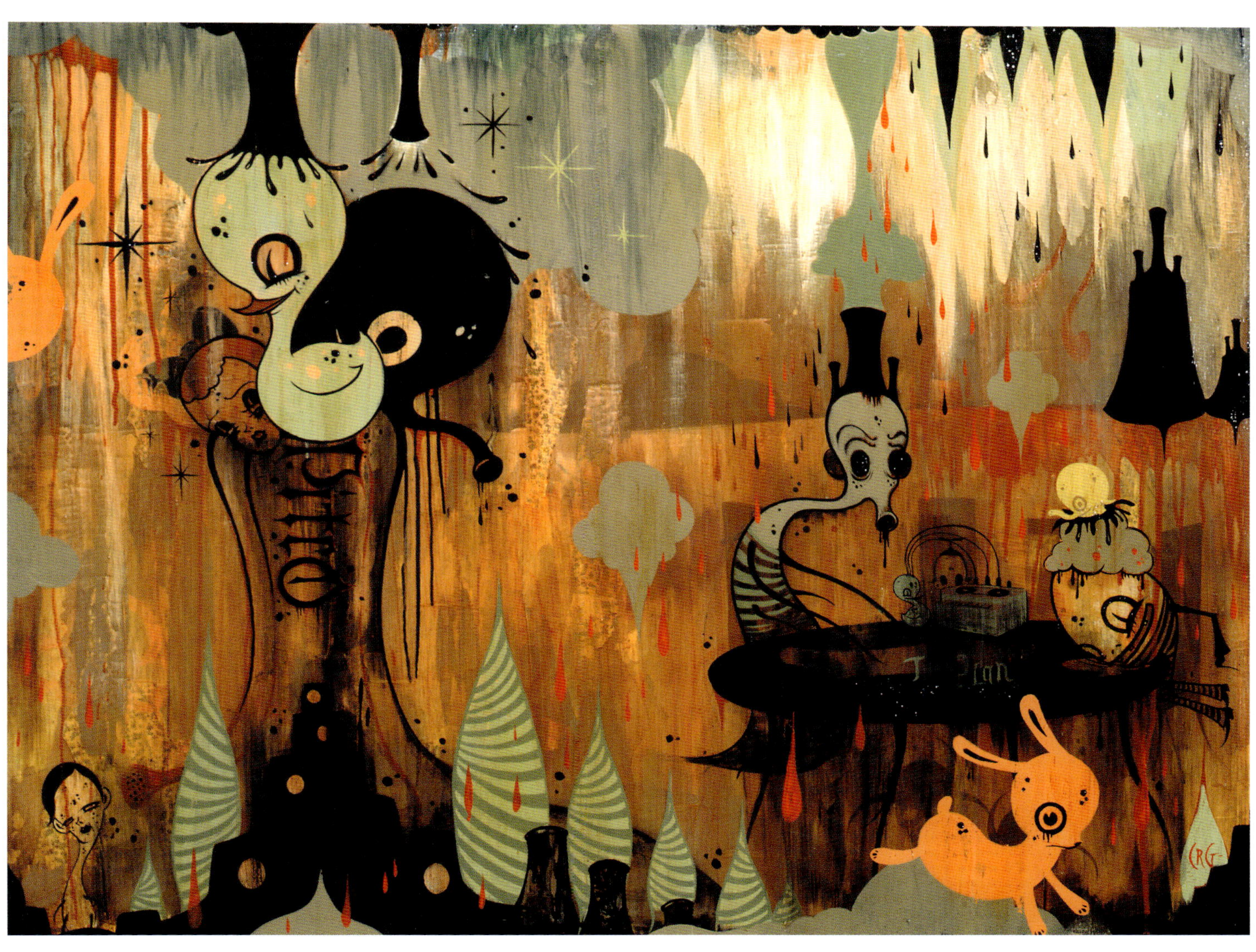


2003, acrylic and glitter on wood, 36" x 48"

THE PLAN

(opposite page) MARY READ AND HER MERMAID ARMY 2002, acrylic and glitter on wood, 36" x 48"

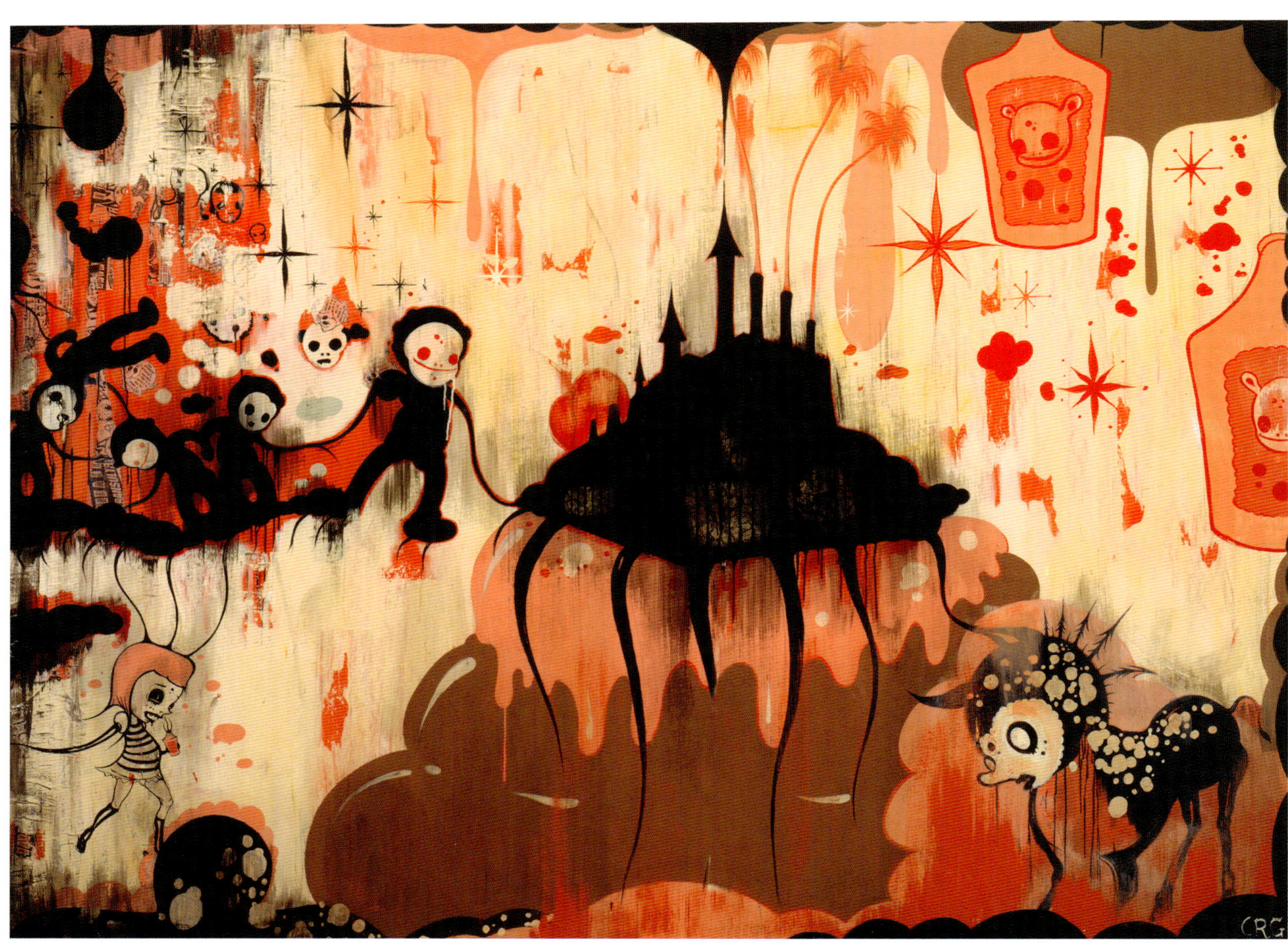



DREAM FACTORY ESCAPE POD

2001, acrylic and glitter on wood, 72" x 96"

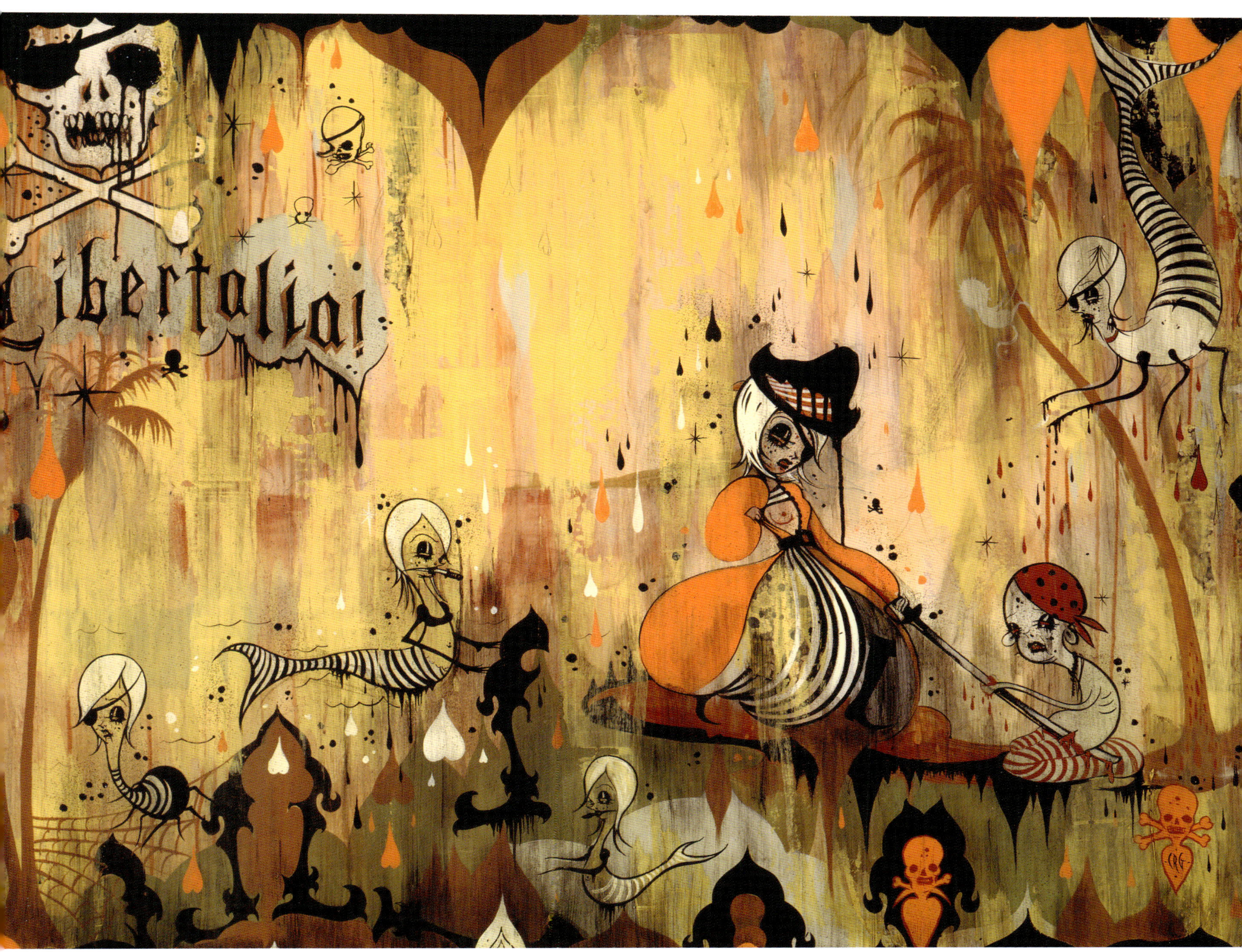
ibertalia!

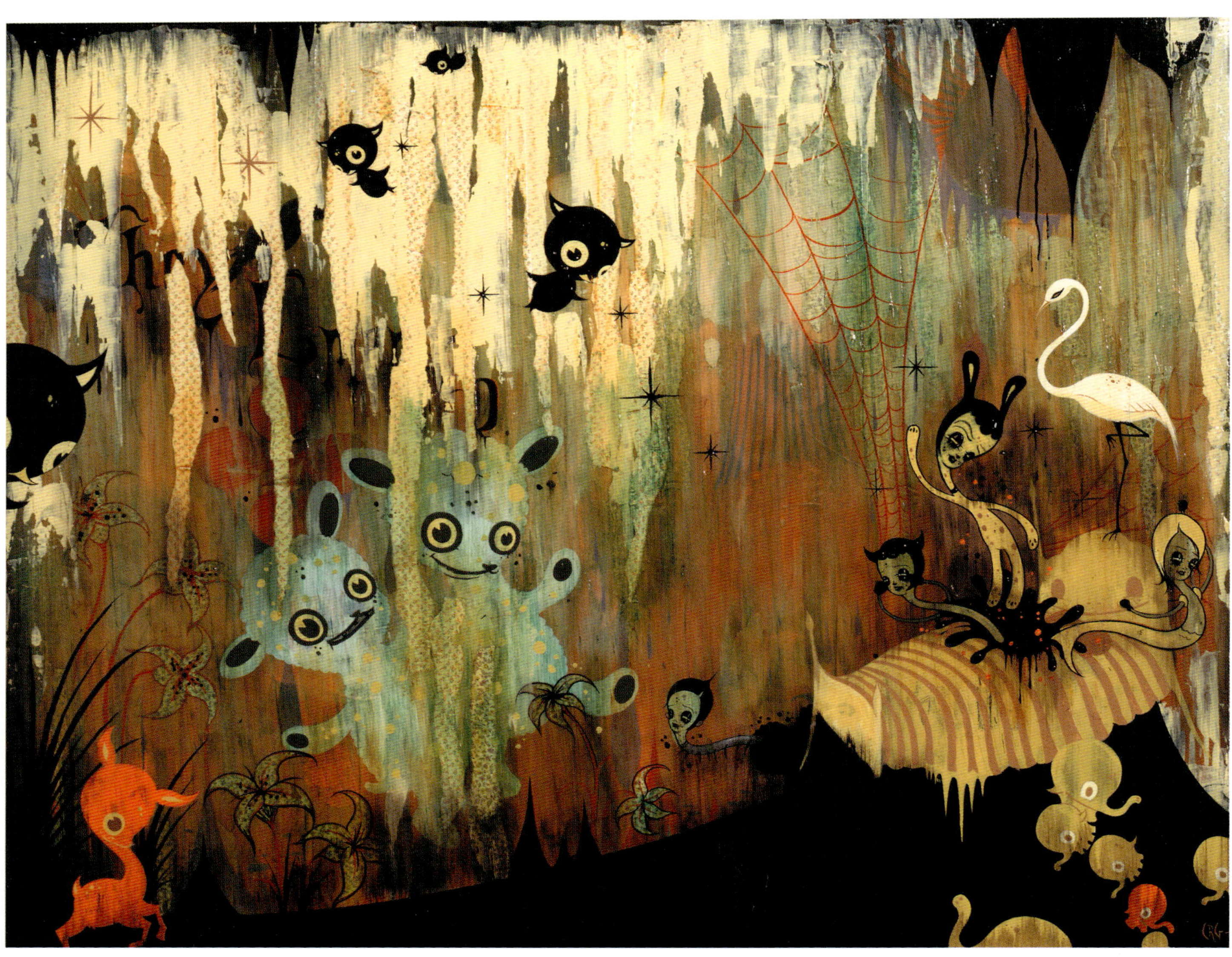

THEY EMERGED FROM A LONG SLUMBER

2003, acrylic and glitter on wood, 48" x 60"

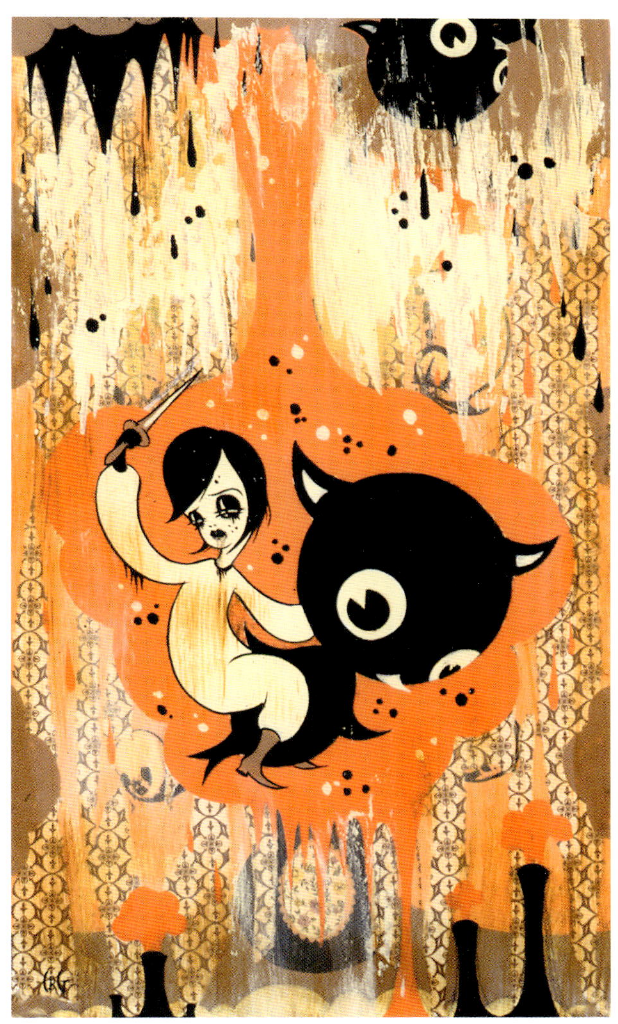

Ariel Forces
2003, acrylic and glitter on paper, 10" x 18"

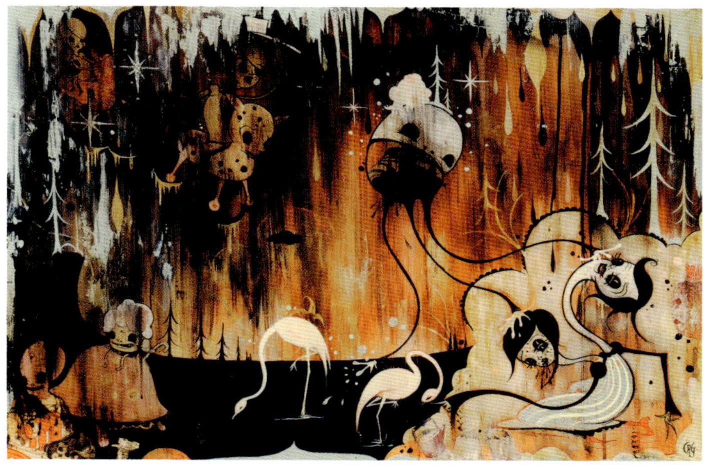

Uranium 238 Comes to Town
2003, acrylic and glitter on wood, 24" x 36"



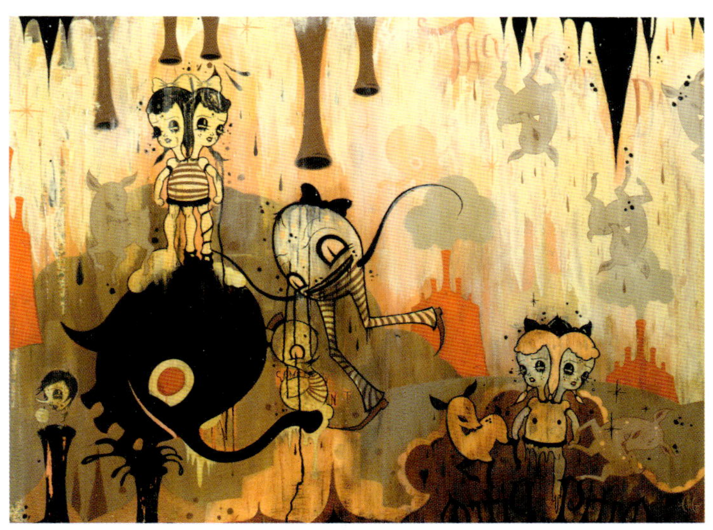

PITCO Production Plant
2003, acrylic and glitter on wood, 36" x 48"

# Alex GROSS

(Los Angeles, California)

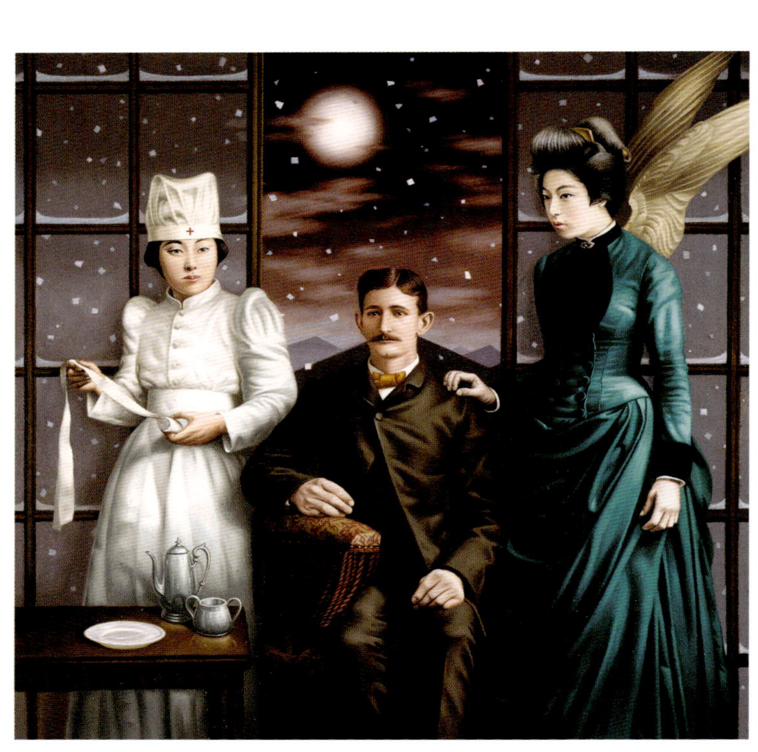

THE SUGAR SICKNESS 2002, oil on panel, 48" x 48"

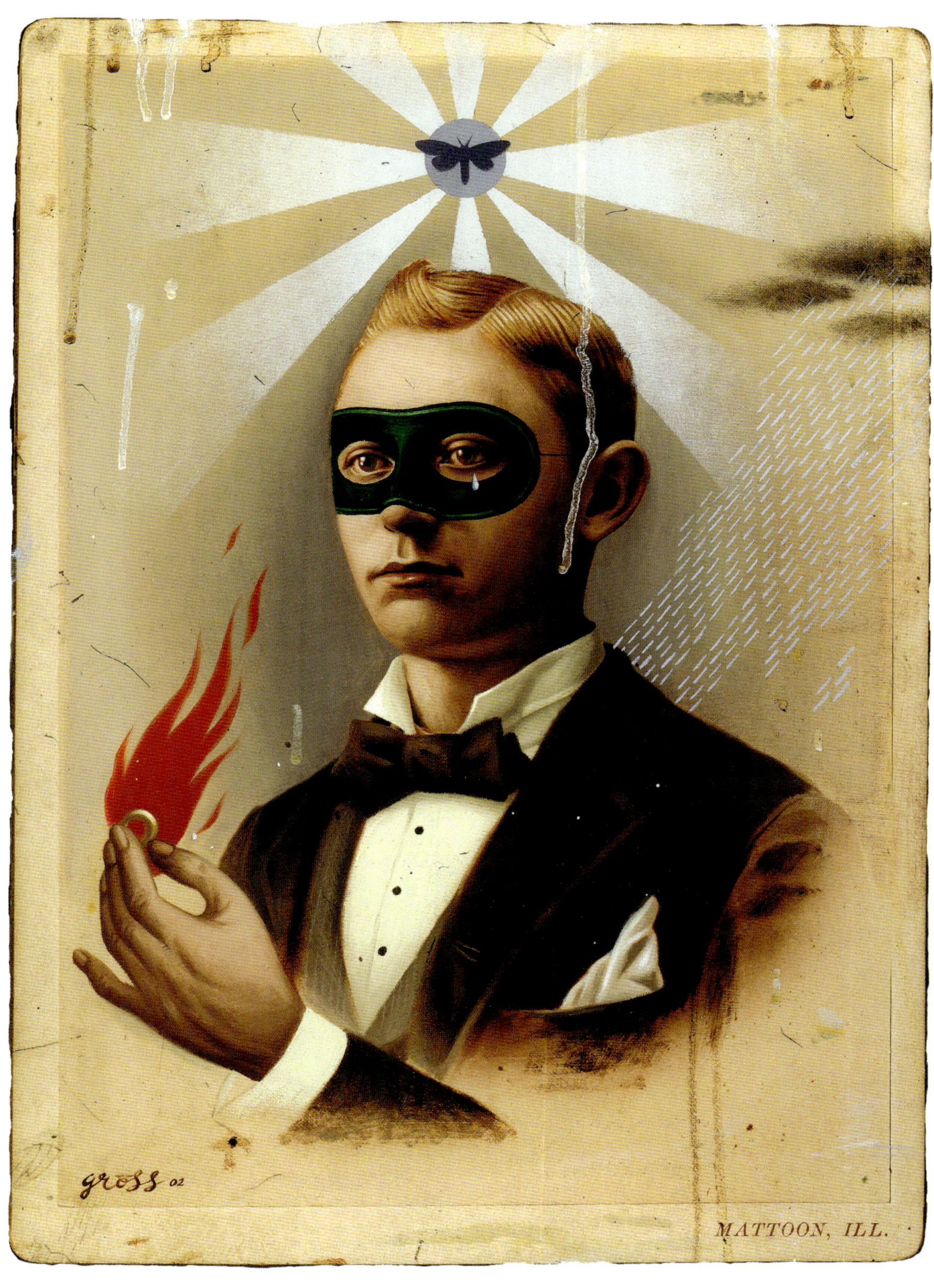


2002, mixed media, oil on paper

THE TRUE ORIGIN OF THE GREEN LANTERN

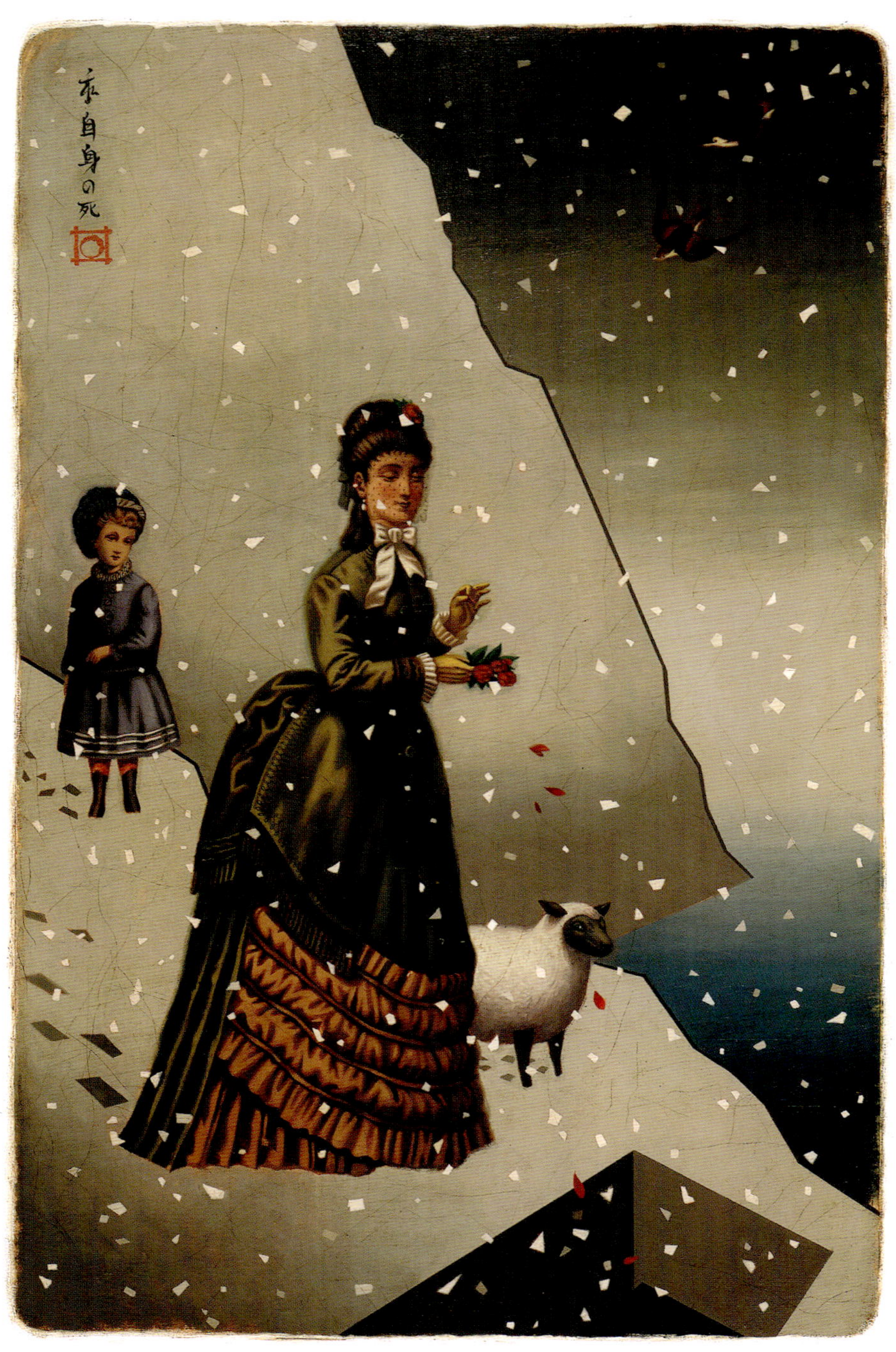


My Own Death 2002, mixed media, oil on panel, 42" x 29"

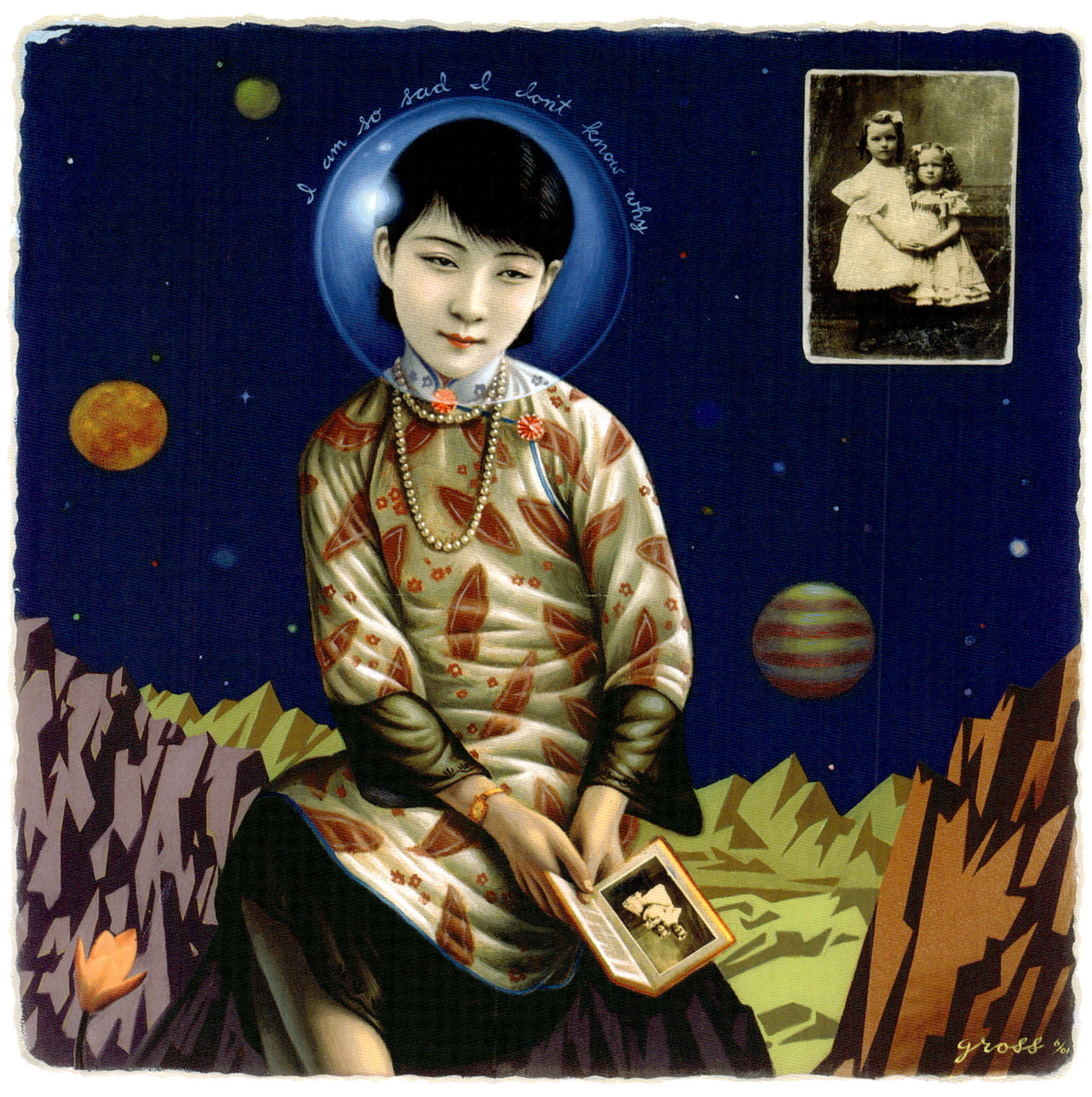


2002, mixed media, oil on paper, 18" x 18"

OUTER SPACE IS A LONELY PLACE

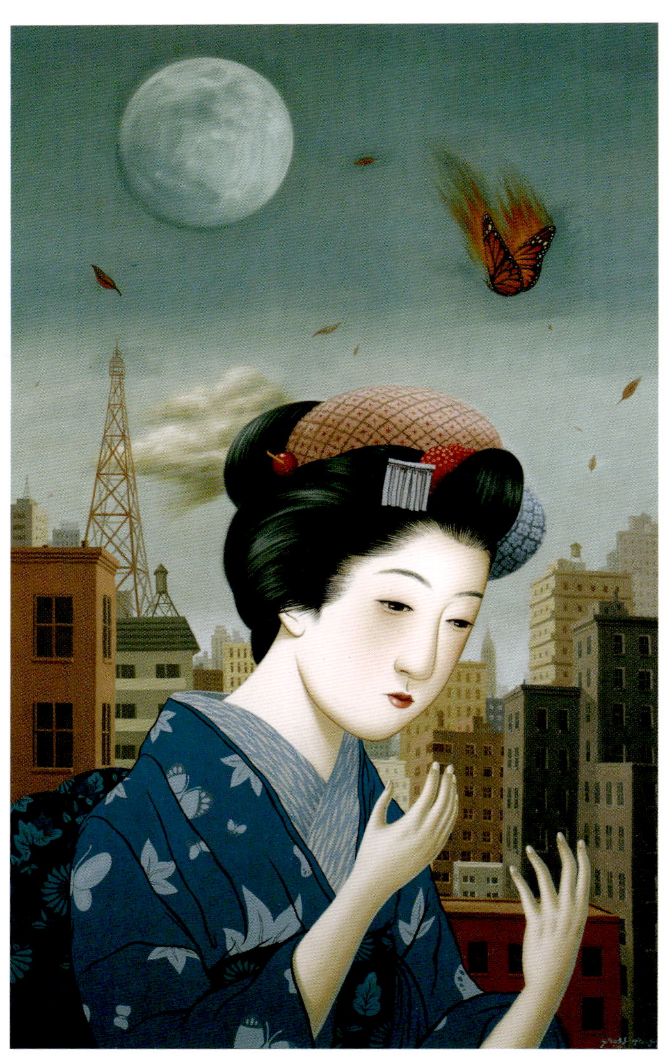

THE MEANING 2003, oil on canvas, 72" x 45"

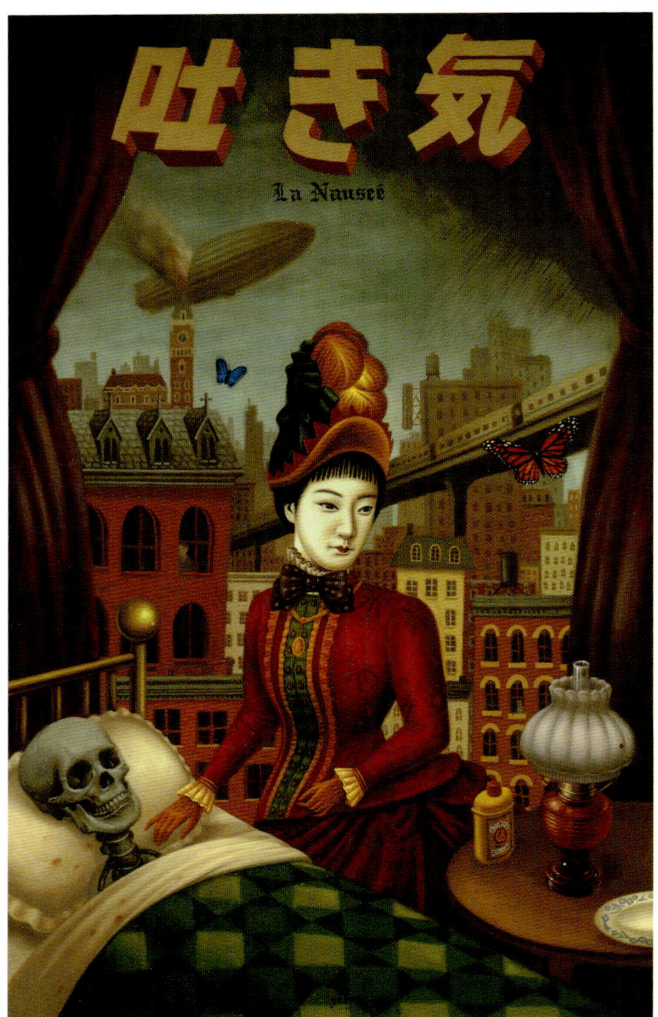


HAKIKE (LA NAUSEE) 2003, oil on panel, 44" x 27.5"

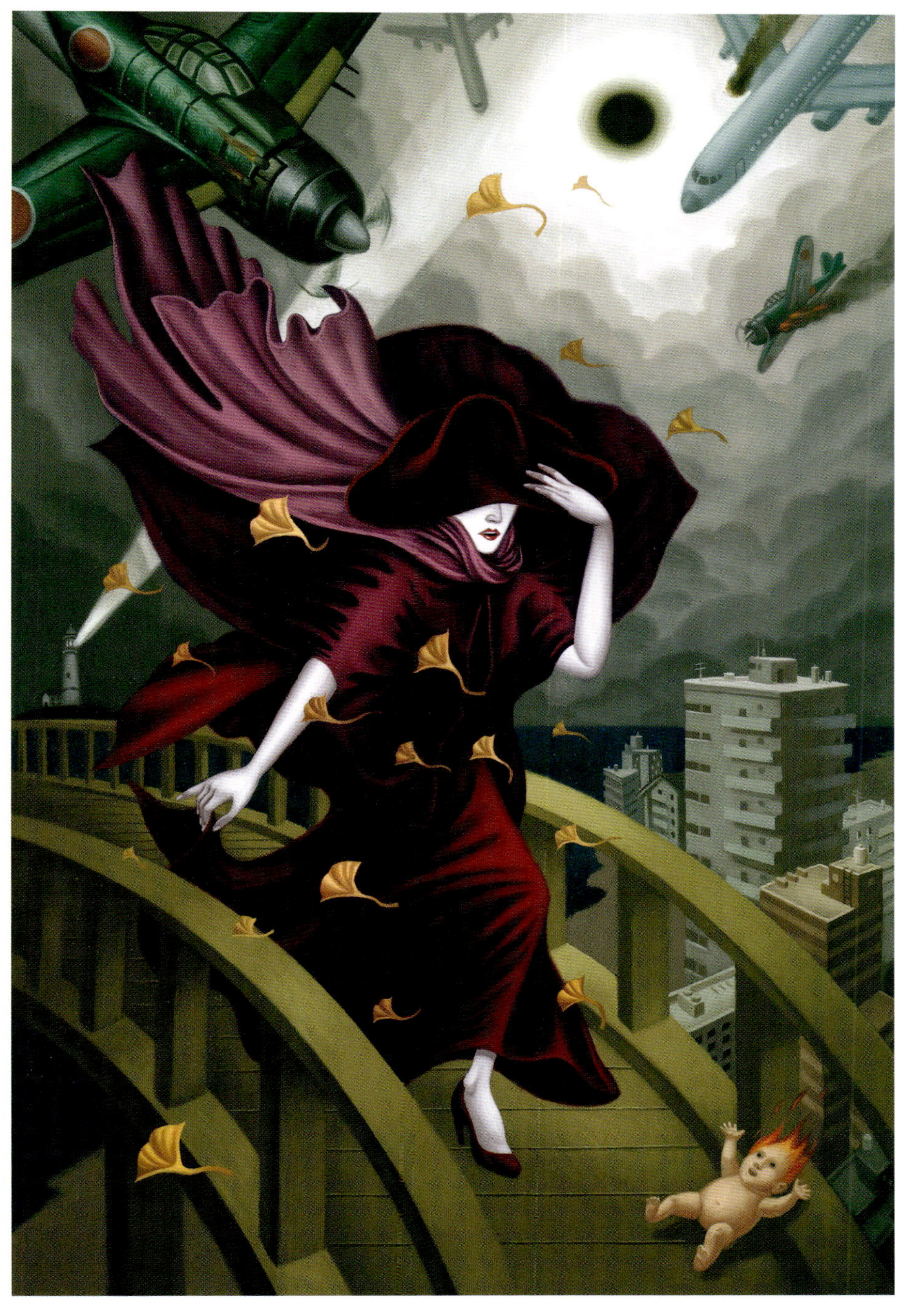

MATASABURO OF THE WIND oil on canvas, 40" x 30"

# Don Ed
# HARDY

(San Francisco, California)

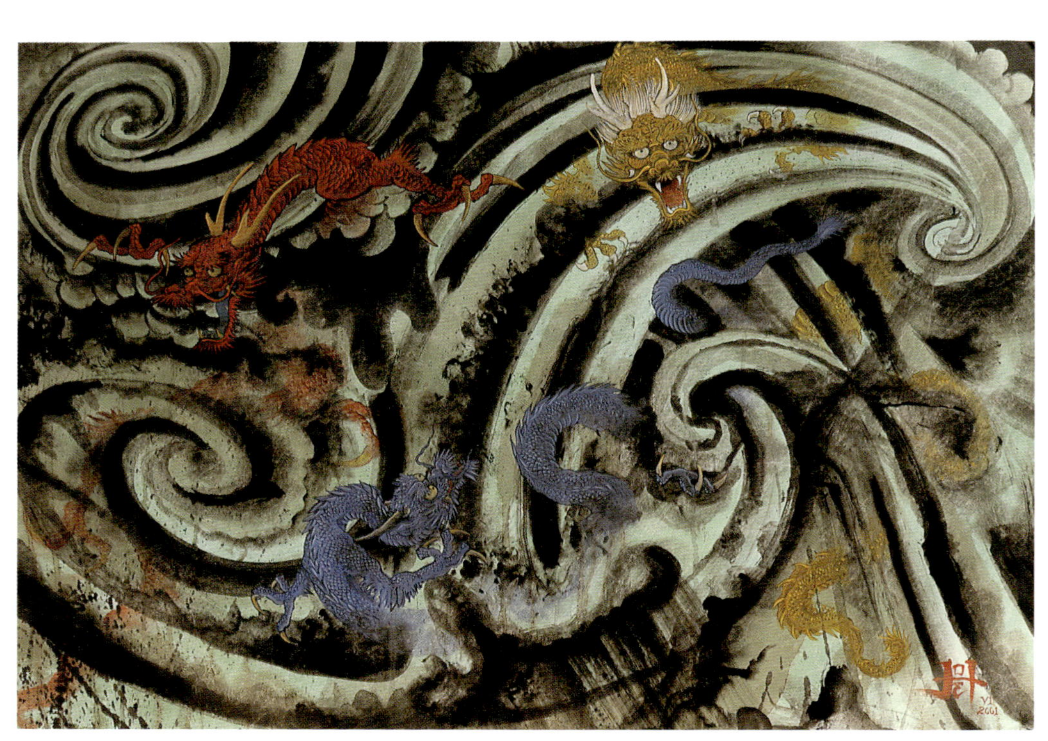

3 Dragons

2001, acrylic, 36" x 51"

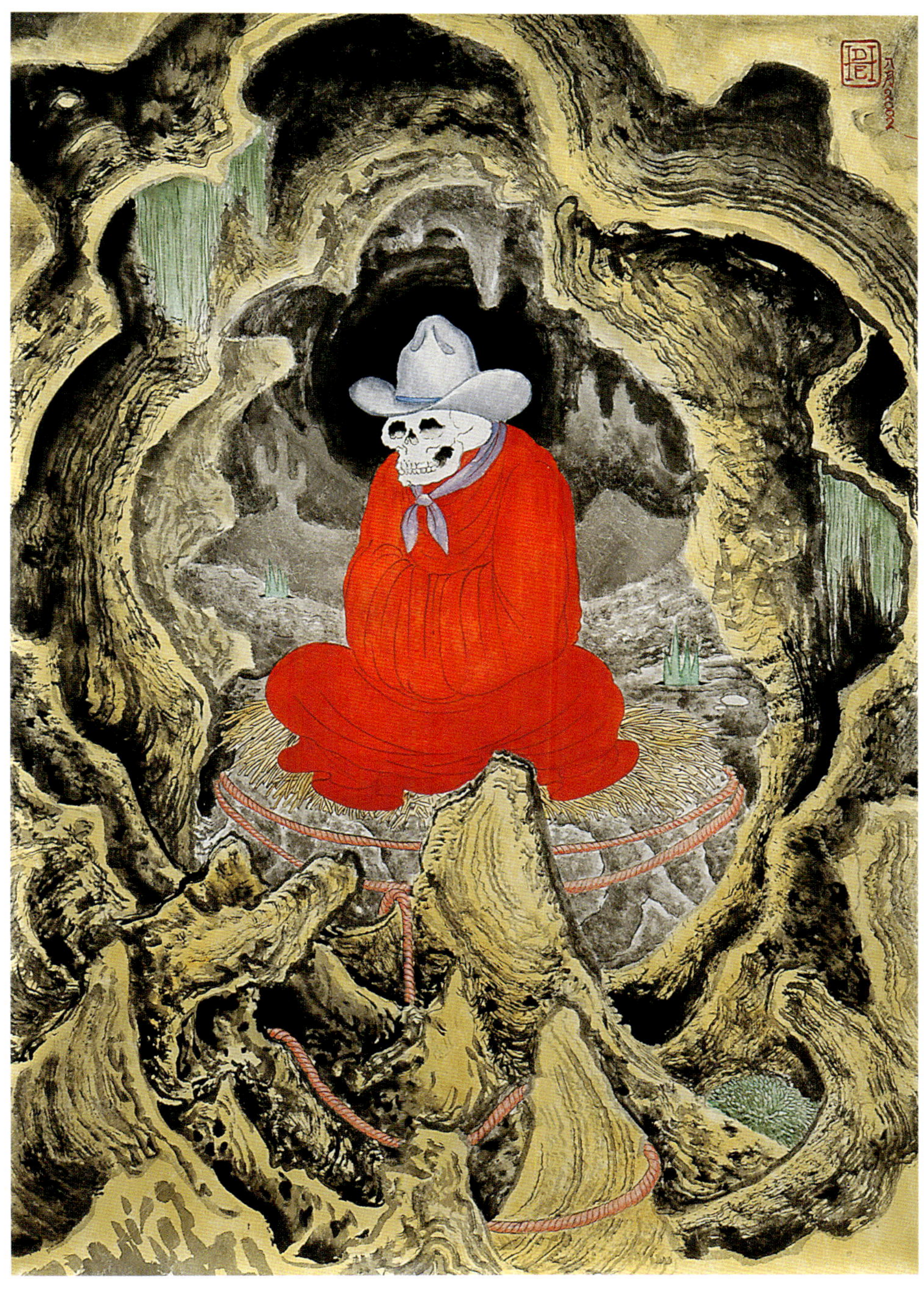

2002, acrylic on synthetic paper and scroll mounted, 51" x 36" HOPPY'S RETREAT

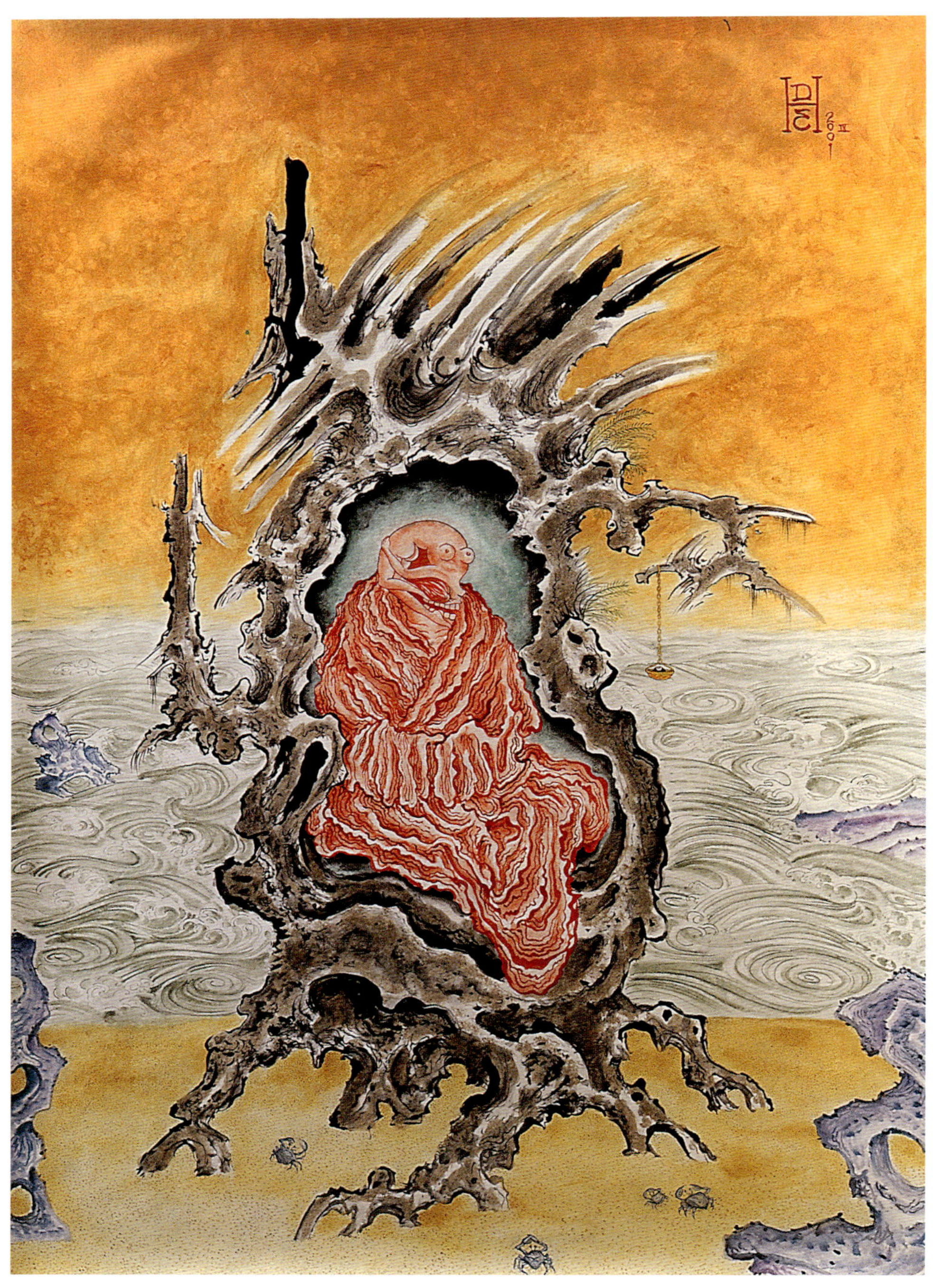

TEACHER'S PET 2001, acrylic on synthetic paper, 73" x 51"

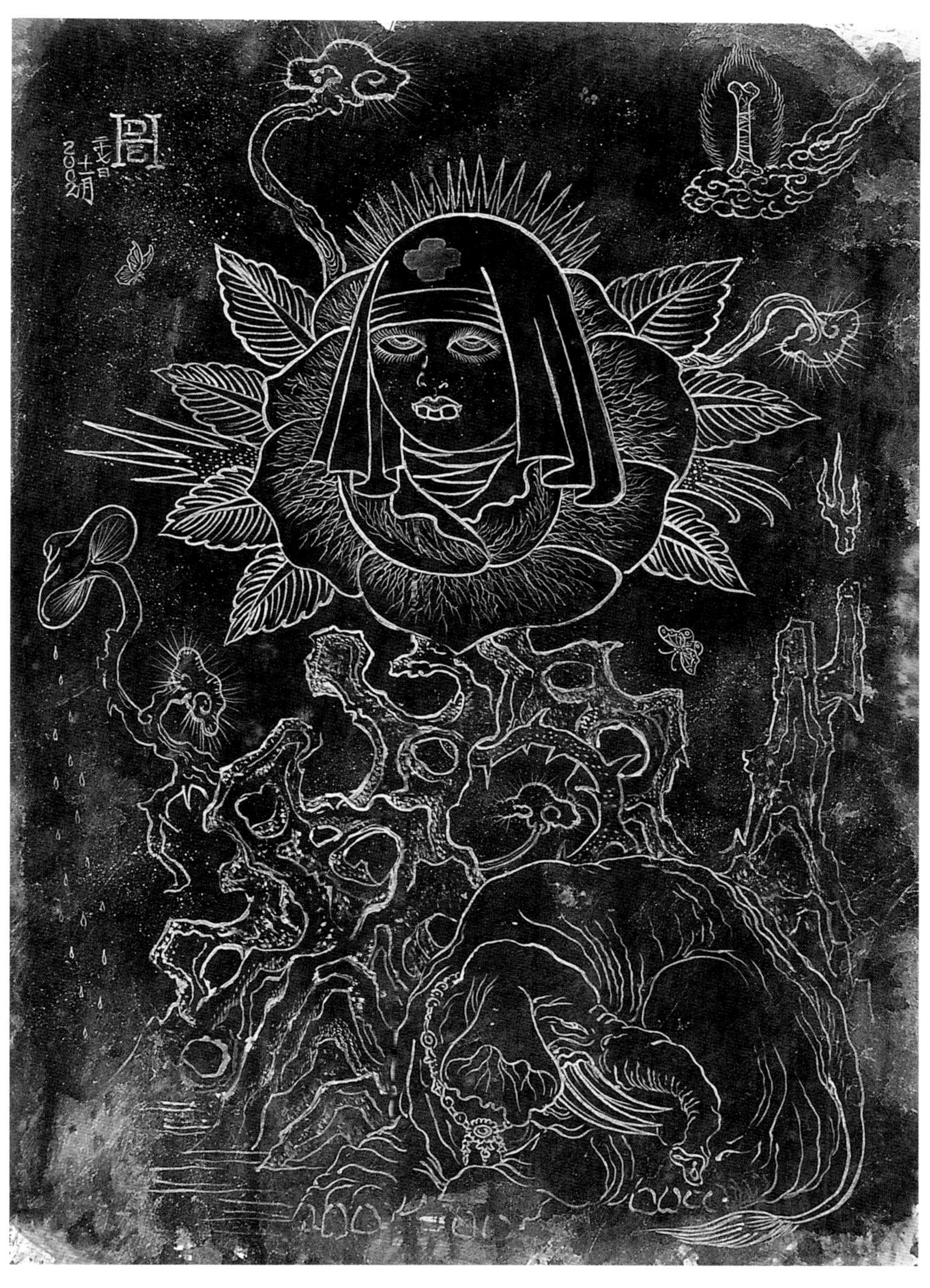

2002, acrylic on synthetic paper, 36" x 25.5"

PETRIFIED PRINCESS #2

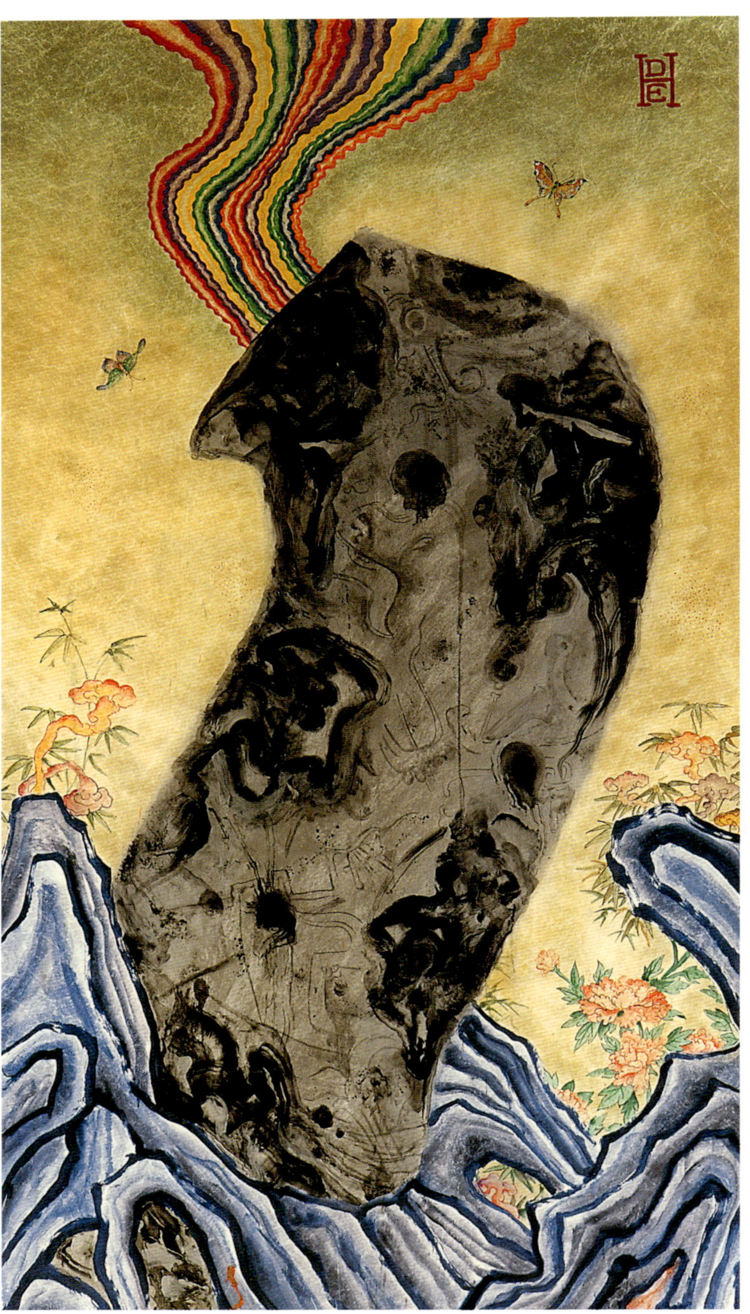

THE ELEPHANT'S GRAVEYARD
2001, acrylic on synthetic paper, 91" x 51"

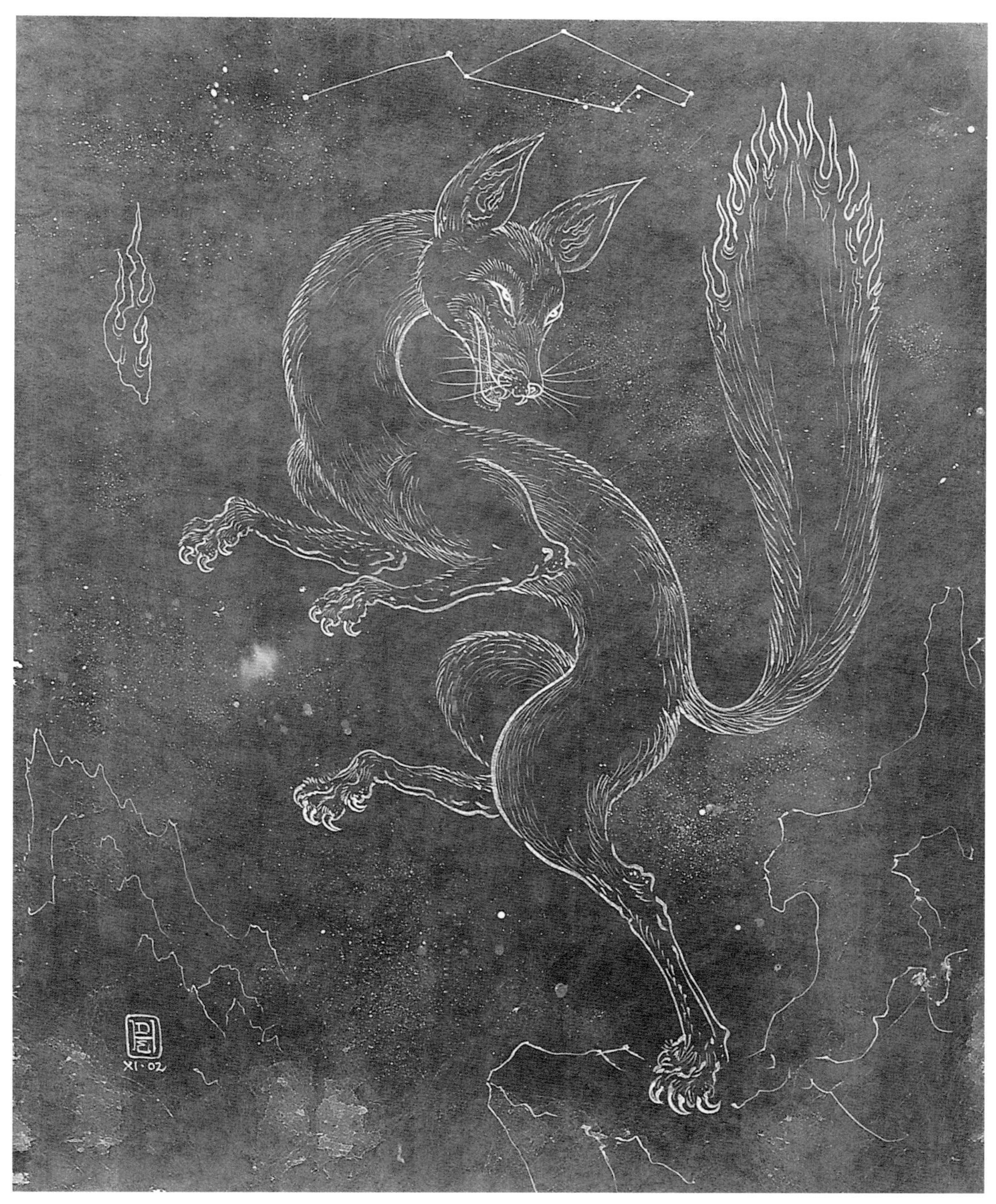


LITTLE EGYPT    2002, acrylic on synthetic paper, 32" x 25.5"

# Charles
# KRAFFT

(Seattle, Washington)

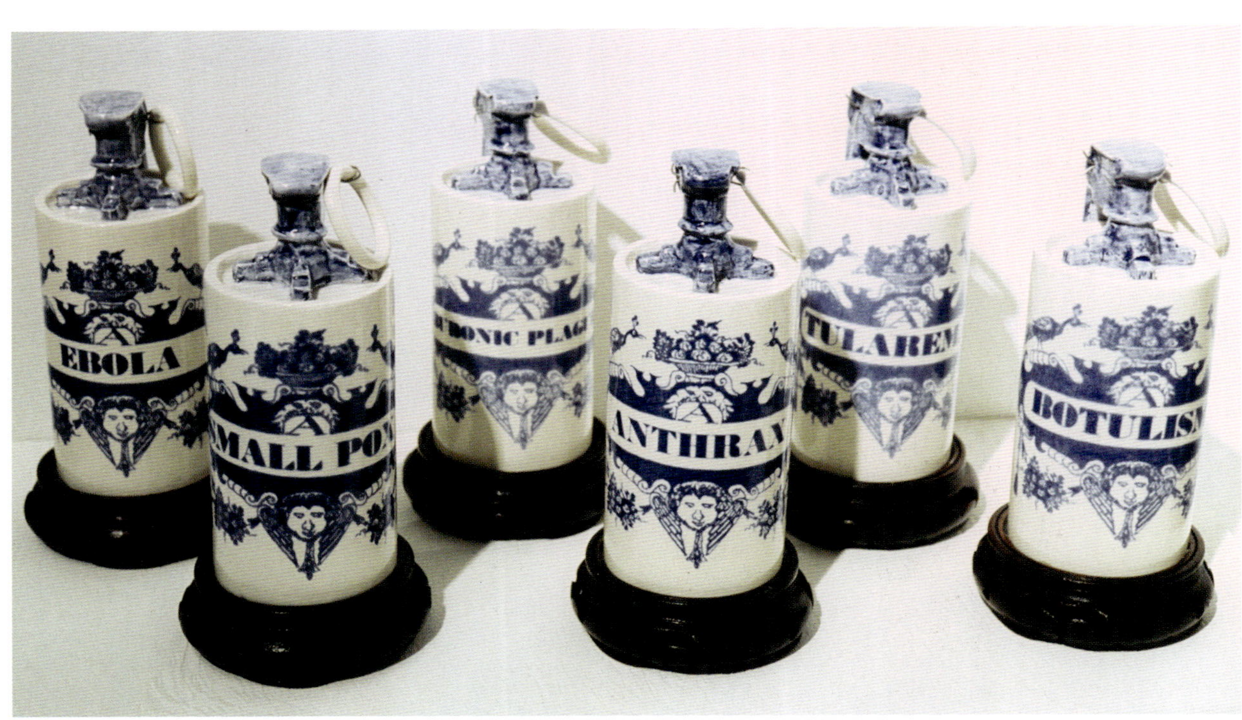


BIOLOGICAL WARFARE CANNISTER GRENADES 2002, hand-painted underglaze and ceramic transfers on porcelain, 4.5" tall

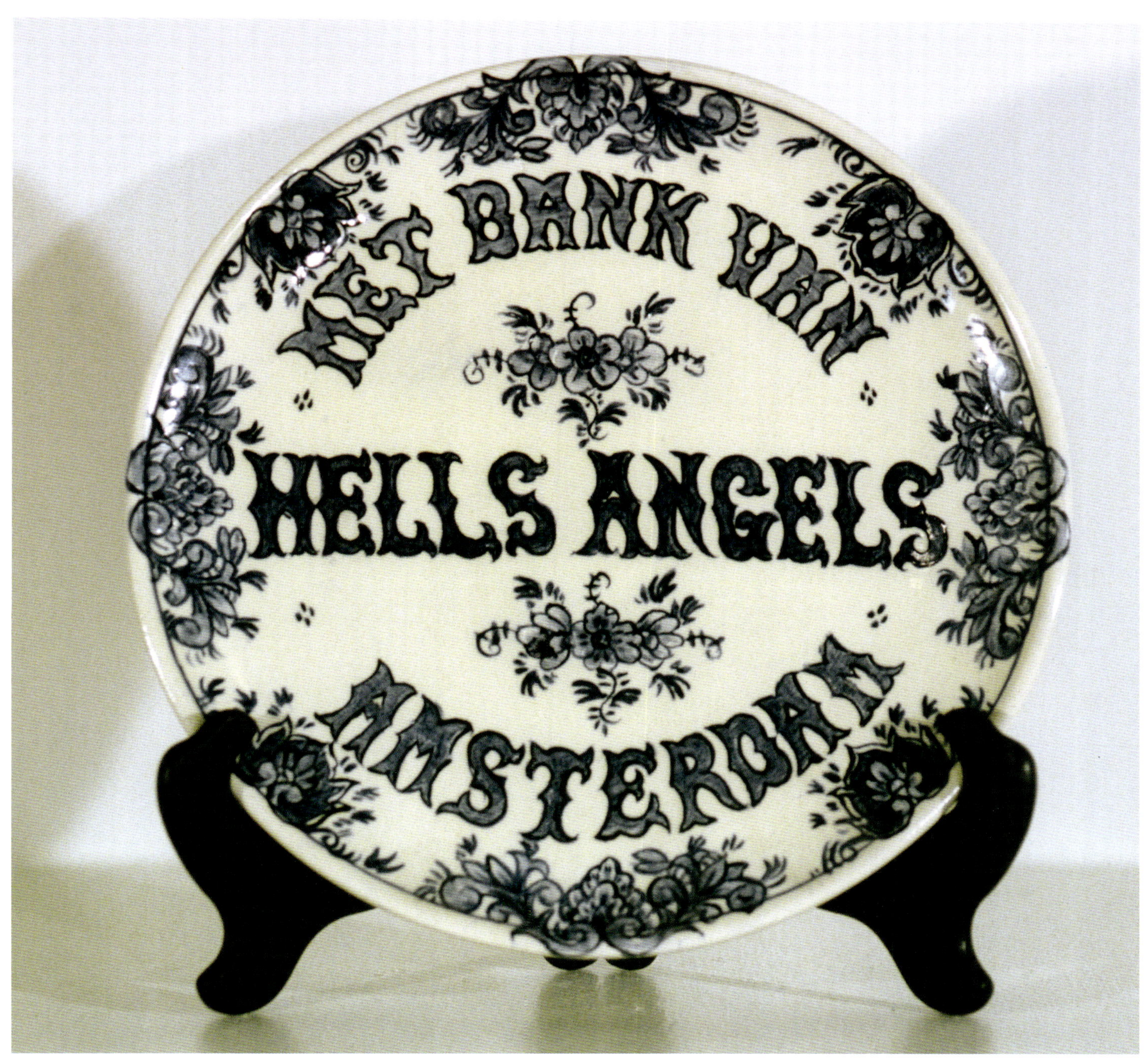


1996, hand-painted underglaze on earthenware, 12" diameter

HELLS ANGELS THANK YOU PLATE

(opposite page) Fragment Grenade 1997, hand-painted underglaze on porcelain, 4.5" tall



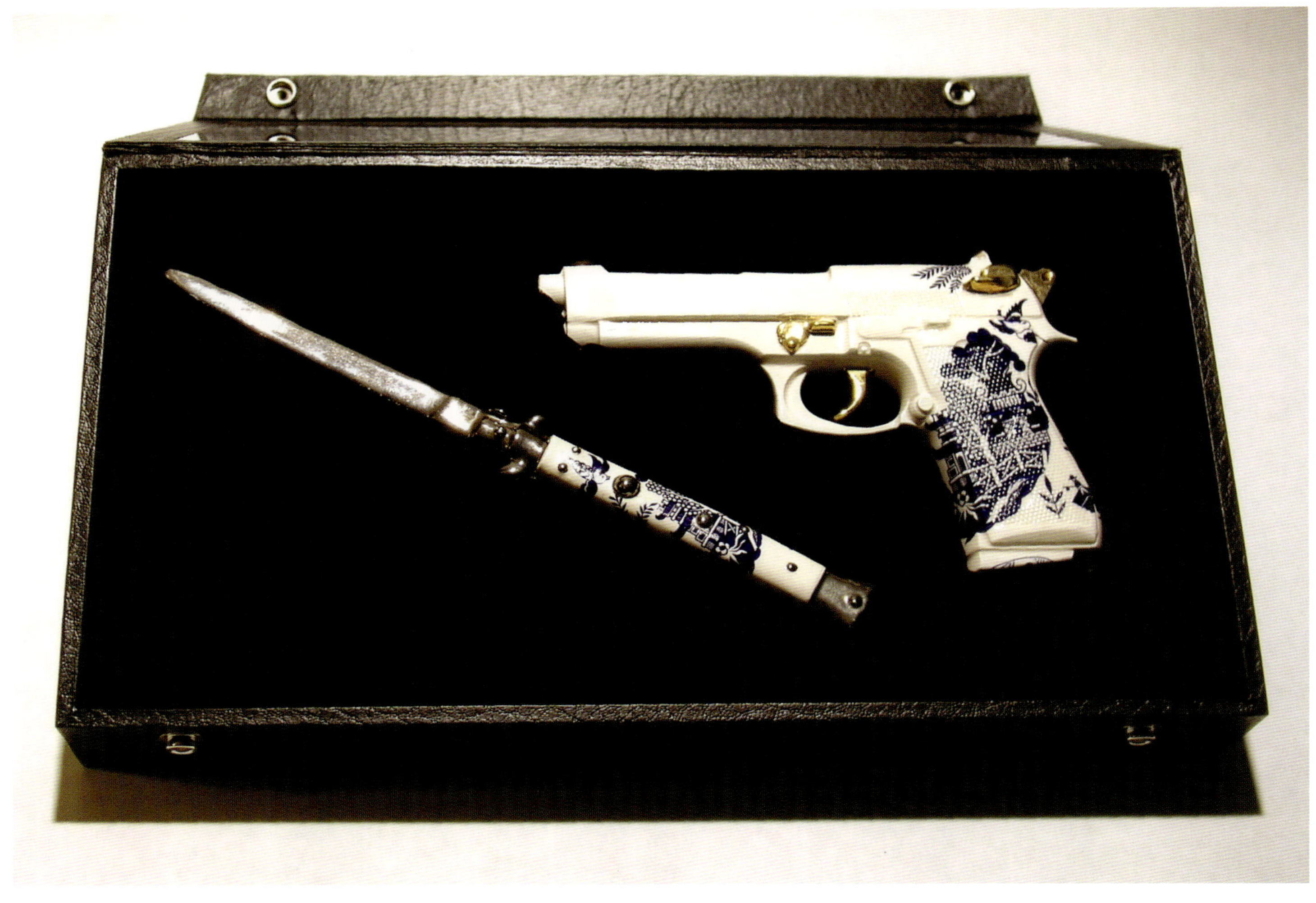

Assassin's Kit (Beretta and Switchblade in Case) 2000, hand-painted underglaze and ceramic transfers, 16" x 12"

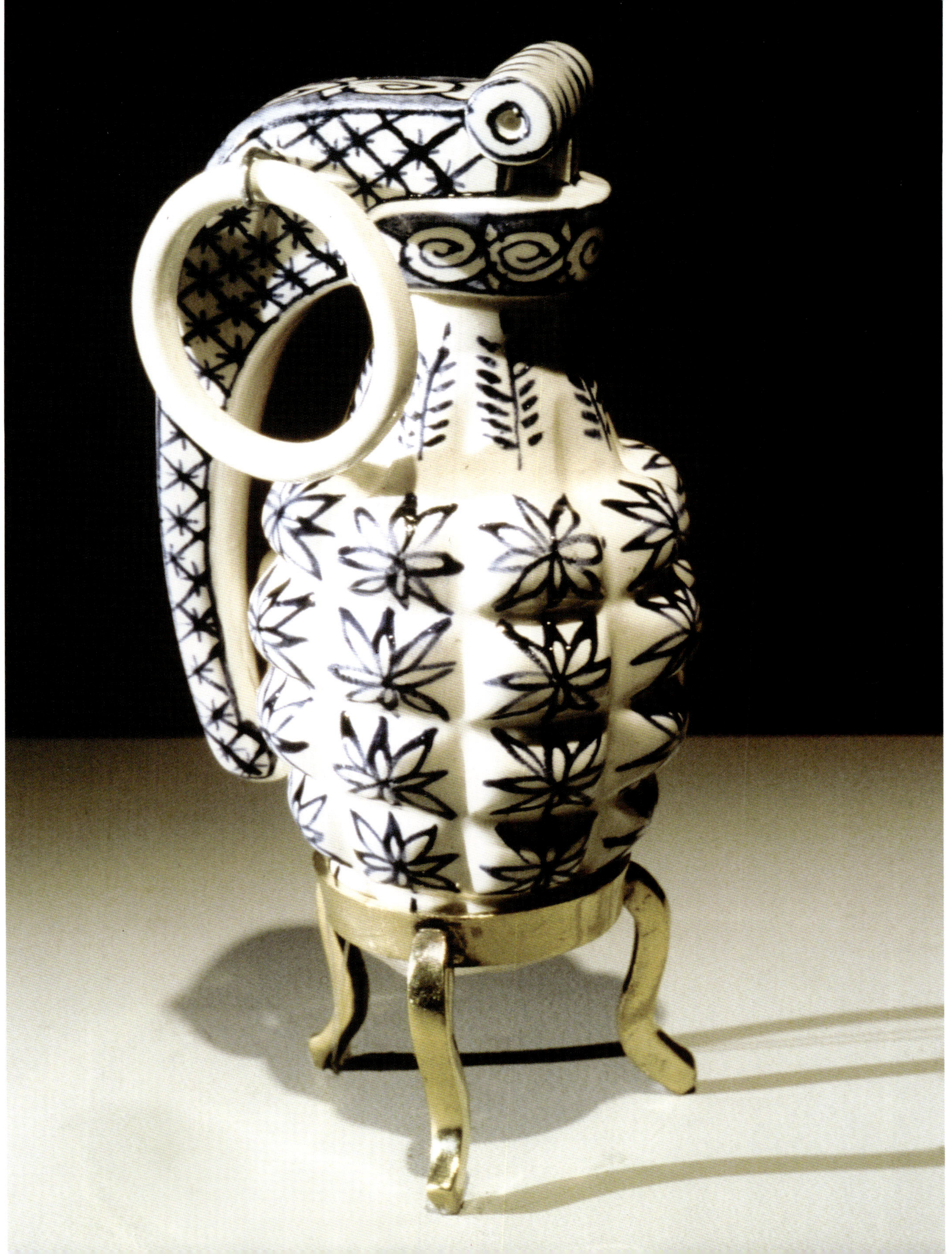

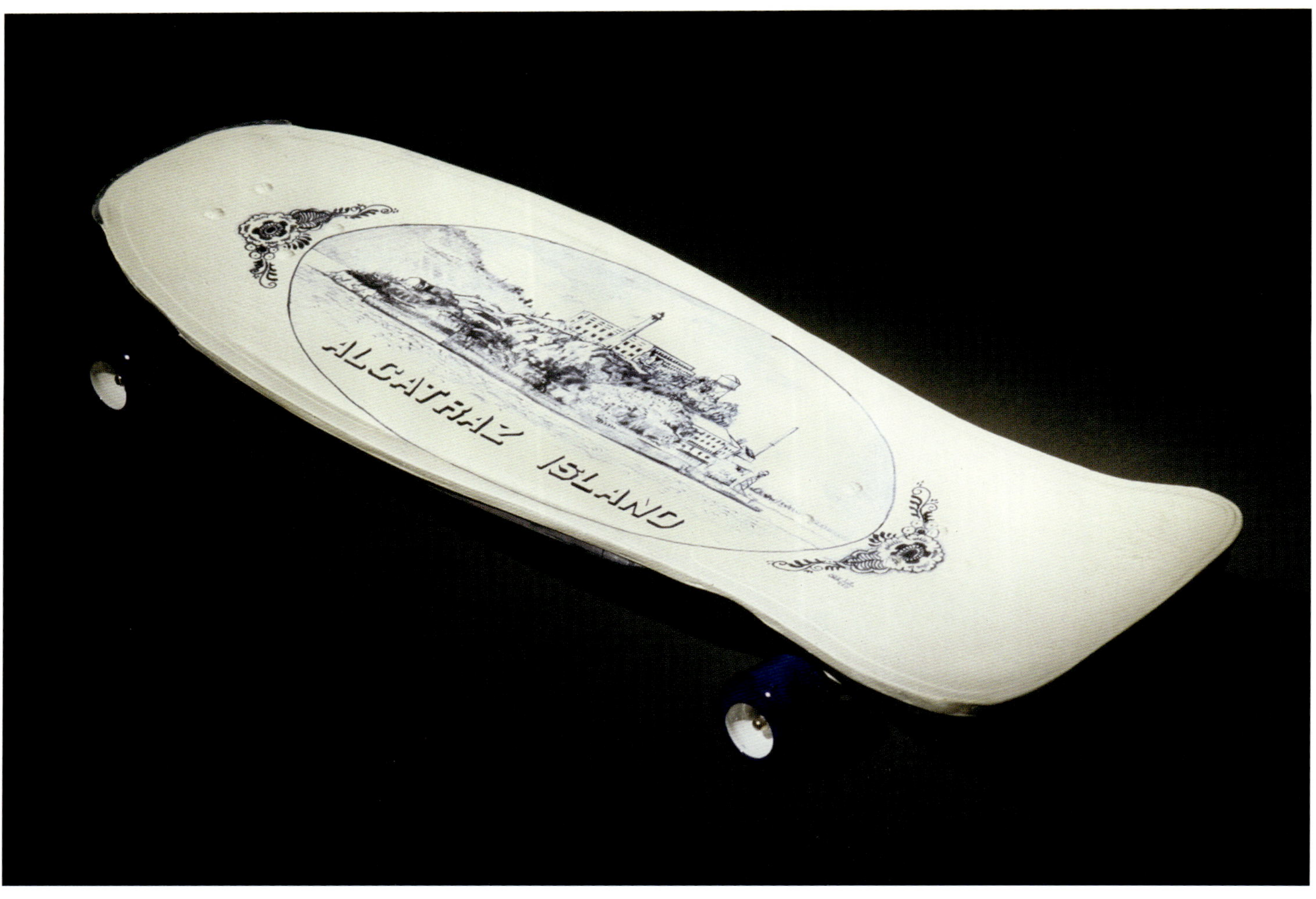


ALCATRAZ ISLAND SKATEBOARD

1999, hand painted underglaze on vitreous porcelain, 30" x 10"

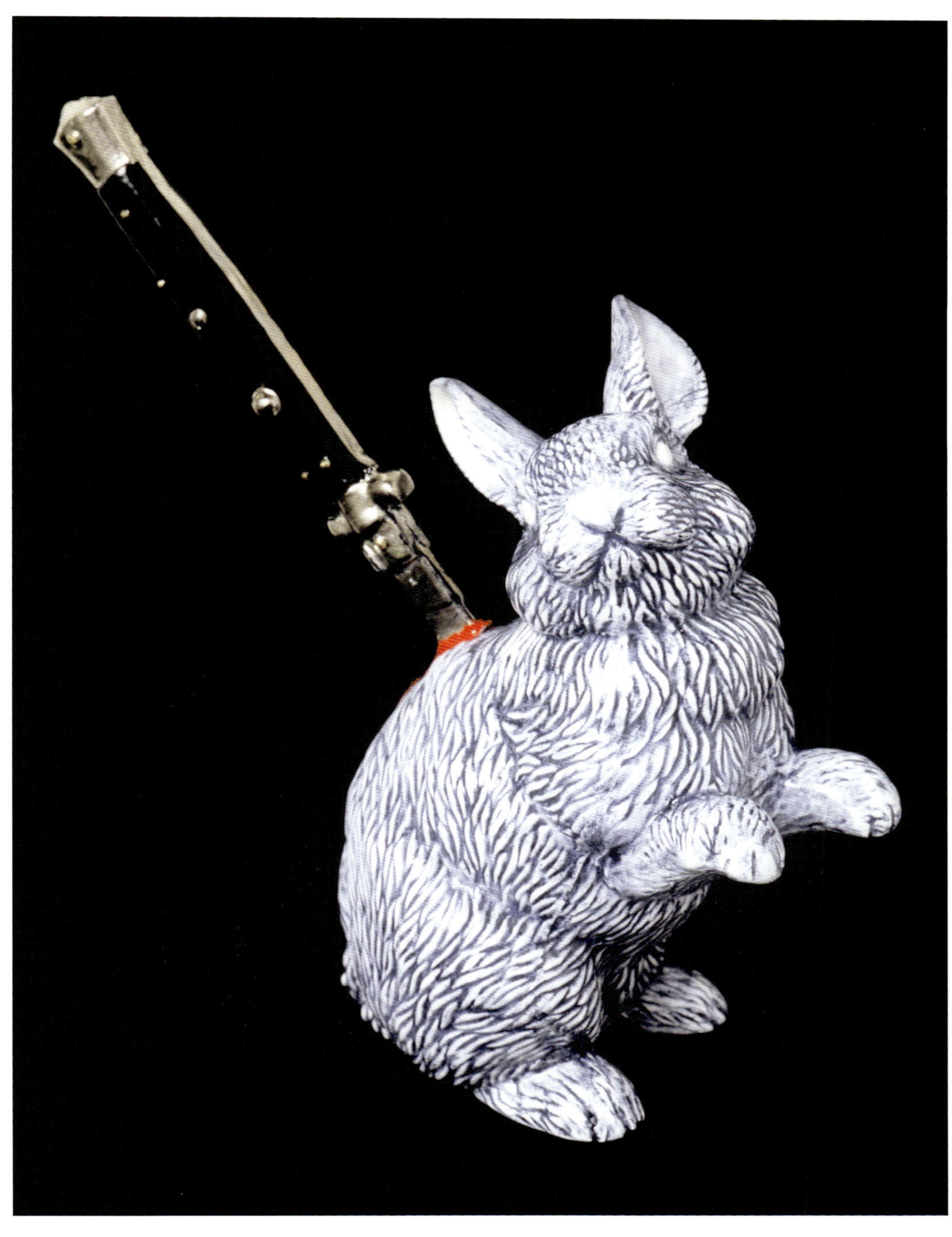

2000, hand-painted underglaze on porcelain, 12" tall

SAL MINEO BUNNY

# Liz McGRATH

(Los Angeles, California)

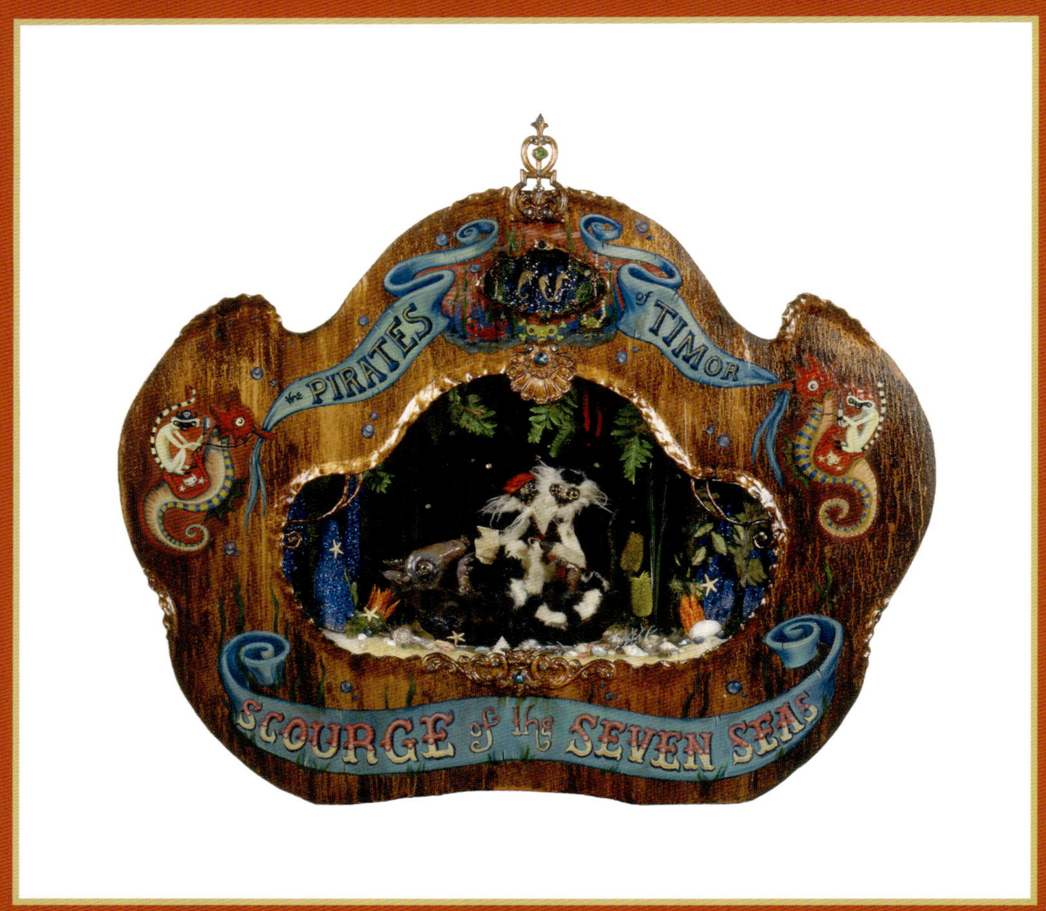


SCOURGE OF THE SEVEN SEAS 2002, mixed media, 32" x 25"

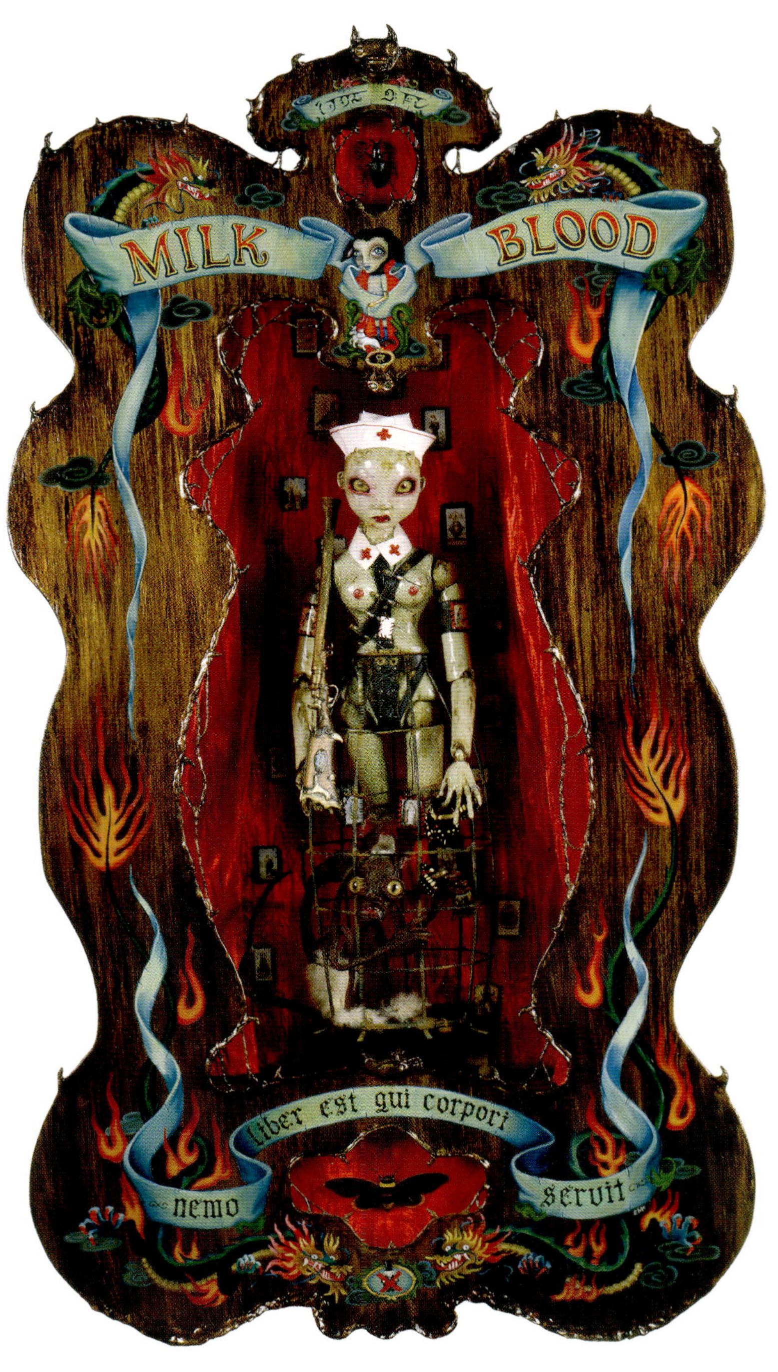


2002, mixed media, 32" x 72"

FRANKIE MACHINE

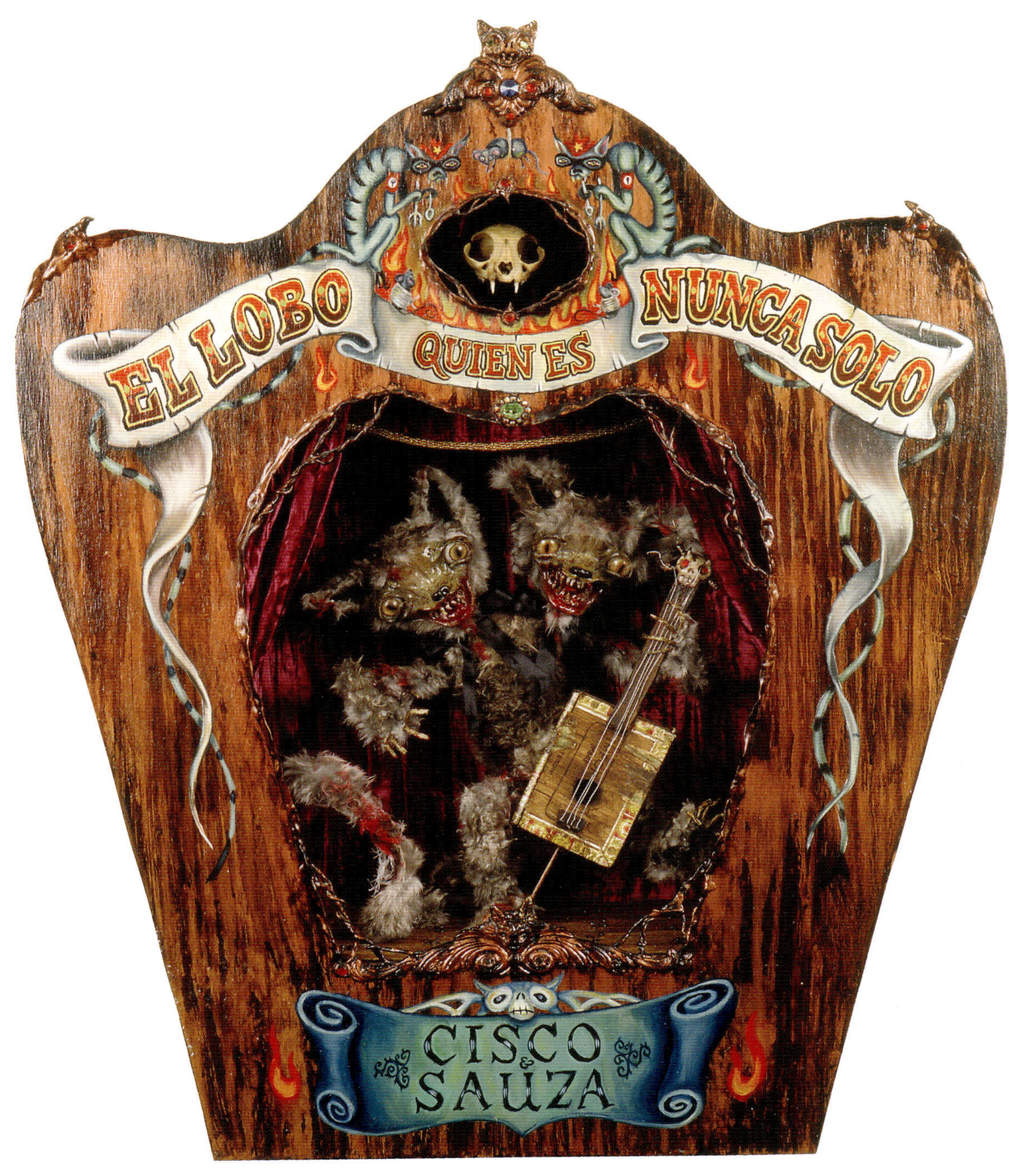


Cisco and Sauza 2003, mixed media, 28" x 24"

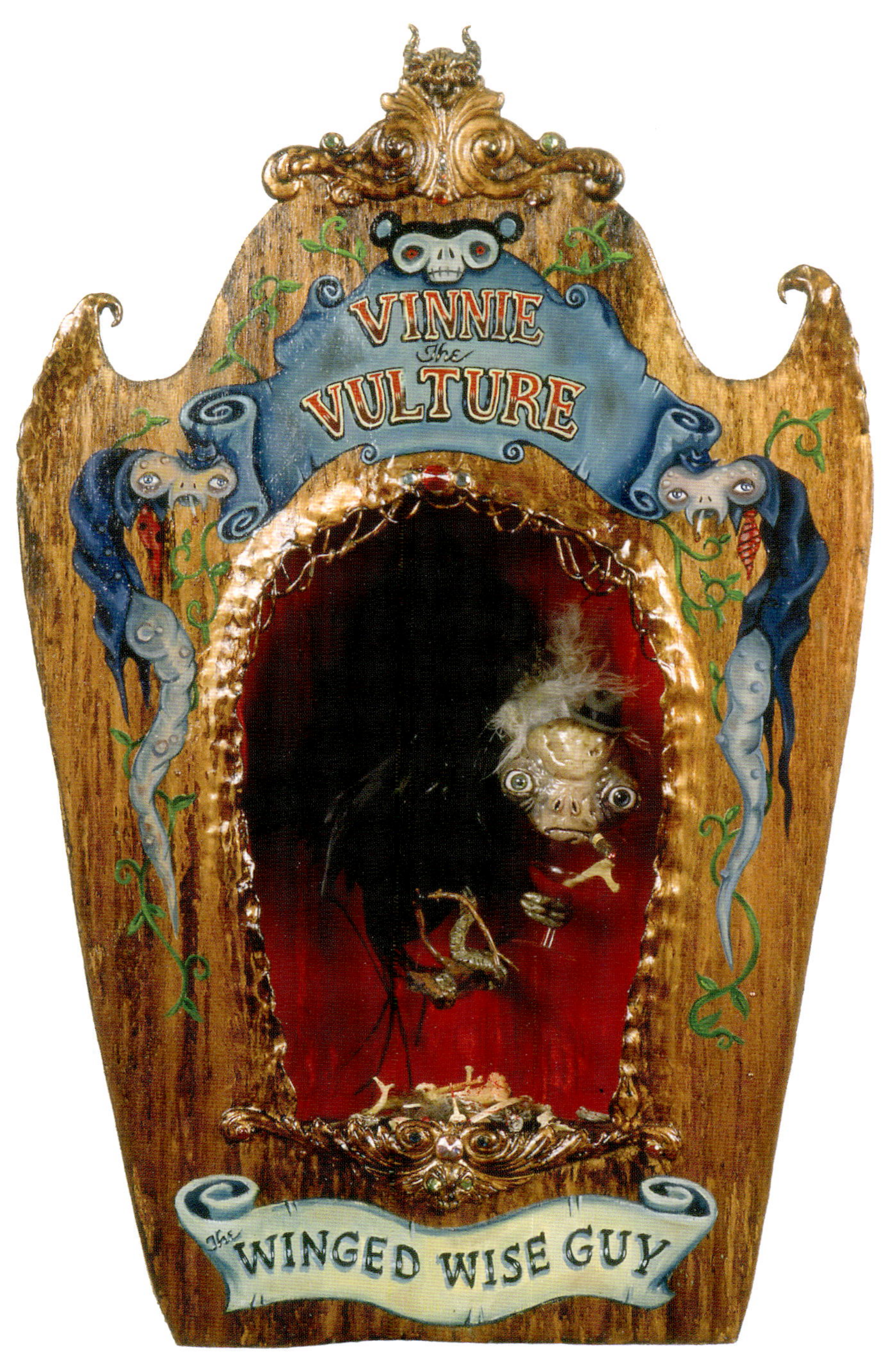


2003, mixed media, 21" x 25"

VINNIE THE VULTURE

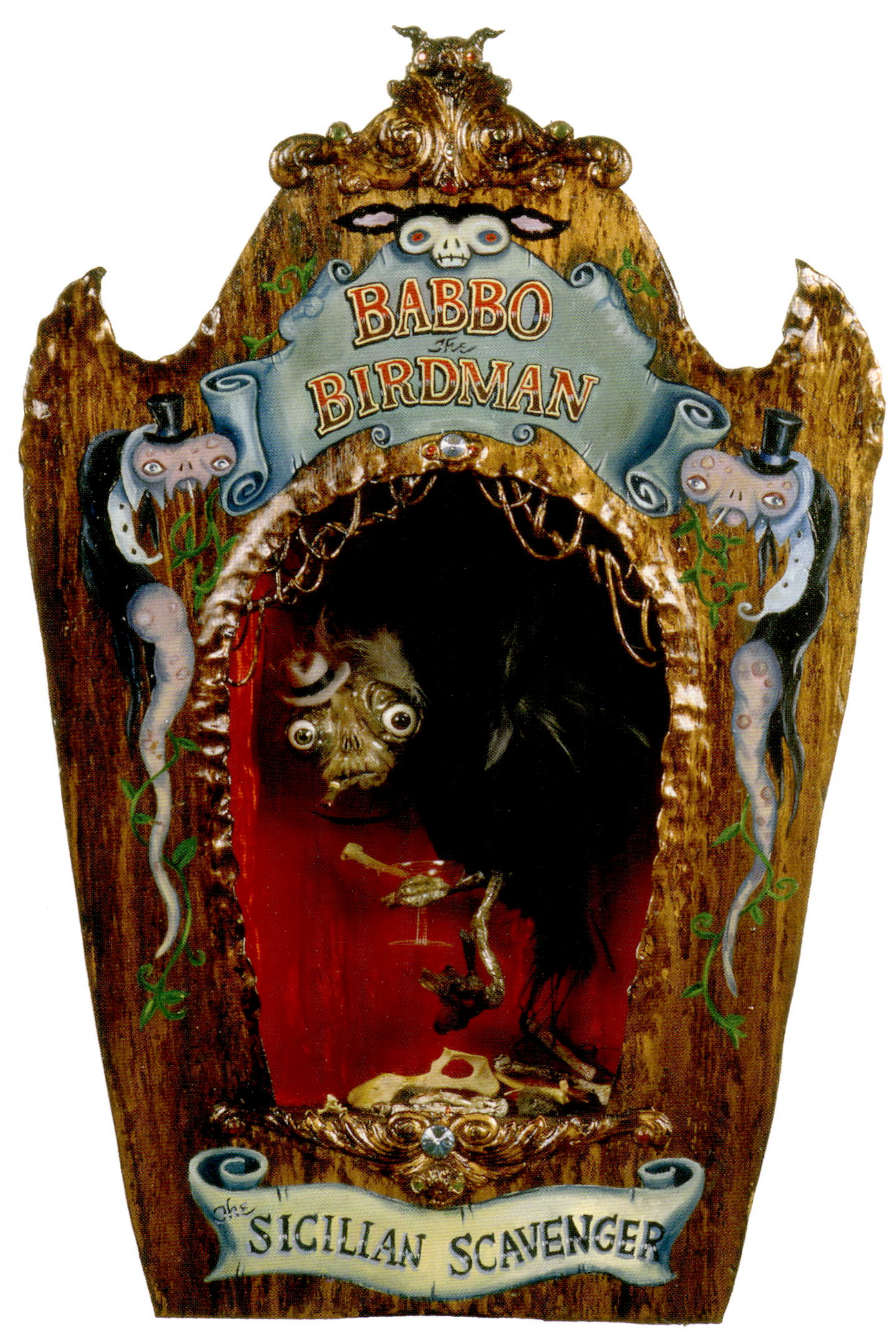


Babo the Birdman 2003, mixed media, 21" x 25"

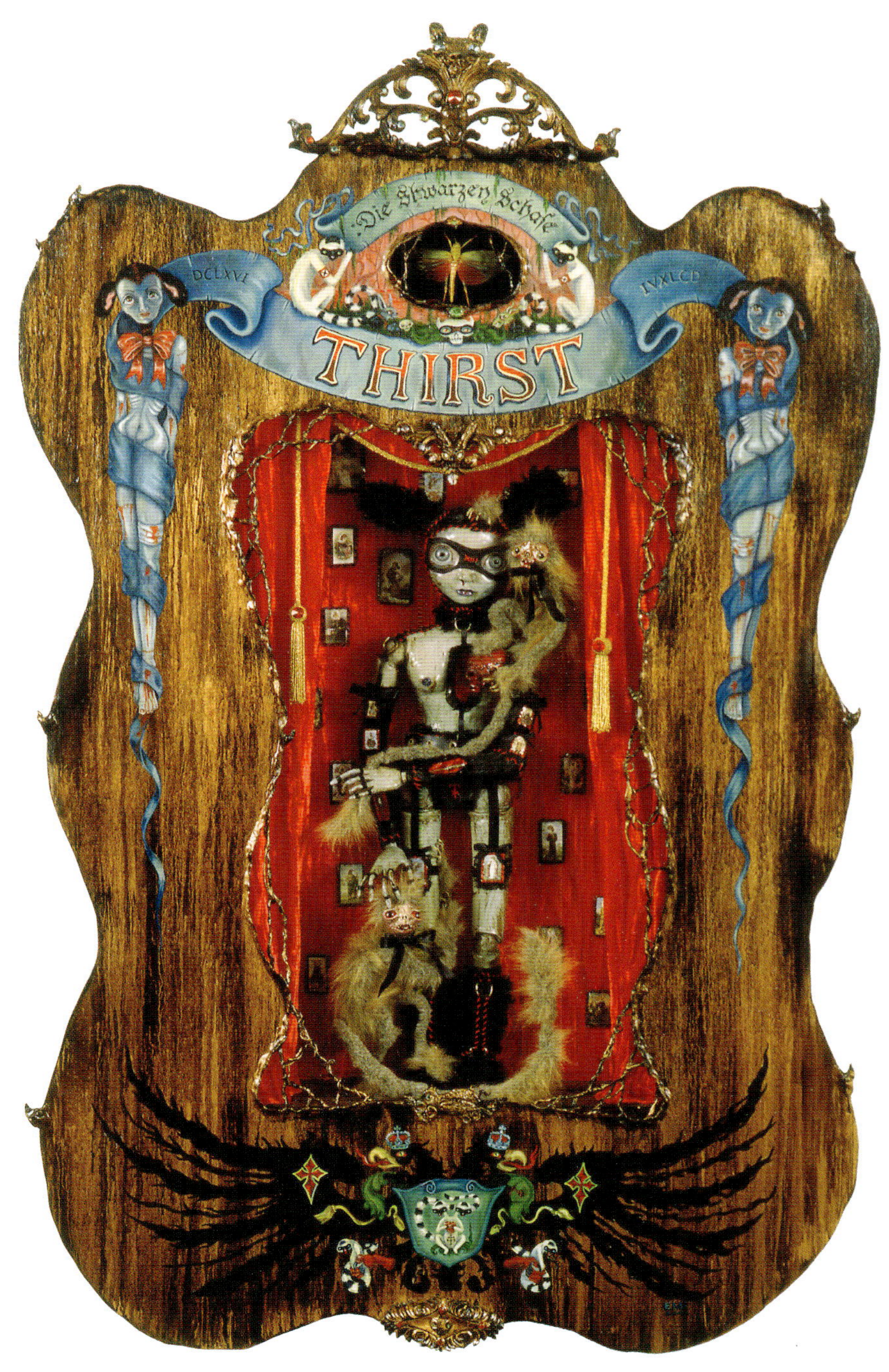


2003, mixed media, 45" x 71" THIRST

# Scott
# MUSGROVE

(Seattle, Washington)

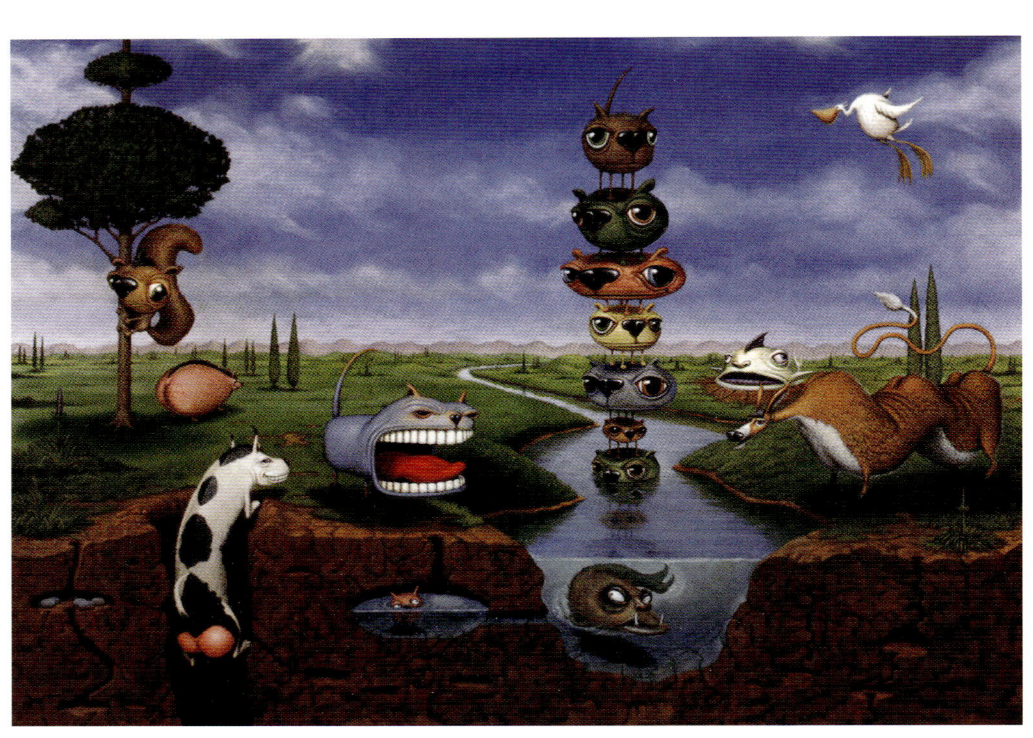

THE LATE FAUNA OF NORTH AMERICA

2002, oil on canvas, 23" x 33"

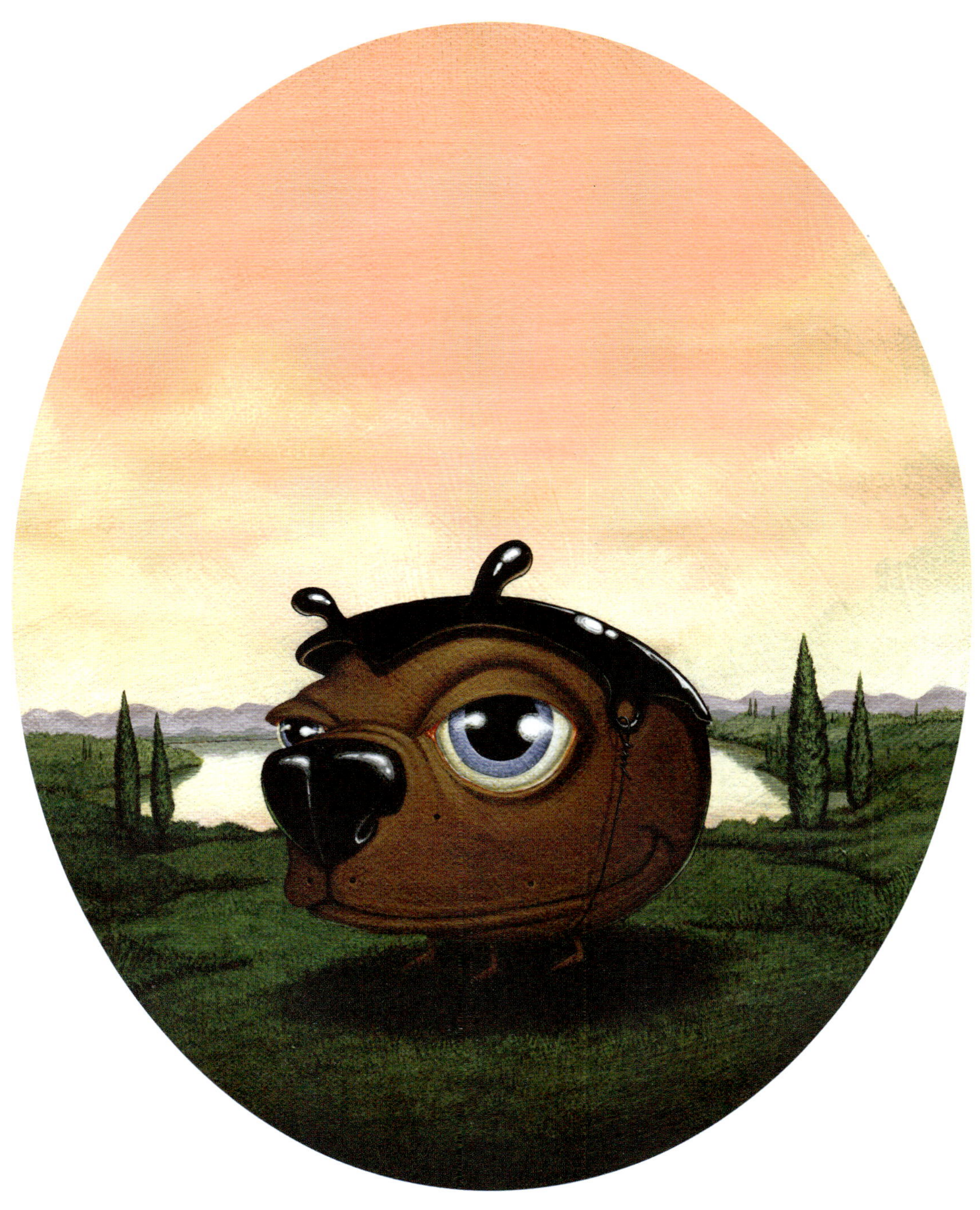

2002, oil on canvas, 13" x 11" oval

Lupus Helmetitus

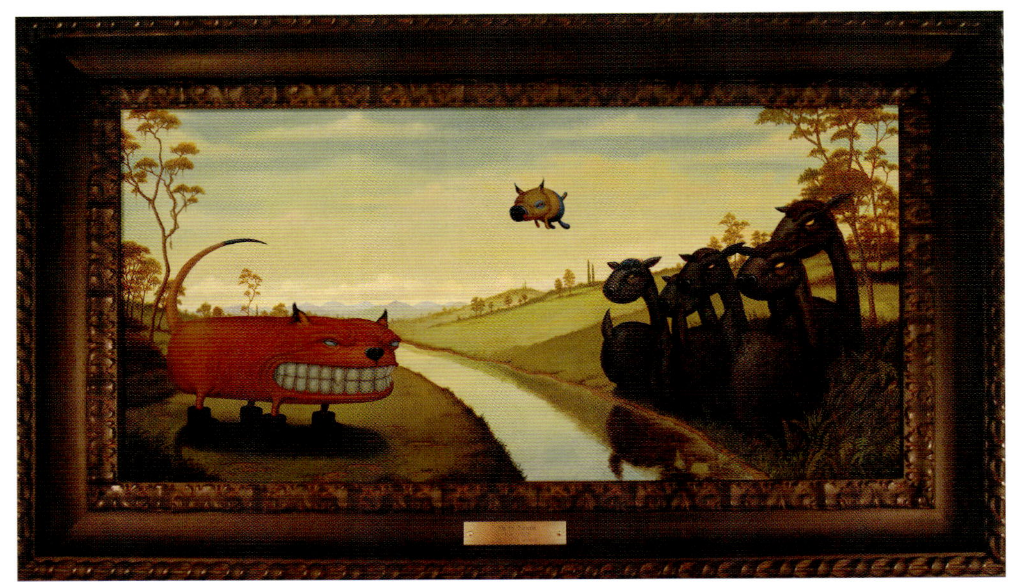

BETE NOIR 2003, oil on canvas, 10" x 20"



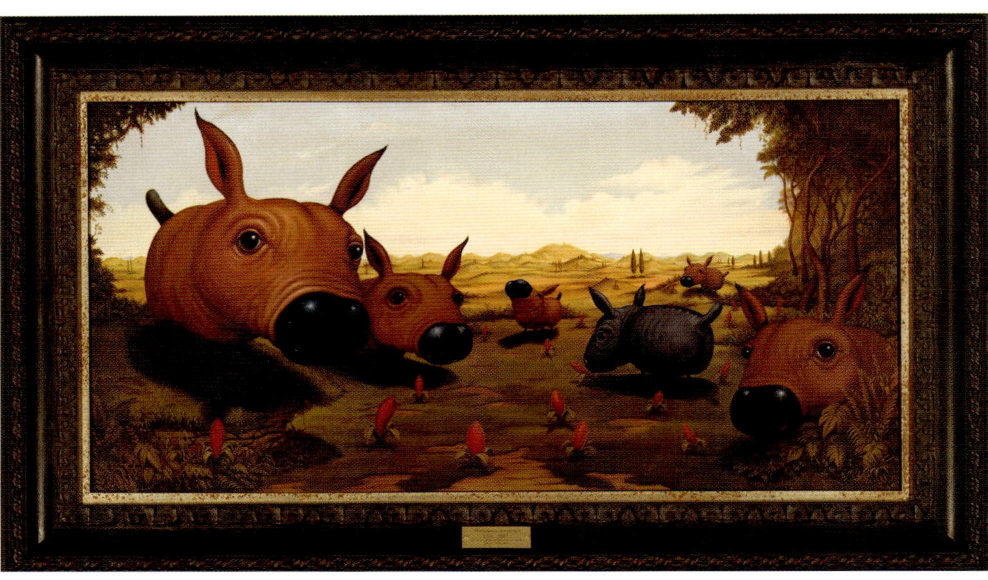

PASTORALIA AMERICANA 2003, oil on canvas, 18" x 30"

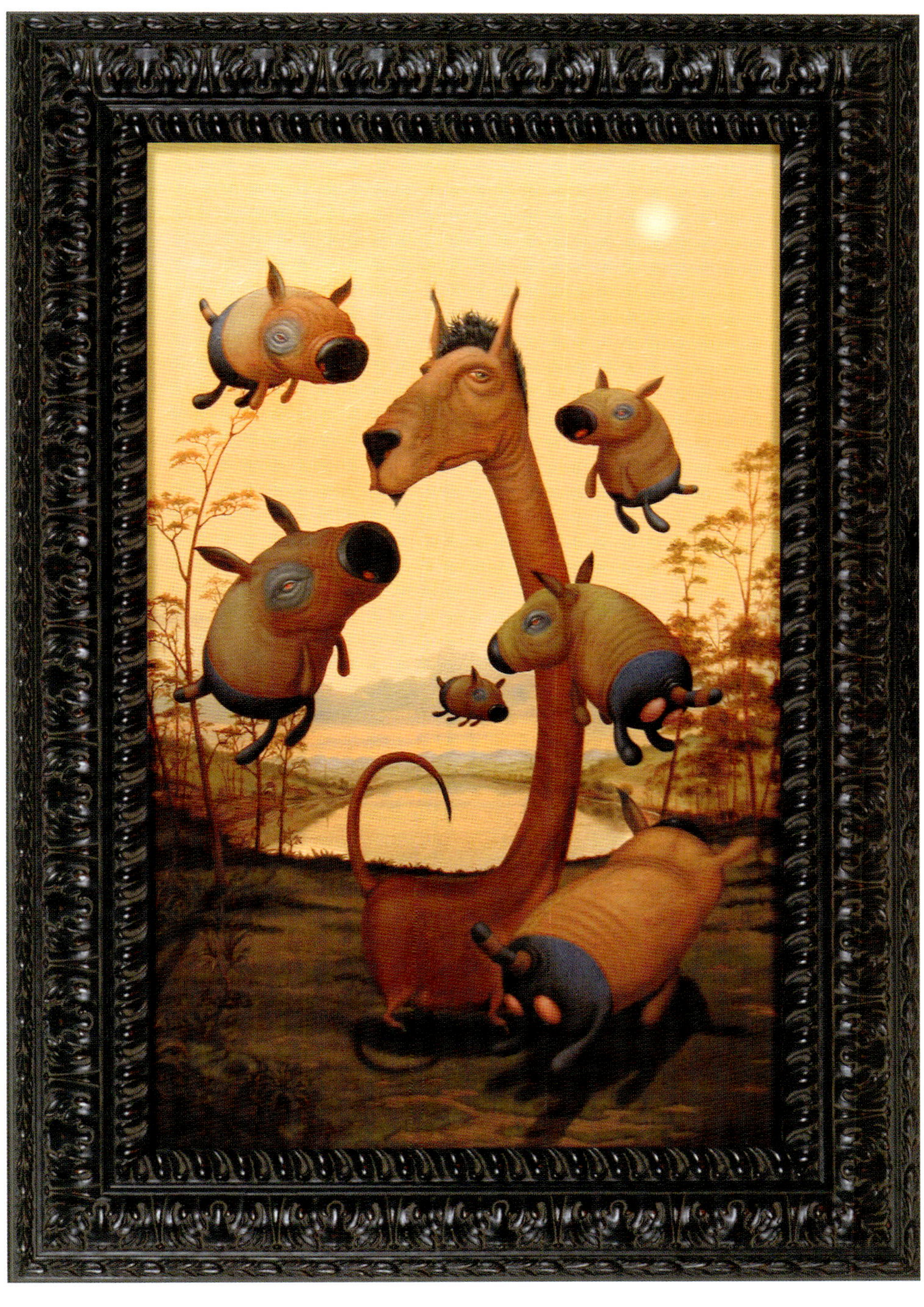

2003, oil on canvas, 26" x 16"

Nimbus

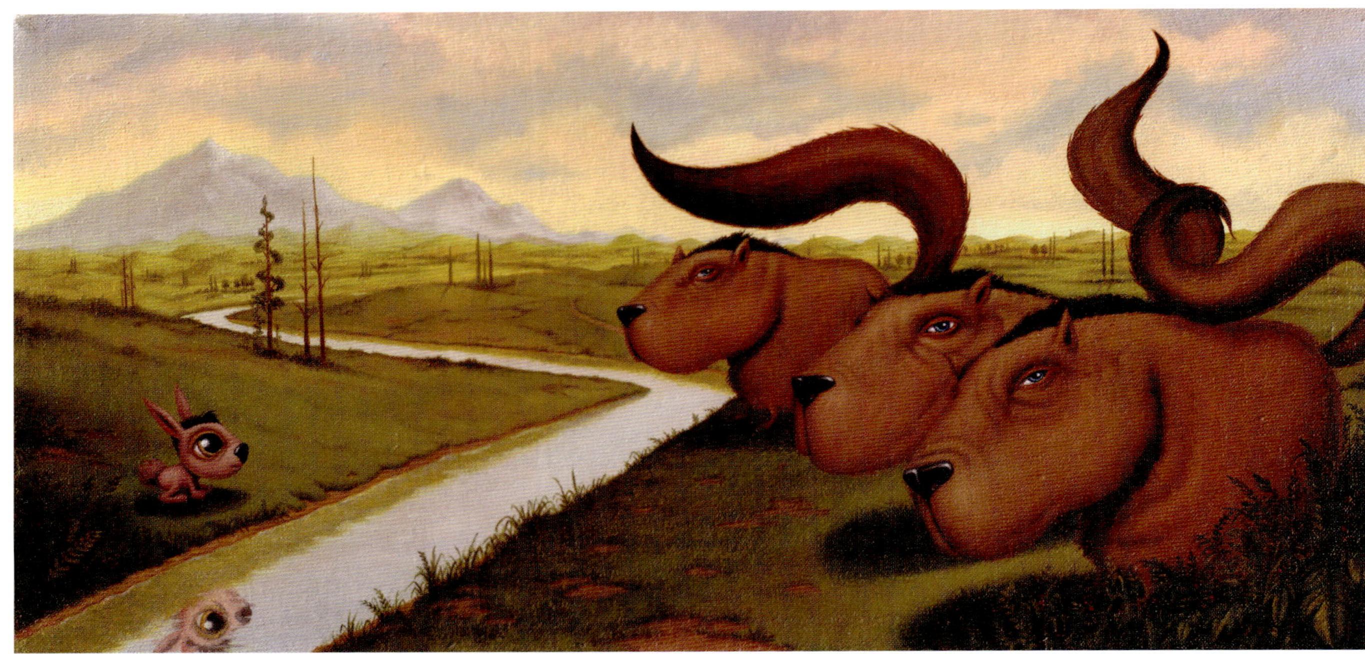

Imbroglio — 2004, oil on canvas, 8" x 16"

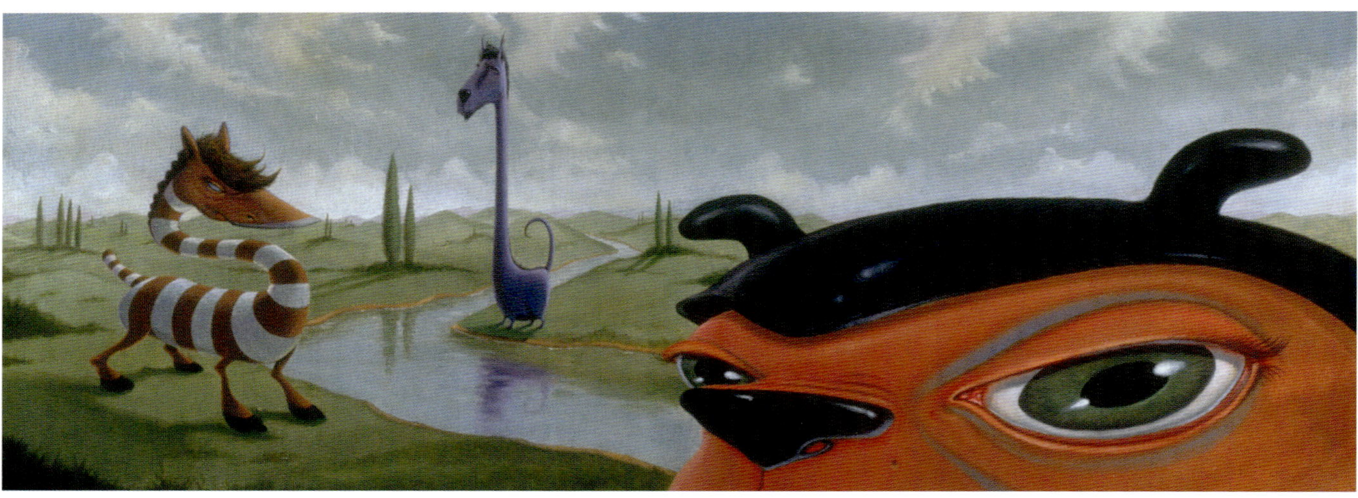

Quiet Time on the Prairie — 2002, oil on canvas, 24" x 10"

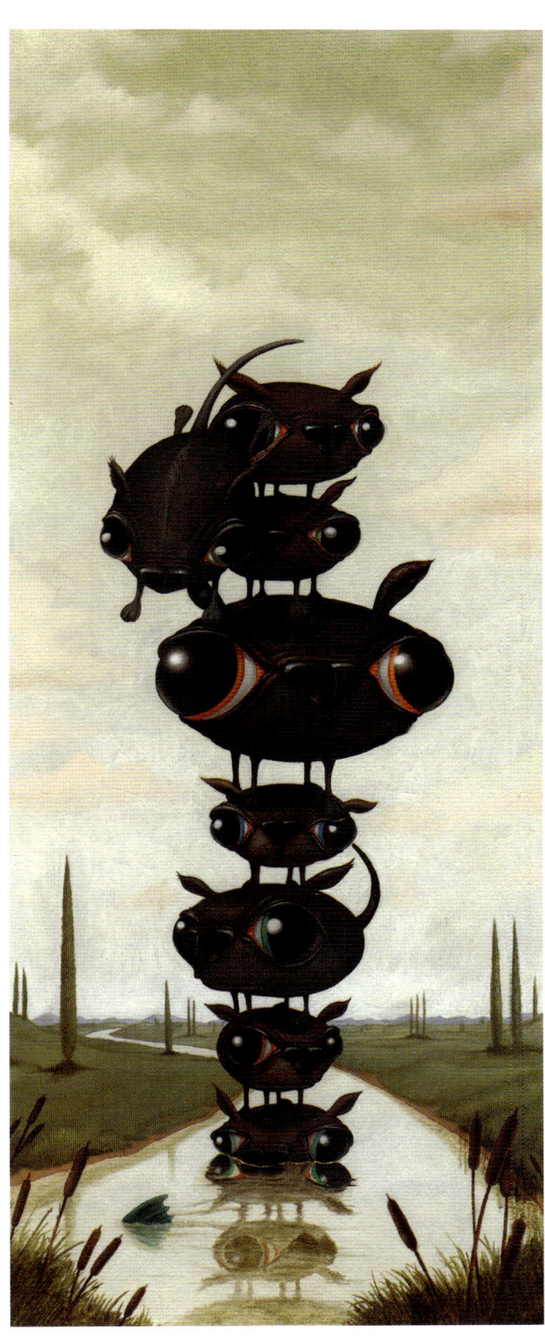

Lupus Aquaticas
2002, oil on board, 15" x 6"

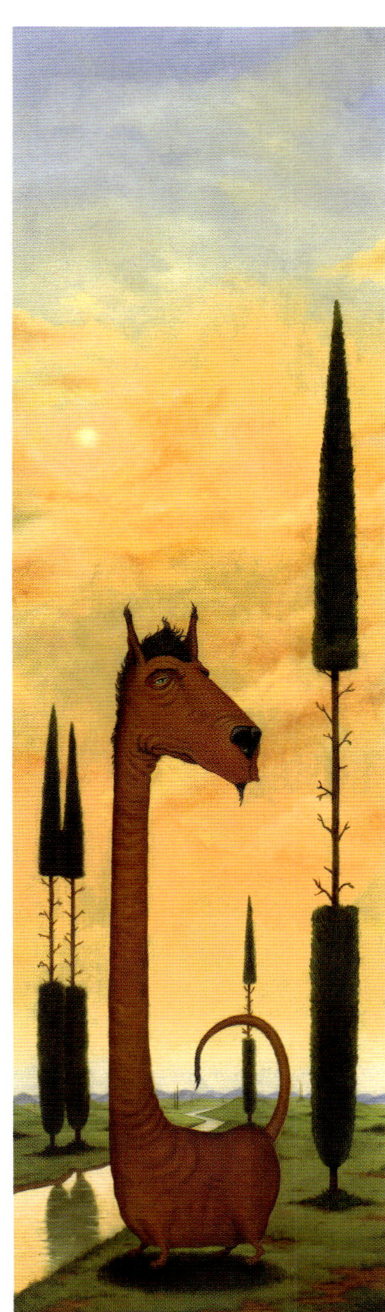

Vegetatus Masticatus
2002, oil on board, 18" x 7"

# NIAGARA

(Detroit, Michigan)

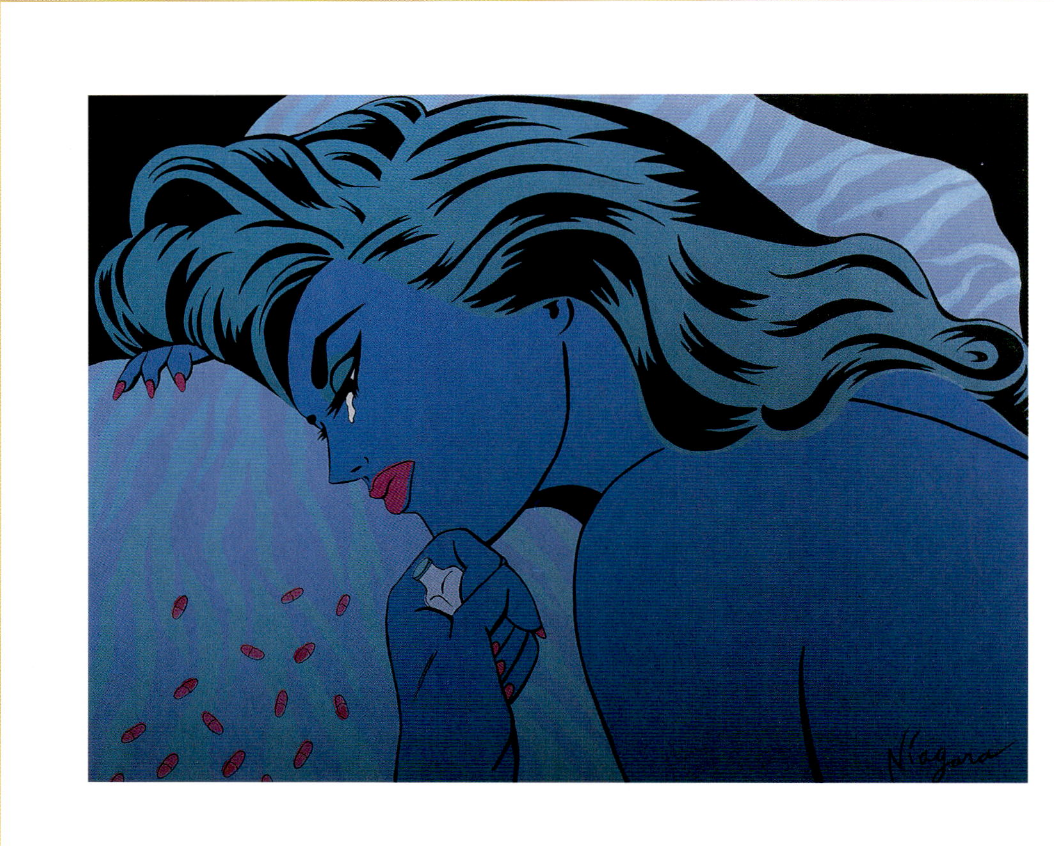


THE PILLS MOTHER GAVE ME DON'T DO ANYTHING AT ALL    2001, acrylic on linen, 24" x 36"

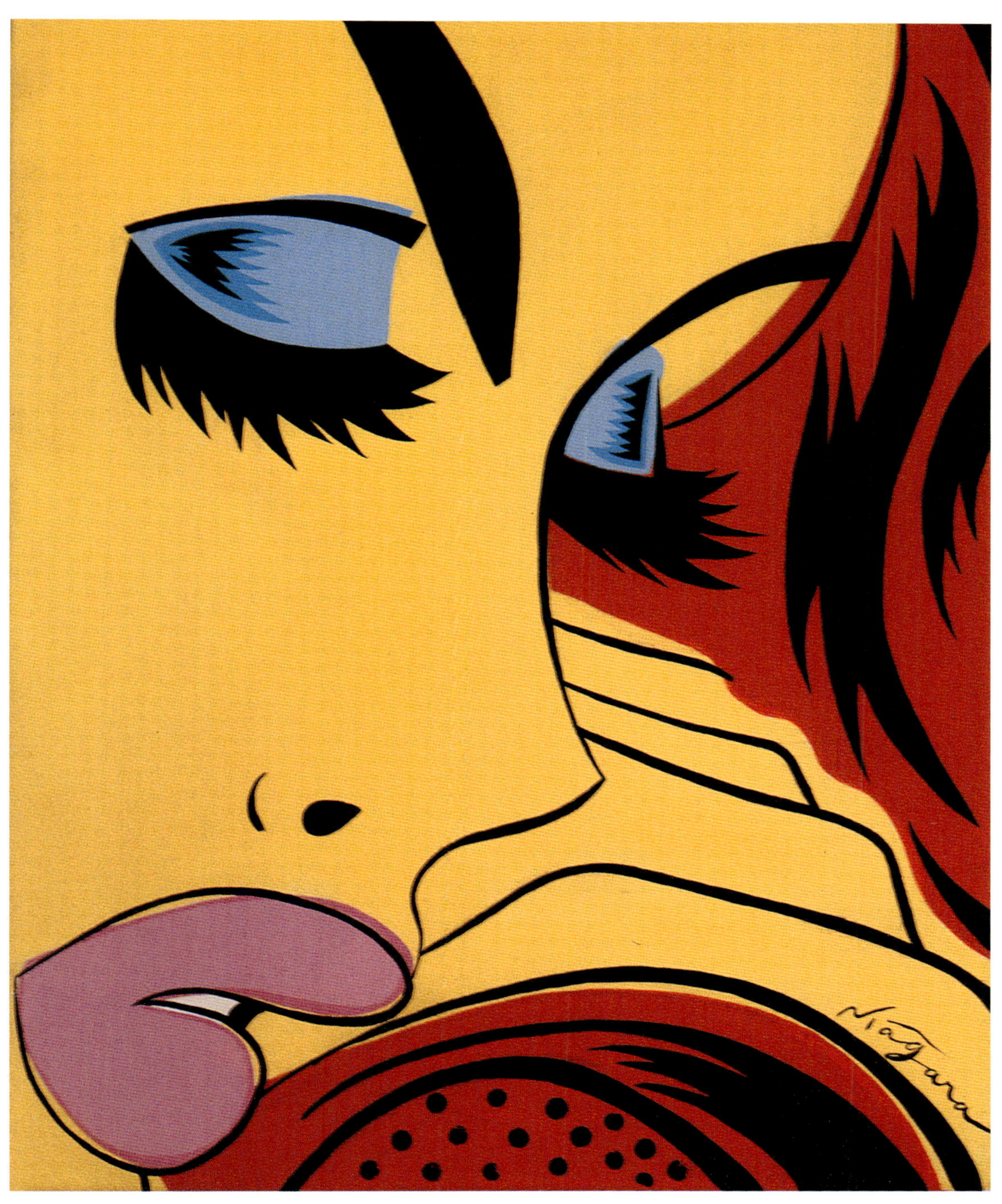


2003, acrylic on linen, 18" x 24"

Sorry Wrong Number

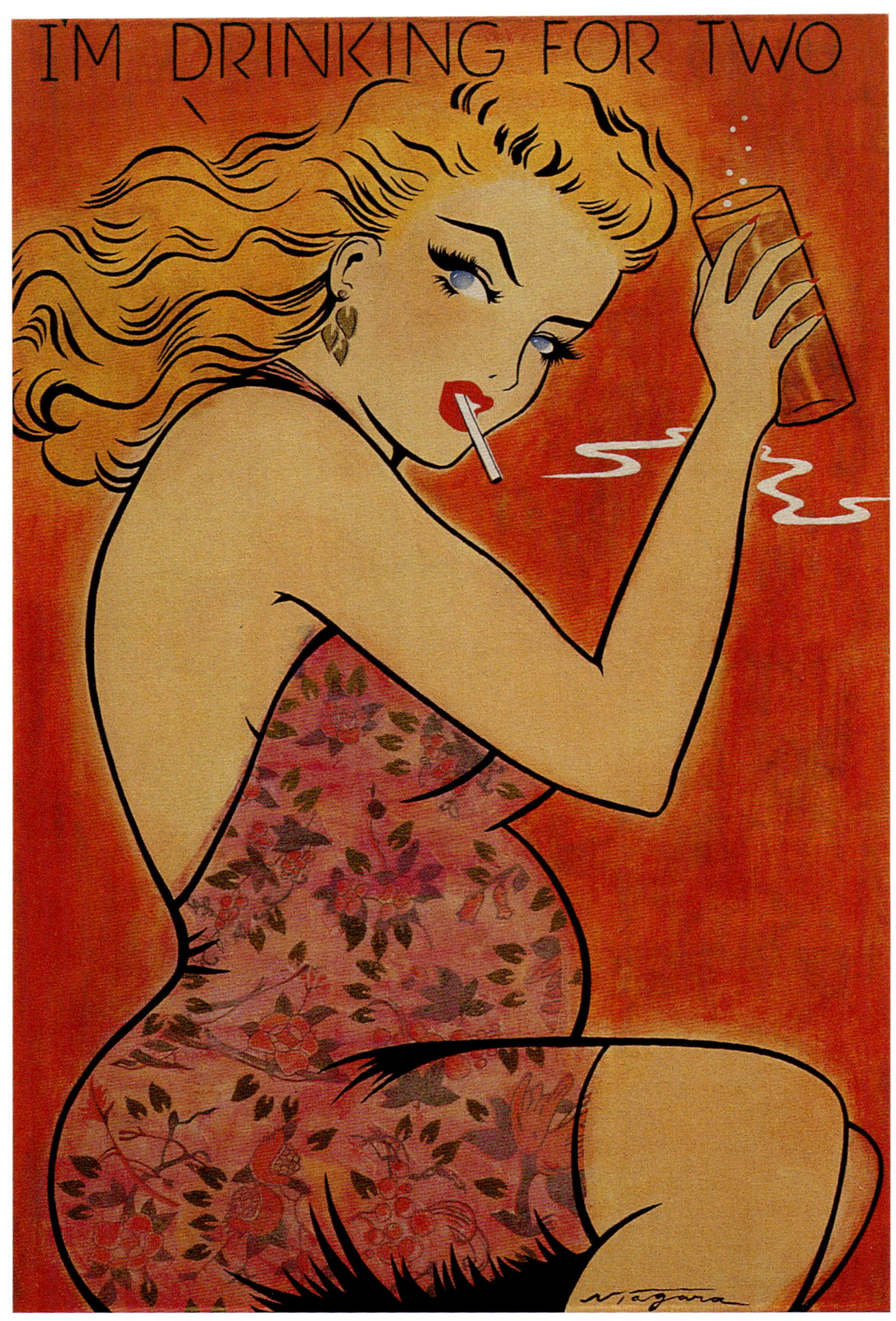


I'M DRINKING FOR TWO 2003, mixed media, 24" x 36"

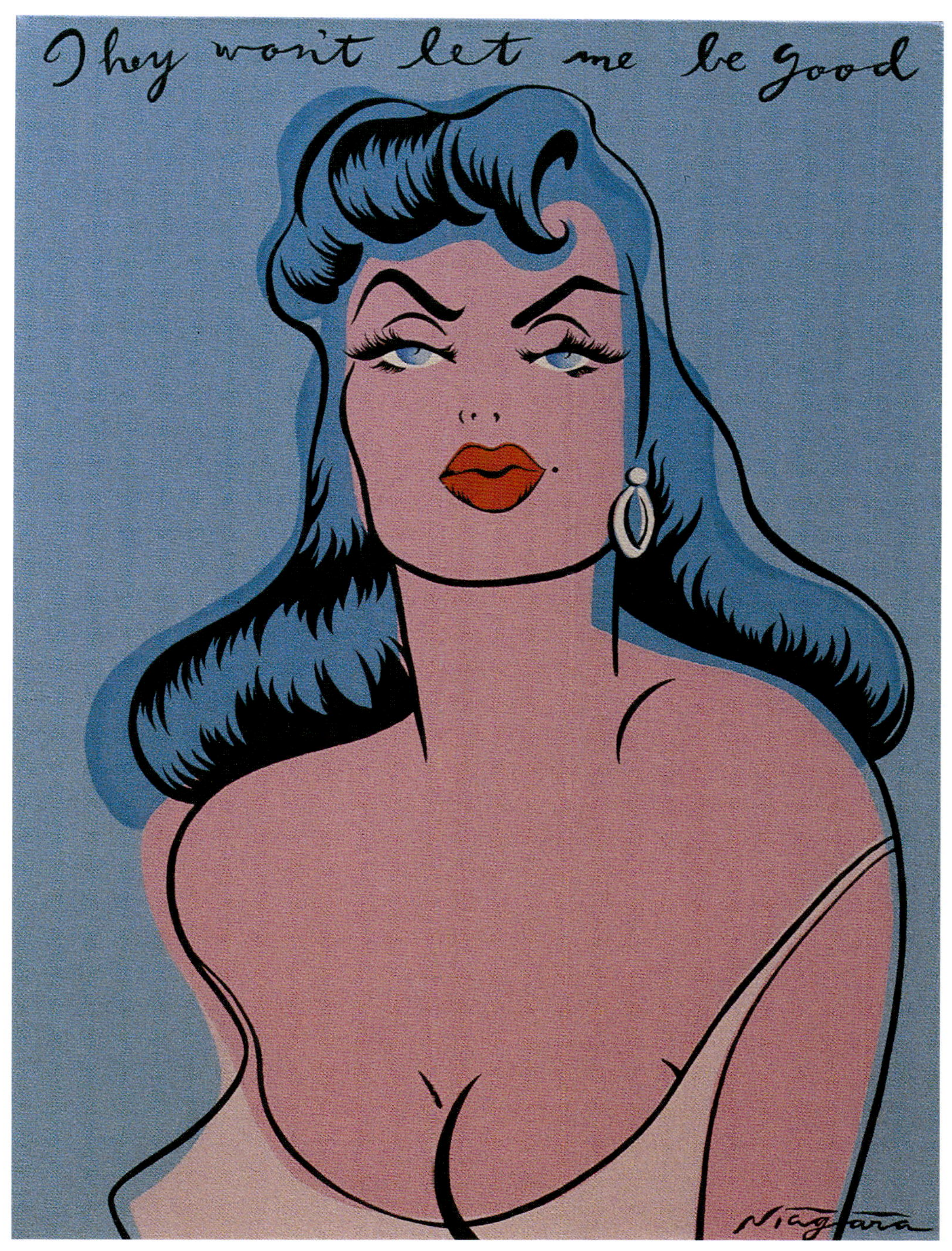


2003, acrylic on linen, 18" x 24"

THEY WON'T LET ME BE GOOD

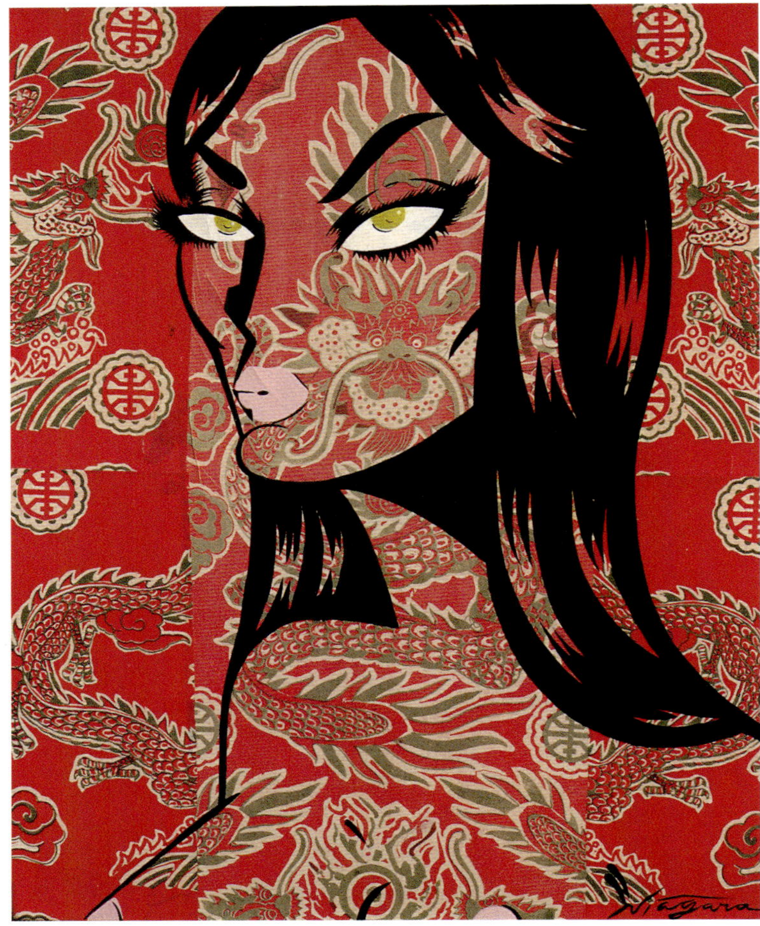

CHASING THE DRAGON #1 of 3
2003, mixed media, 18" x 24"

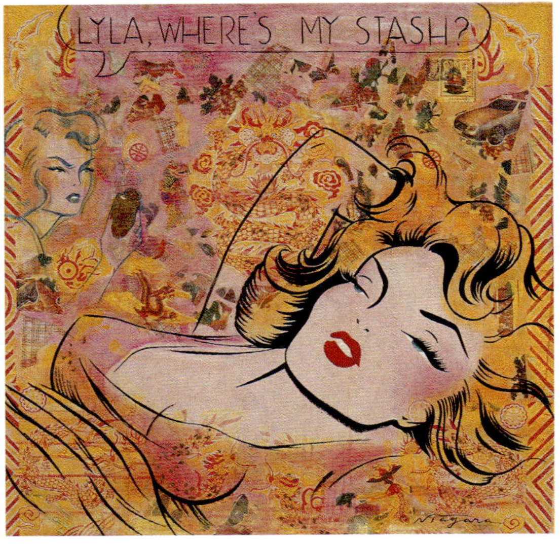


LYLA, WHERE'S MY STASH
2003, mixed media, 36" x 36"

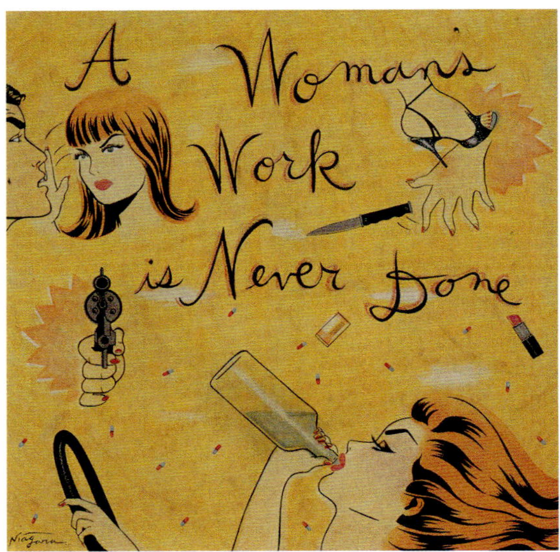


A WOMAN'S WORK IS NEVER DONE
2003, acrylic and oil on linen, 36" x 36"

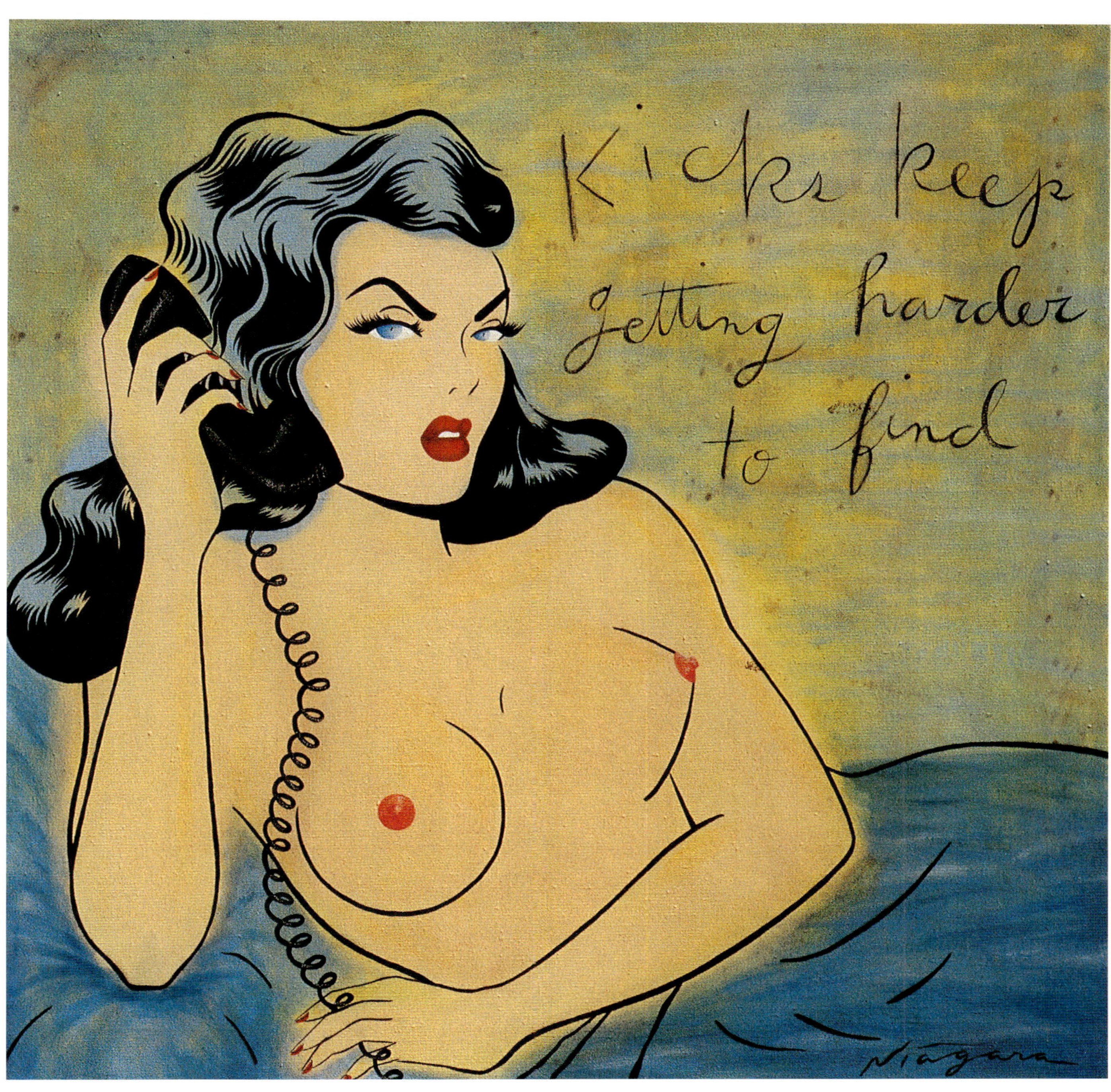


2003, acrylic on linen, 36" x 36"

KICKS KEEP GETTING HARDER TO FIND

# Marion
# PECK

(Seattle, Washington)

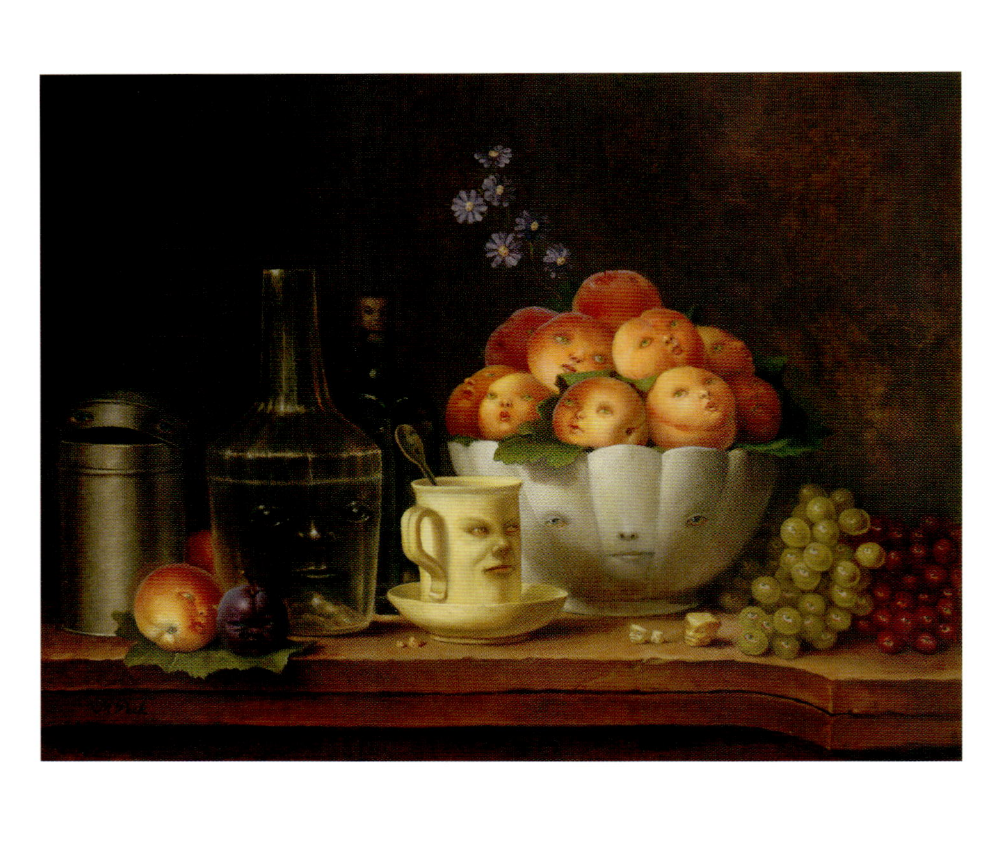

STILL LIFE WITH DRALAS (AFTER HENRI-NORACE ROLAND DE LA PORTE) 2003, oil on canvas, 16" x 20"

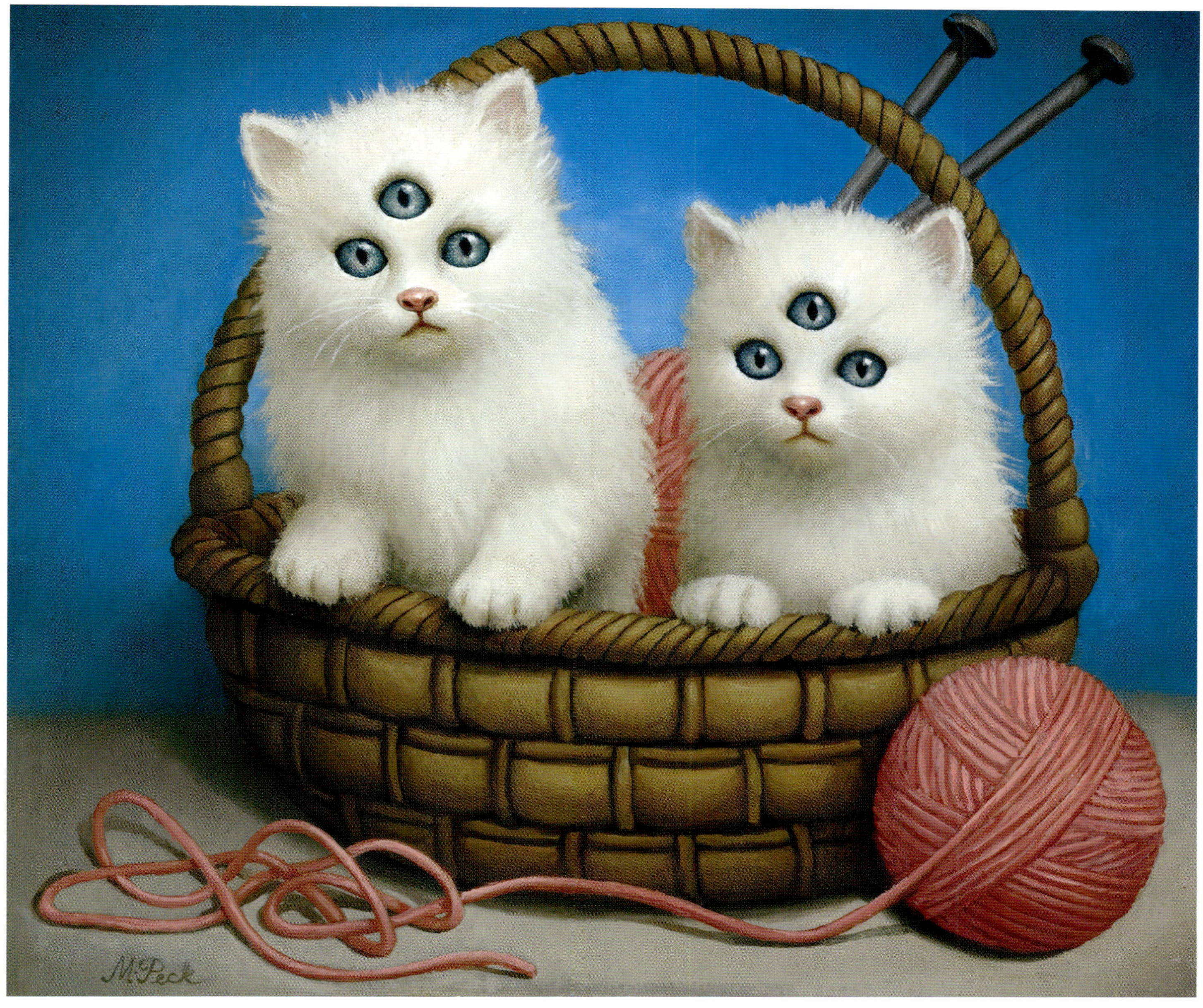

2003, oil on panel, 12" x 14"

Kittens

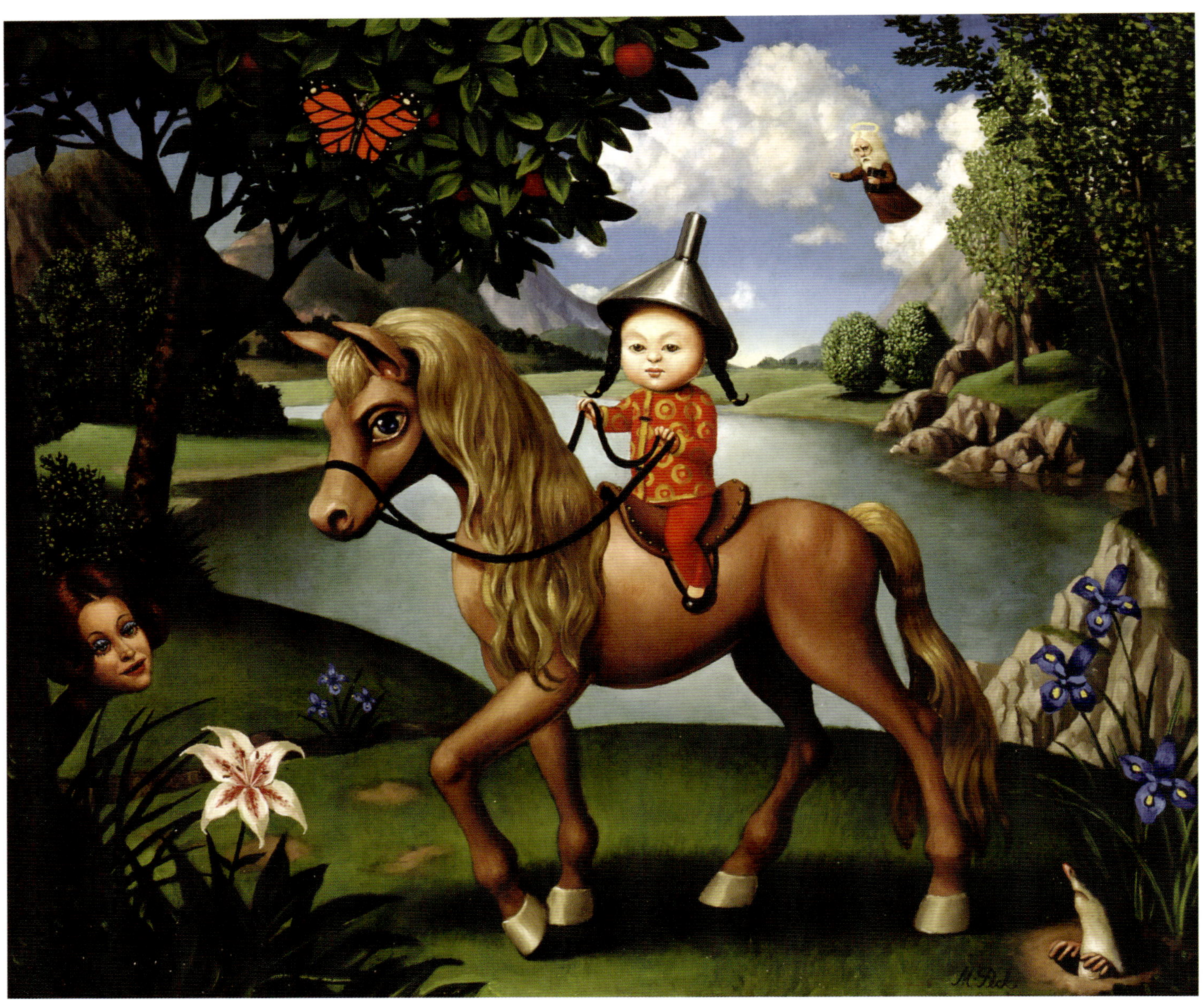

Lili Ridin' Through the Garden of Eden 2002, oil on panel, 32" x 38"

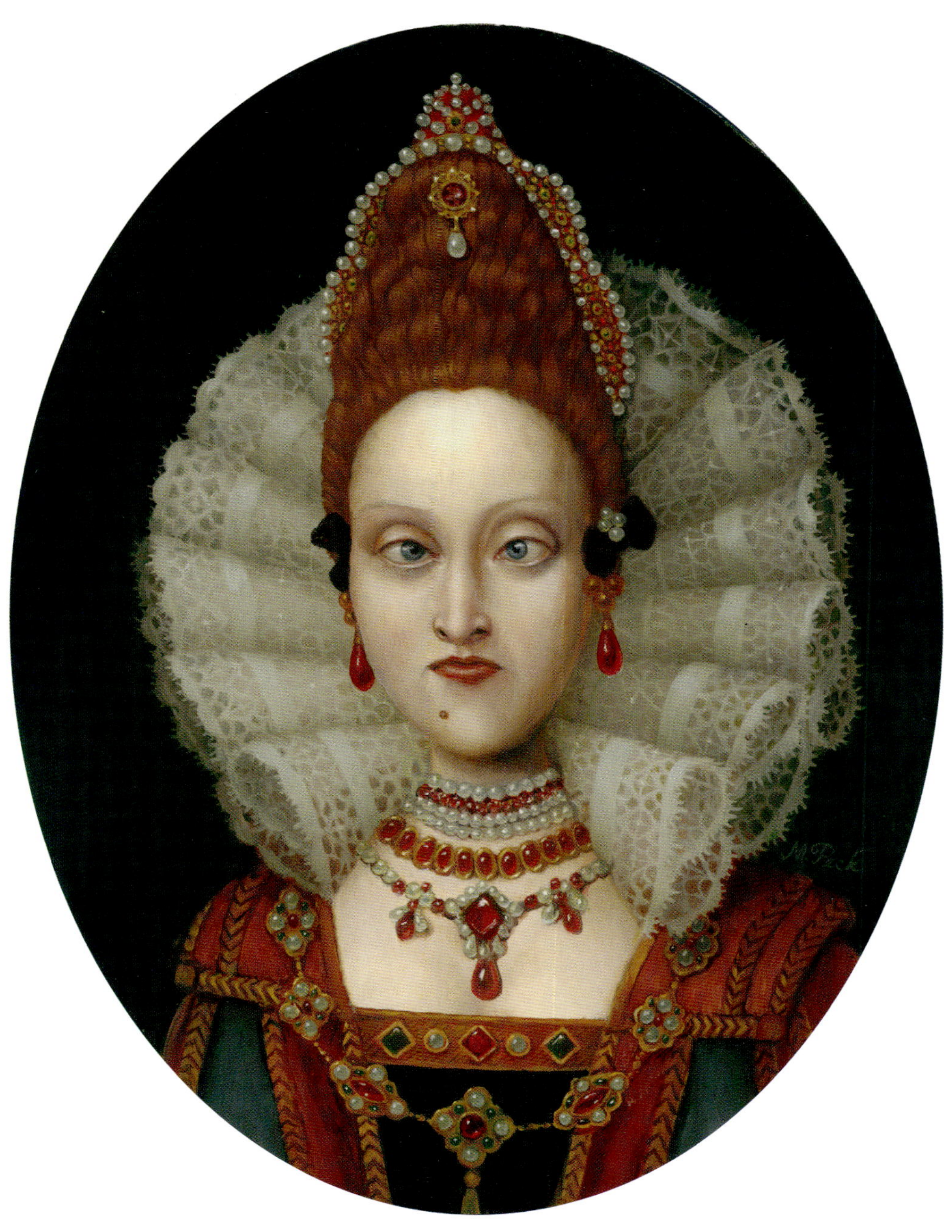

Lady Henrietta Swaneshald, Mistress of Ethelred the Unready
(Later To Become Queen Charles of Wessex)
2003, oil on panel, 14" x 11" oval

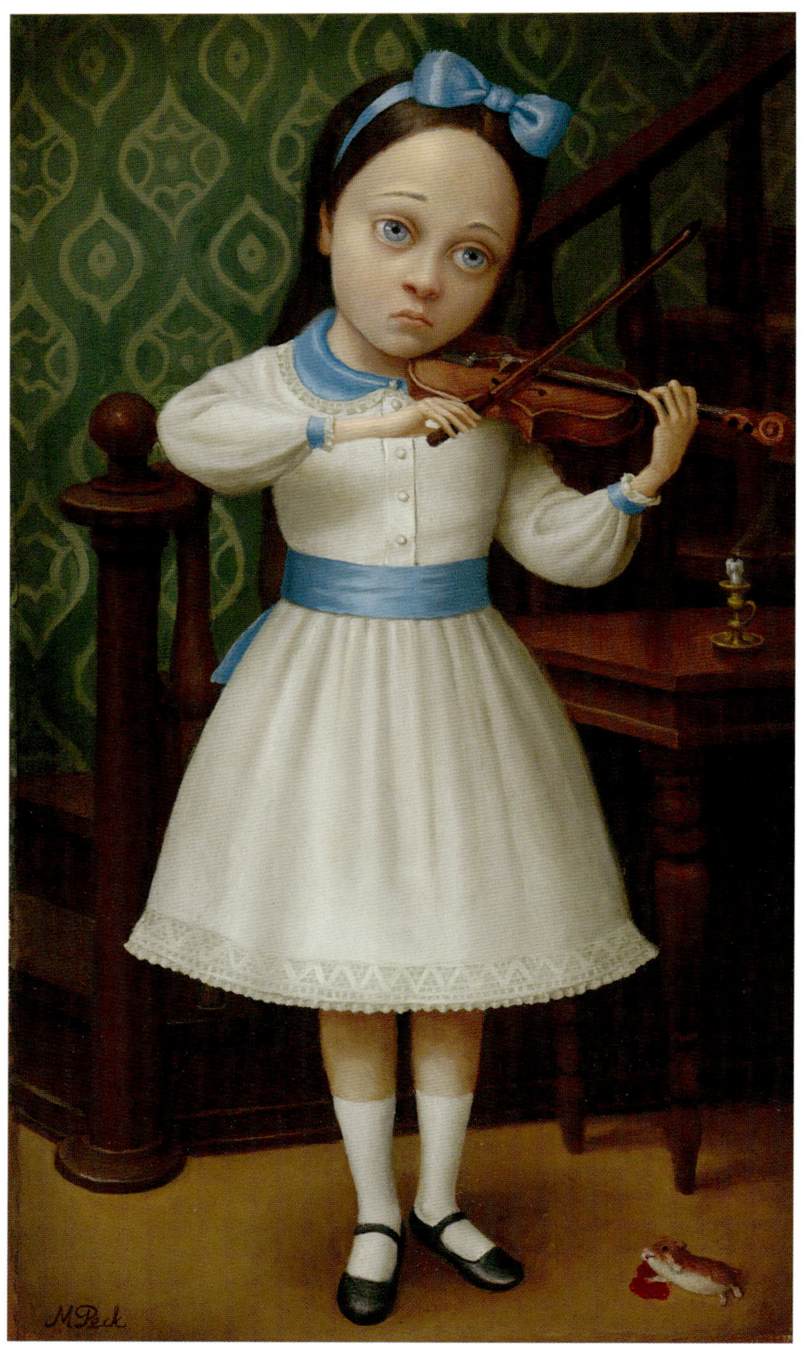

ALBERT'S SONG 2003, oil on panel, 14" x 24"

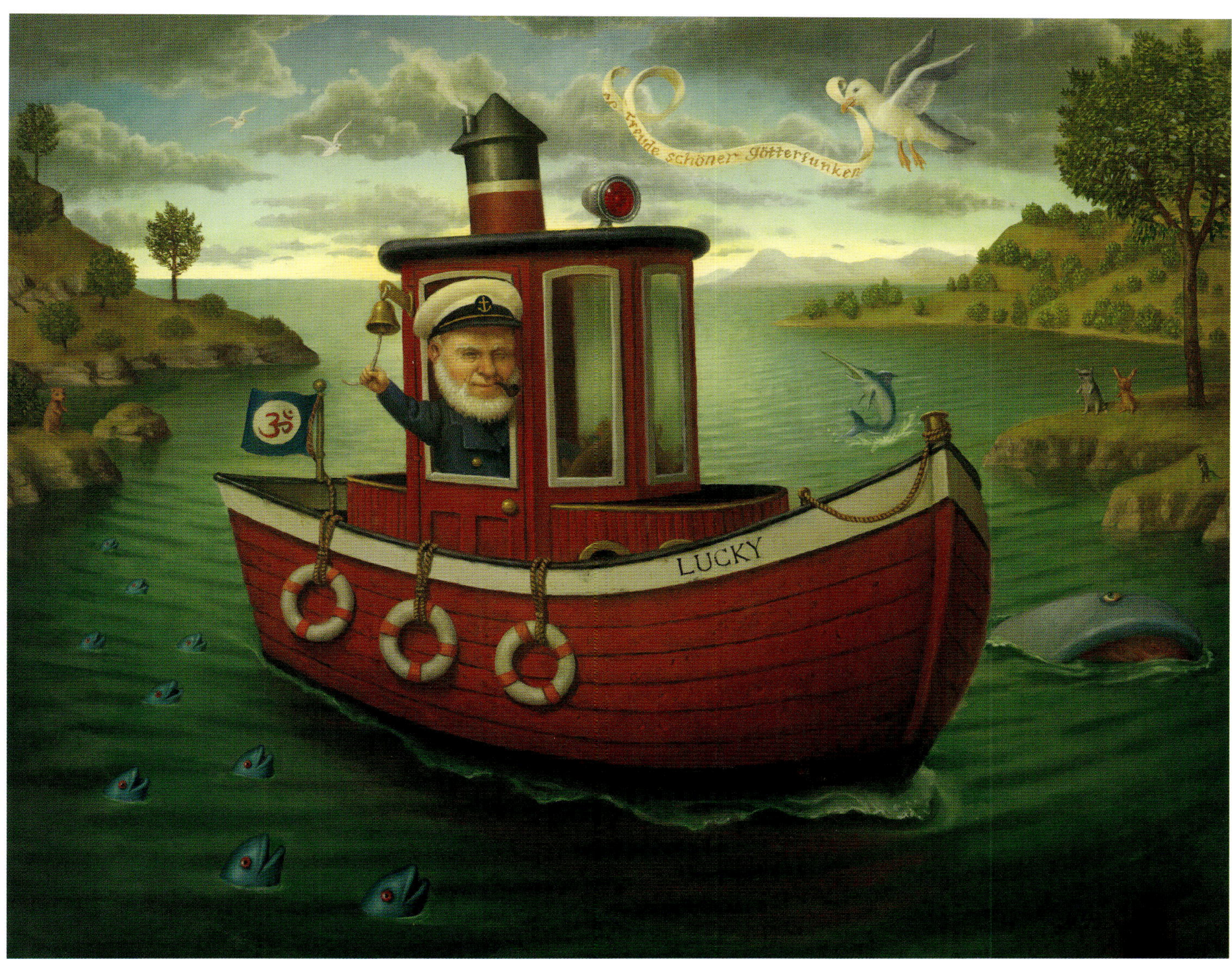


2003, oil on panel, 19" x 24"

THE HAPPY CAPTAIN

# Lisa PETRUCCI

(Seattle, Washington)

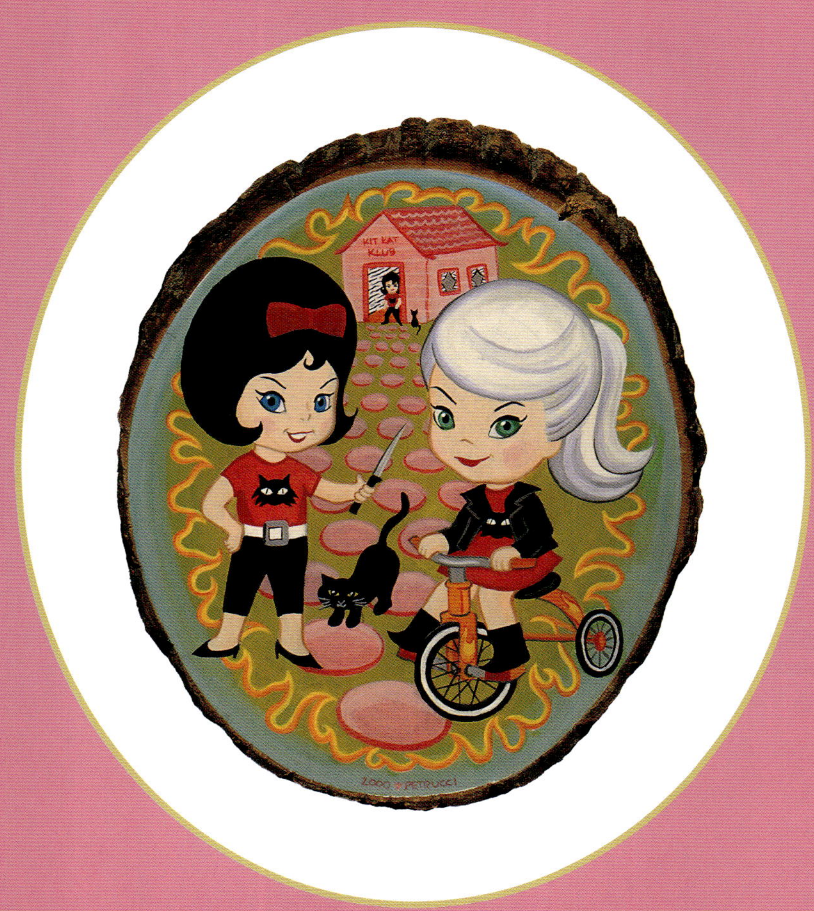


KIT KAT KLUB 2000, acrylic, envirotex on wood, 11" x 9"

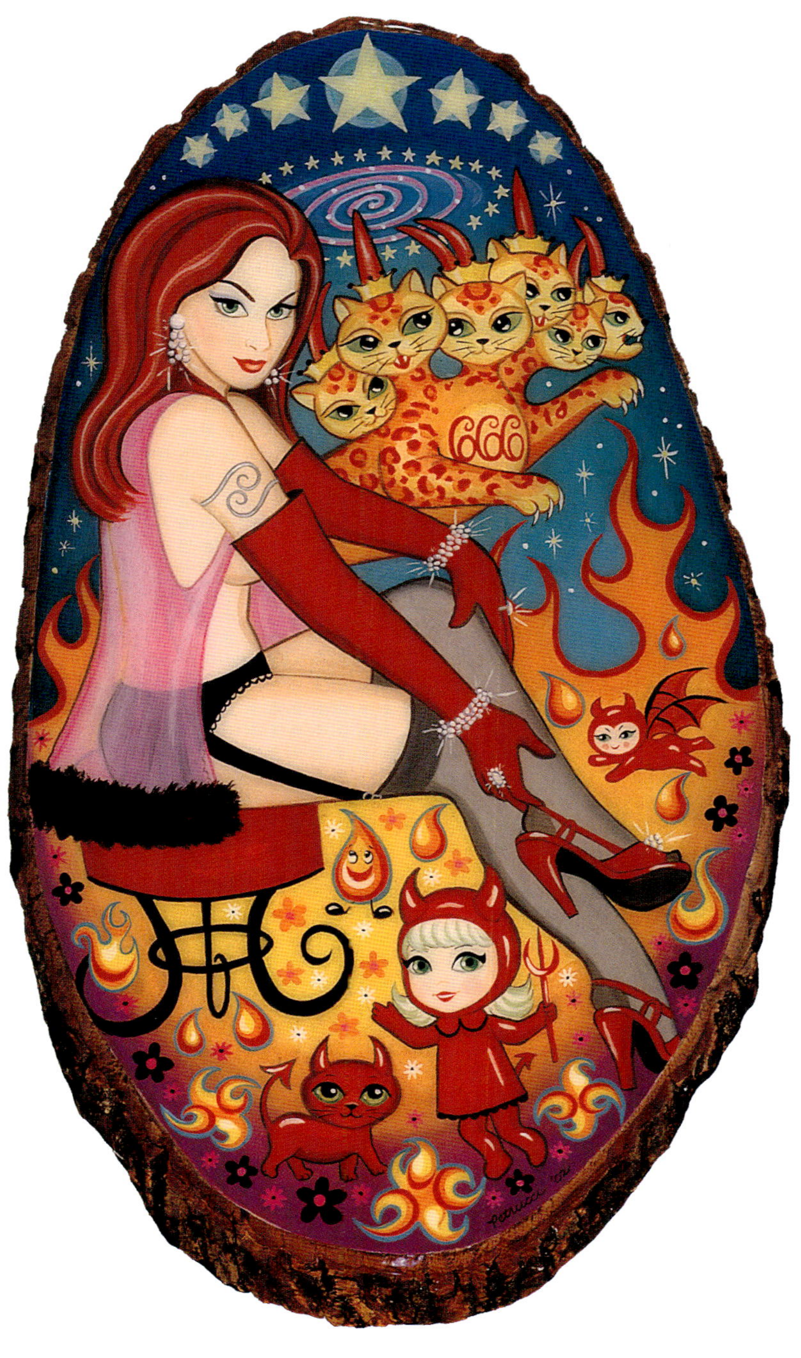

2002, acrylic, envirotex on wood 14" x 11"    THE DEVIL'S PLAYGROUND

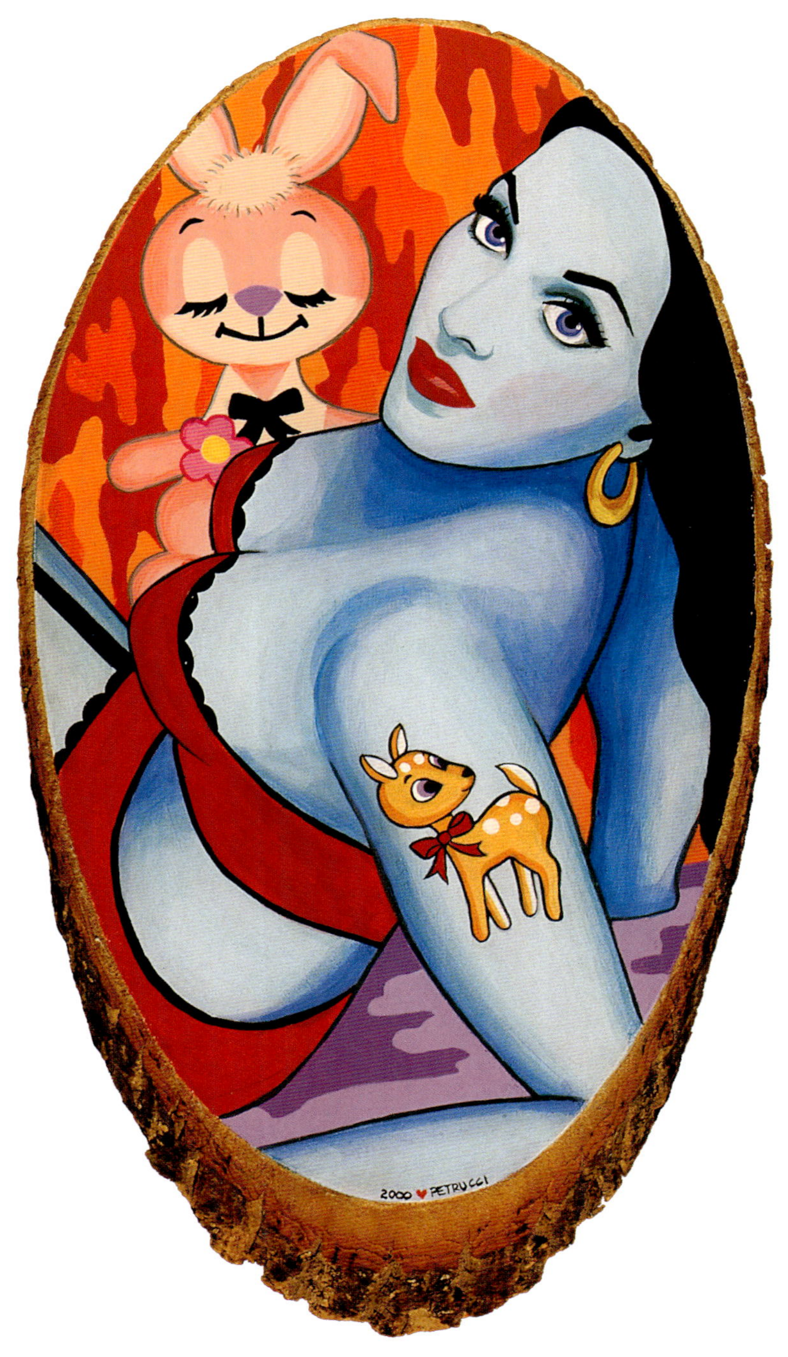


DREAM PET 2001, acrylic, envirotex on wood, 6" x 12"

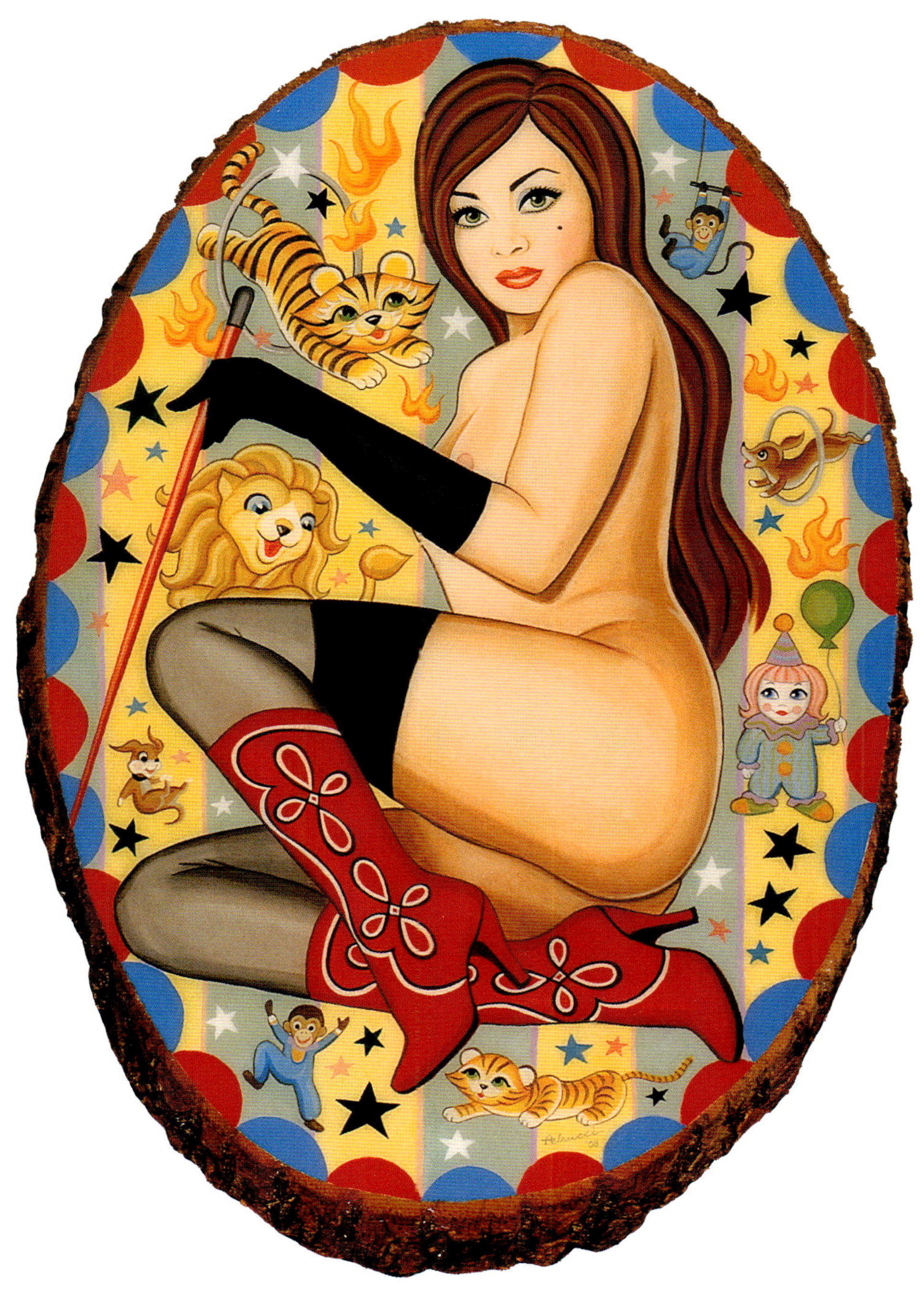

2003, acrylic, envirotex on wood, 17" x 11"

Big Top Beauty

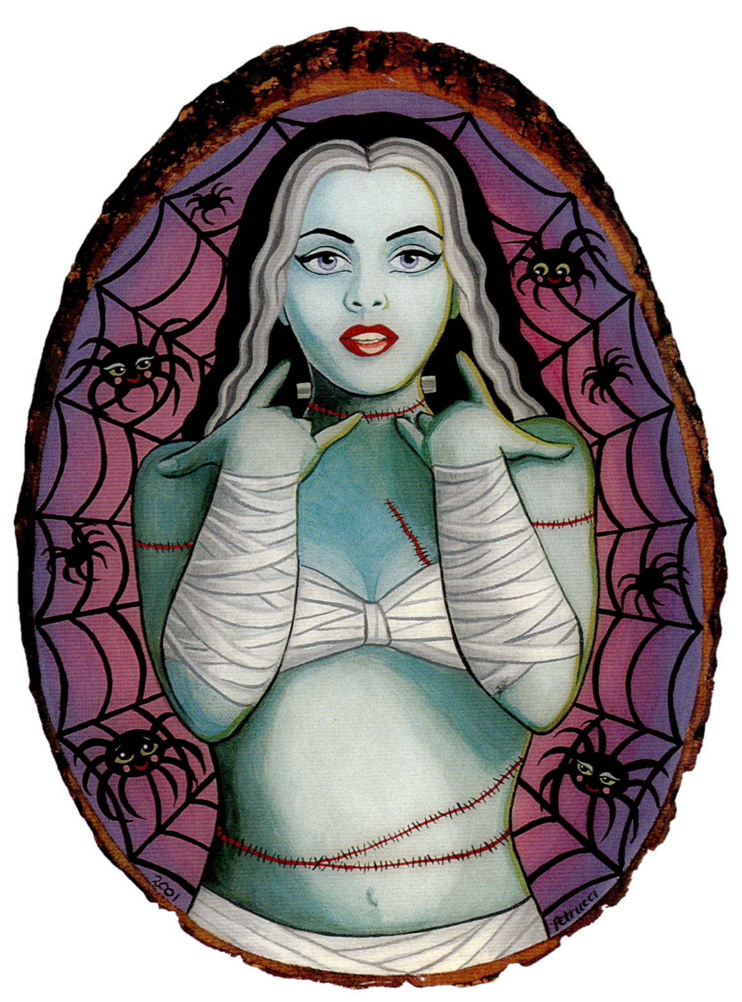

Miss Monster
2002, acrylic, envirotex on wood, 10" x 8"

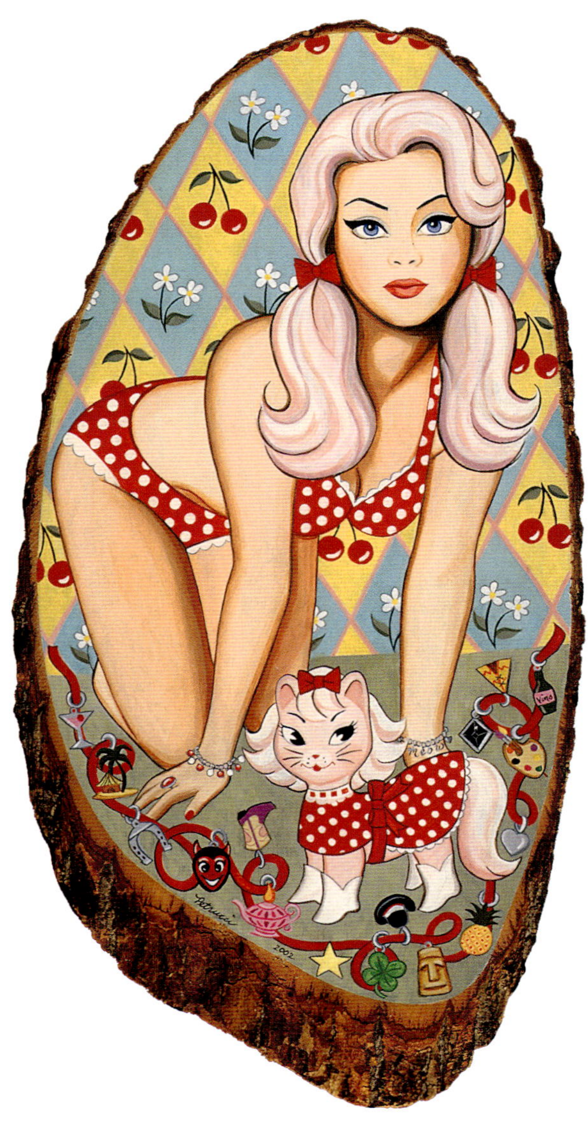

Charmed and Dangerous
2002, acrylic, envirotex on wood, 17" x 8.5"

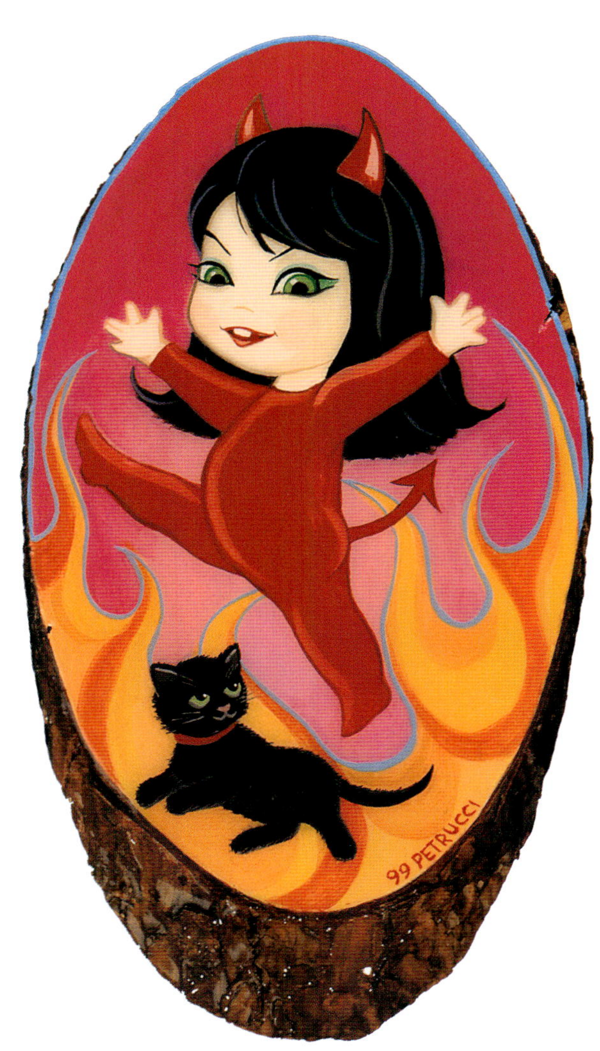


NAUGHTY (A)
1999, acrylic, envirotex on wood, 8" x 4"

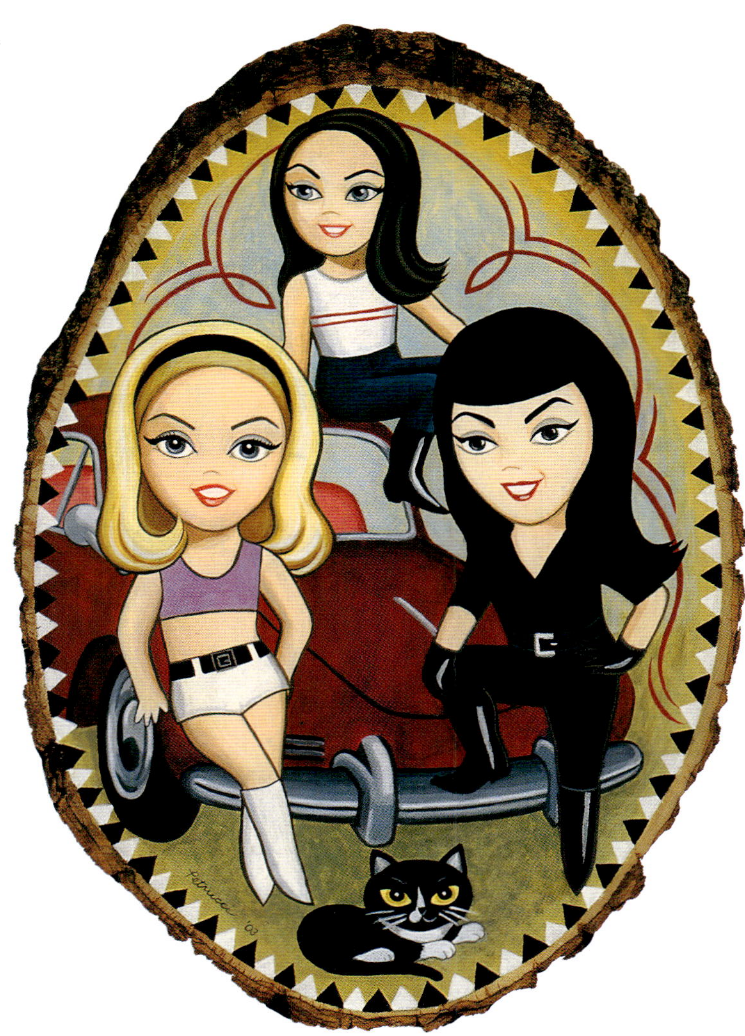

FASTER PUSSYCAT KIDDLE KIDDLE
2003, acrylic, envirotex on wood, 11" x 9"

# The PIZZ

(Los Angeles, California)

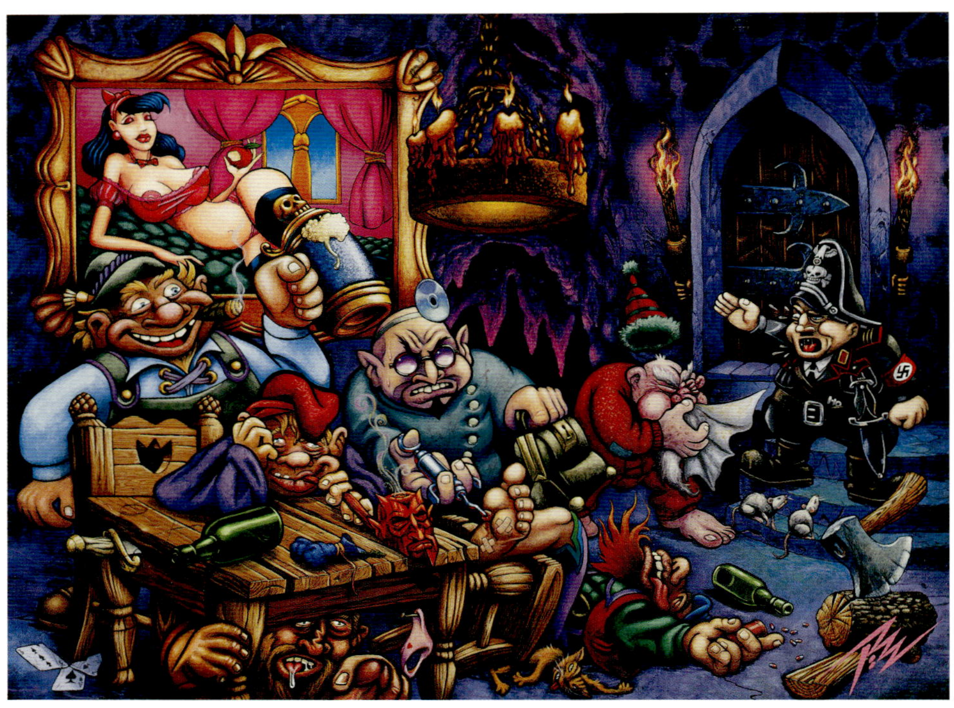

7 DWARVES

1999, acrylic on canvas, 30" x 40"

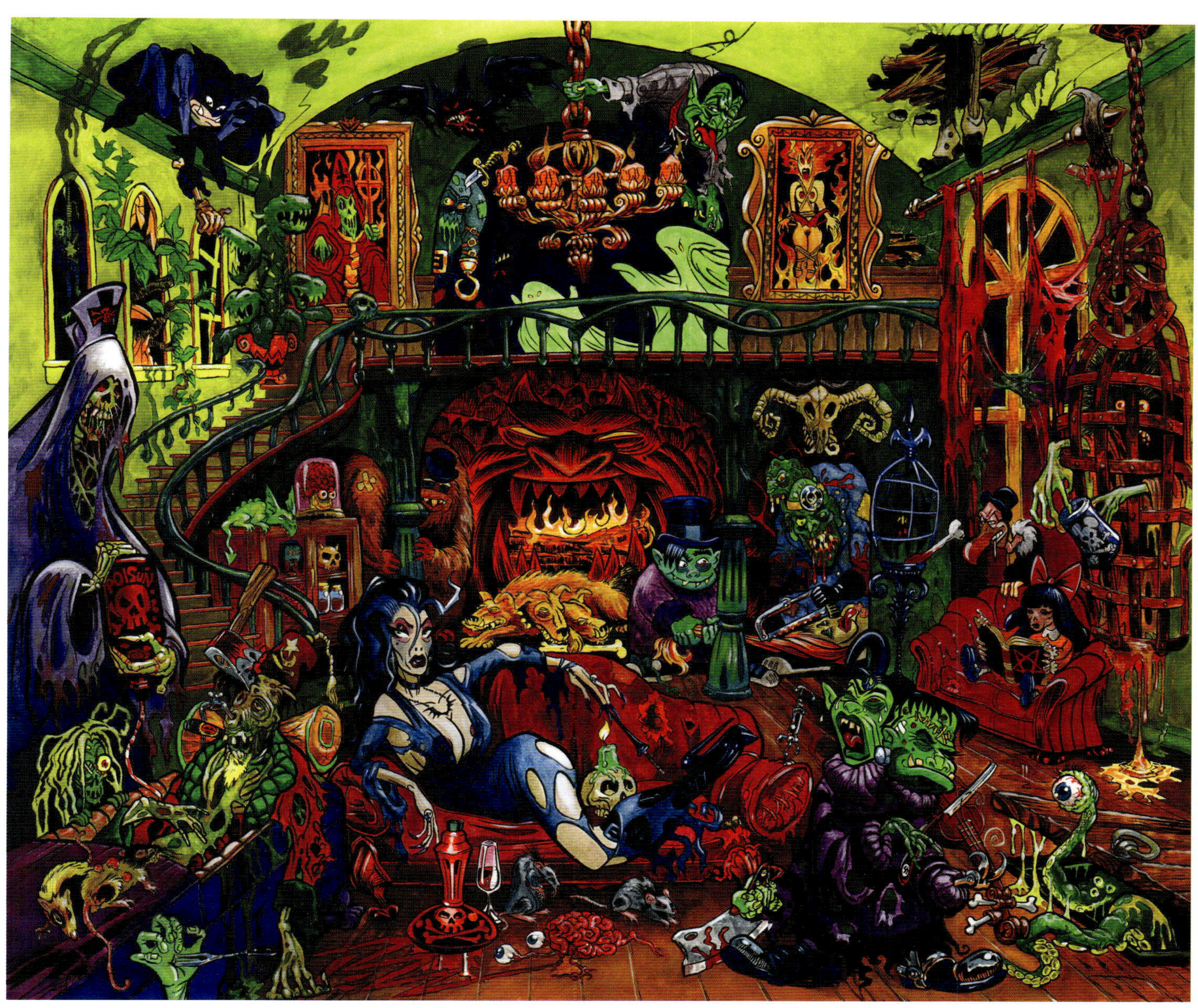


2000, aquatint, watercolor on paper, 18" x 24"

HAUNTED HOUSE

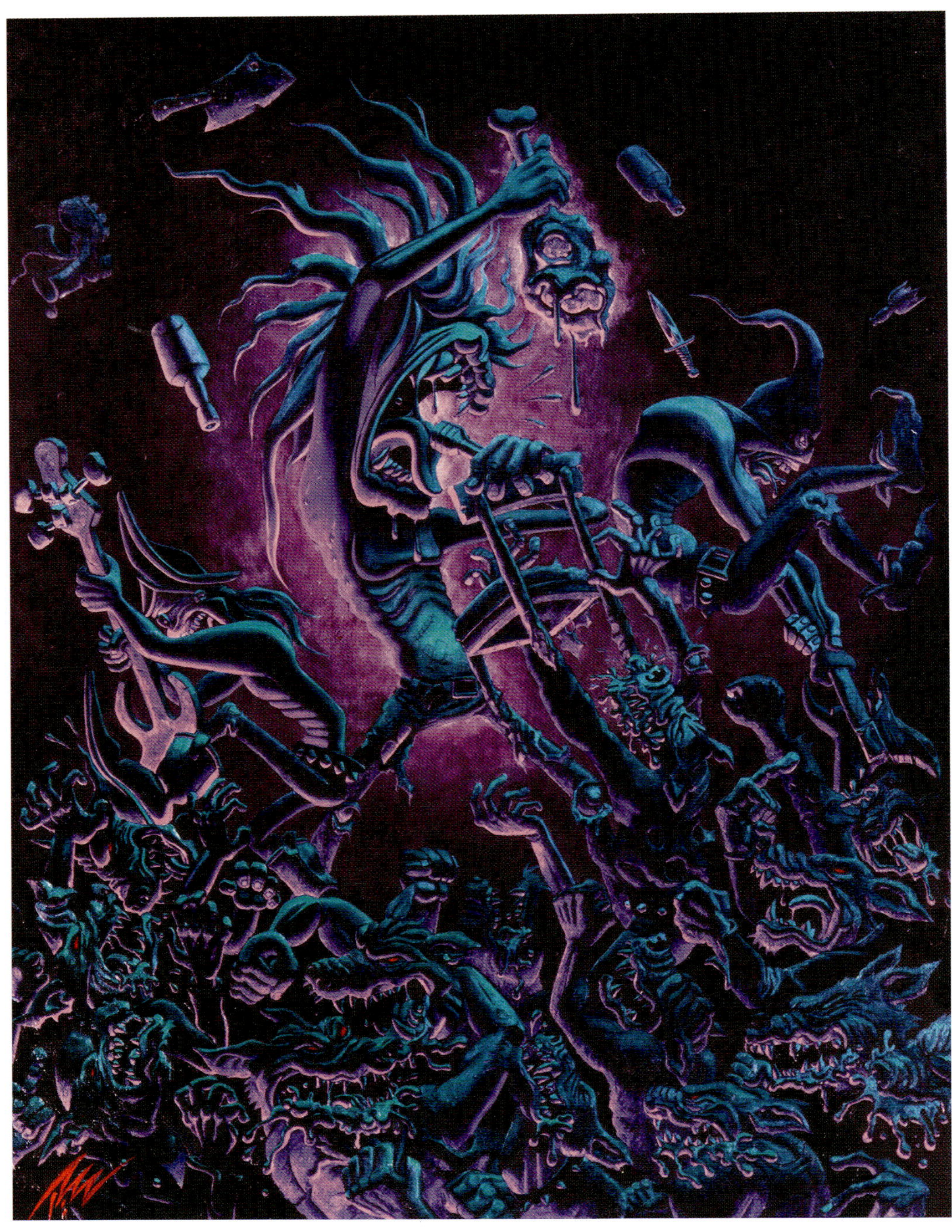

Atavistic Avatar 1987, acrylic on canvas, 36" x 48"

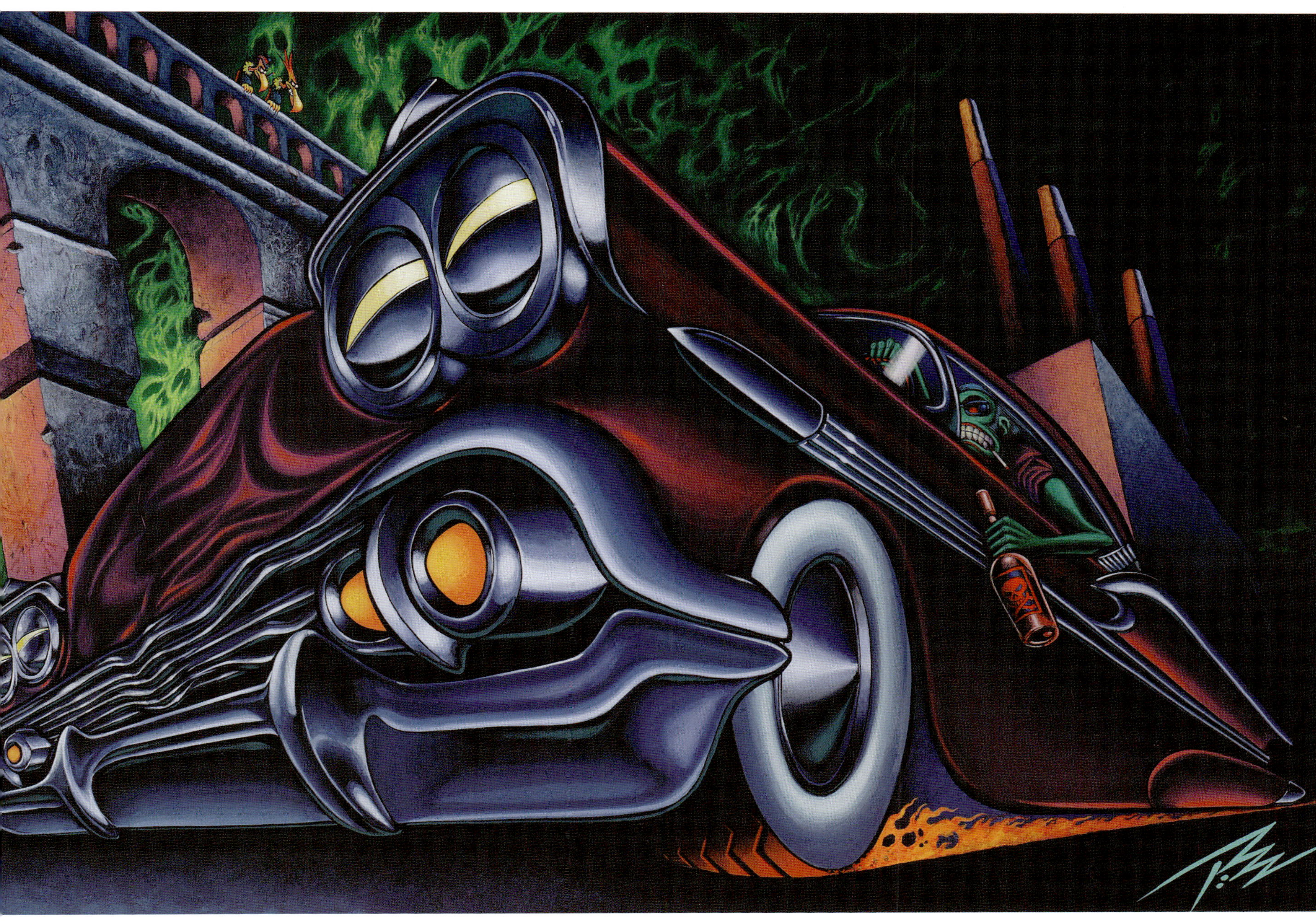

1999, acrylic on canvas, 28" x 56"

Death Takes a Holiday

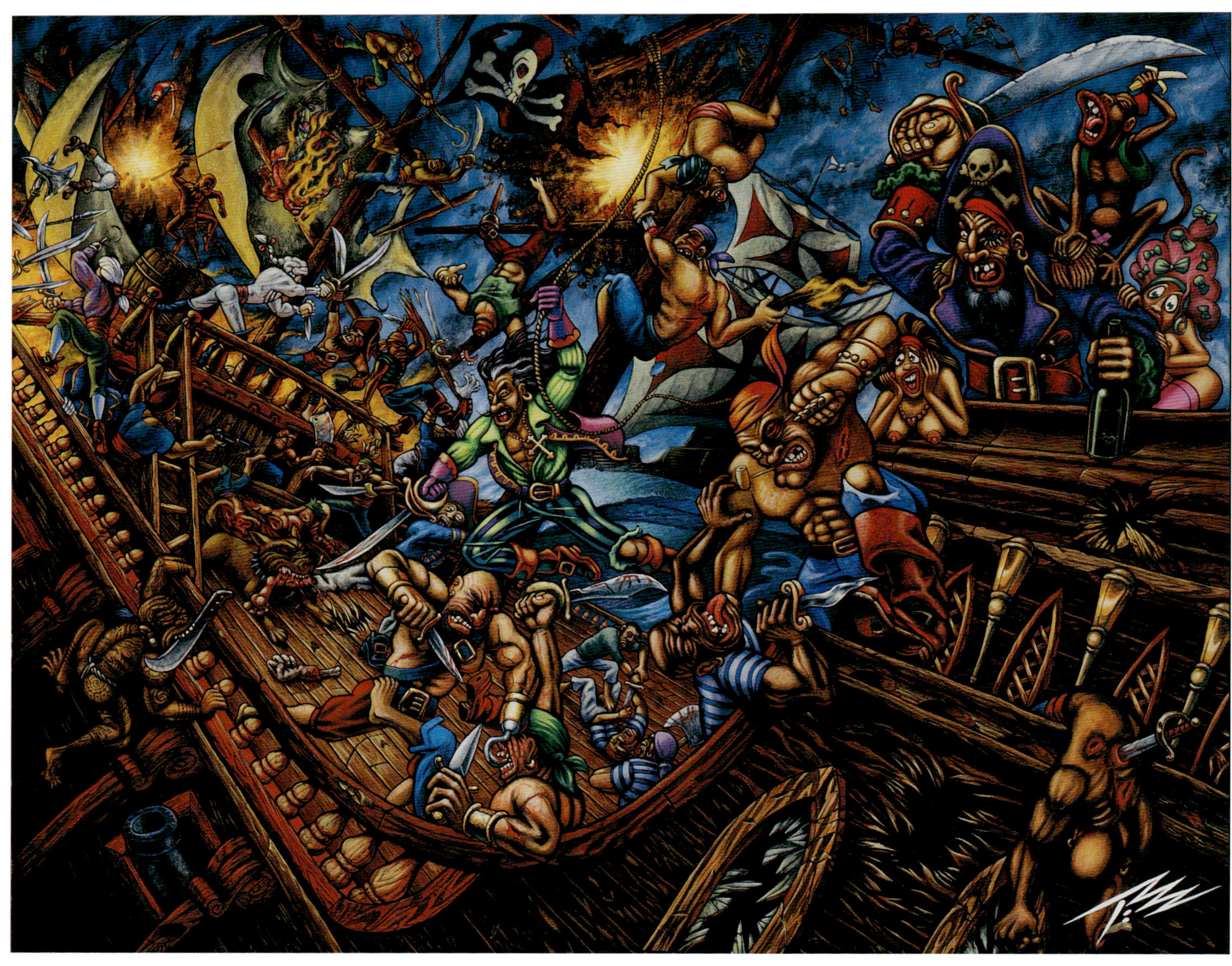

Aye For an Aye

2000, acrylic on canvas, 36" x 48"

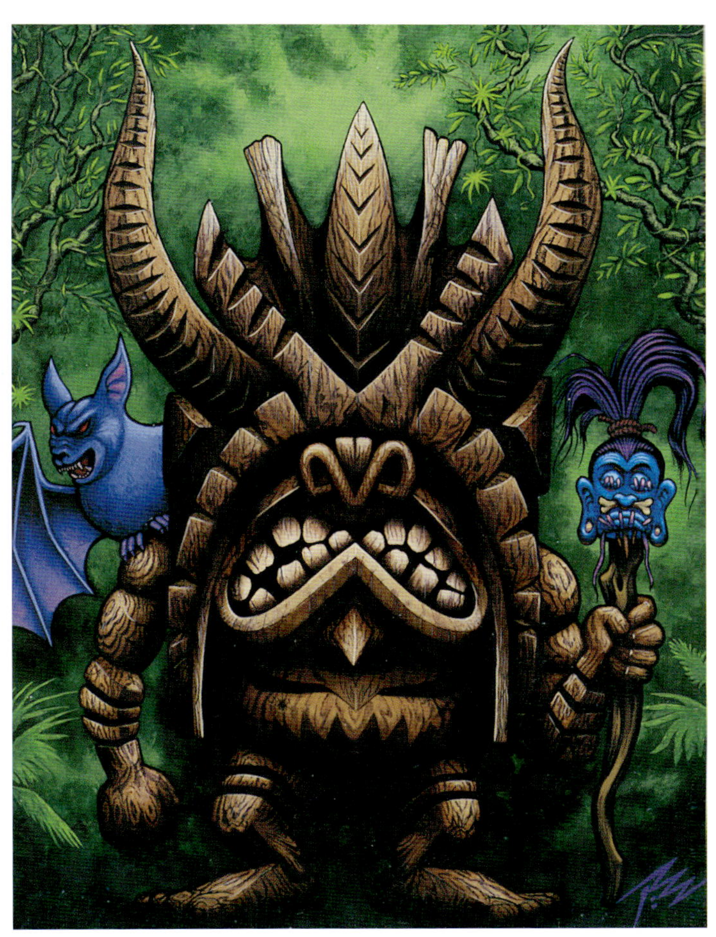

1998, acrylic on canvas, 16" x 20"

Badass Tiki

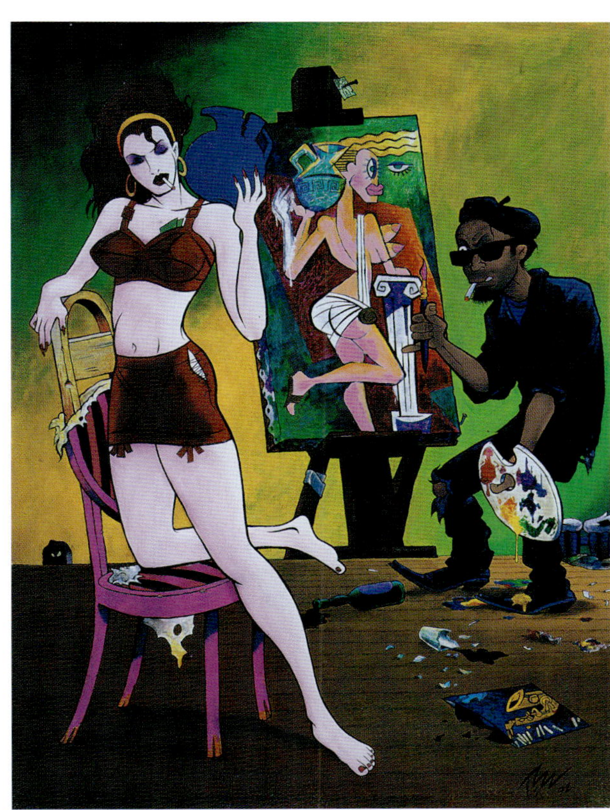

Working With Cheap Materials
1992, mixed media on canvas, 36" x 42"

# Mark RYDEN

(Los Angeles, California)

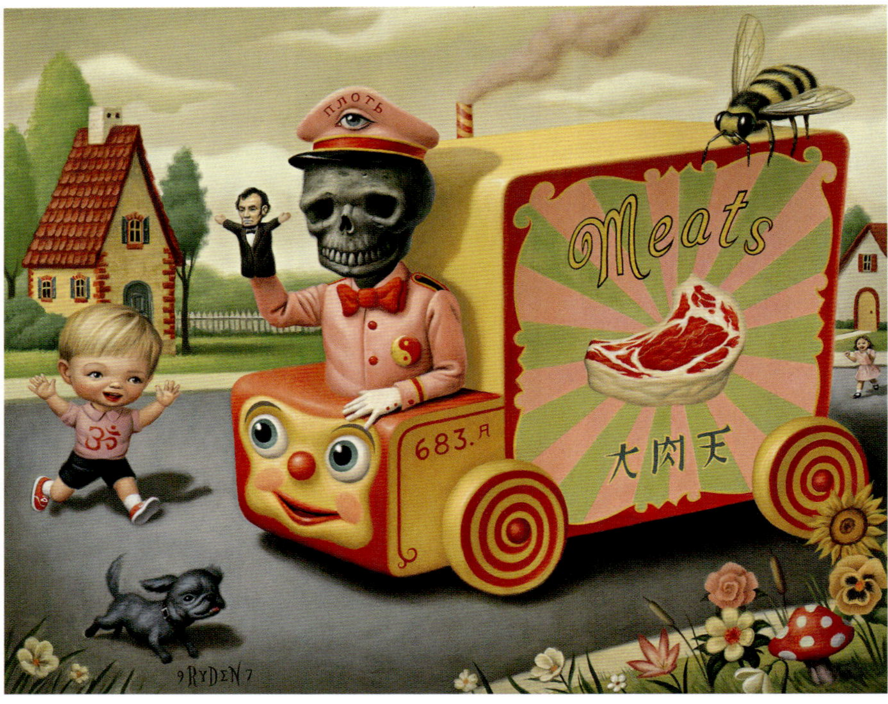


THE MEAT MAGI

1997, oil on canvas, 20" x 24"

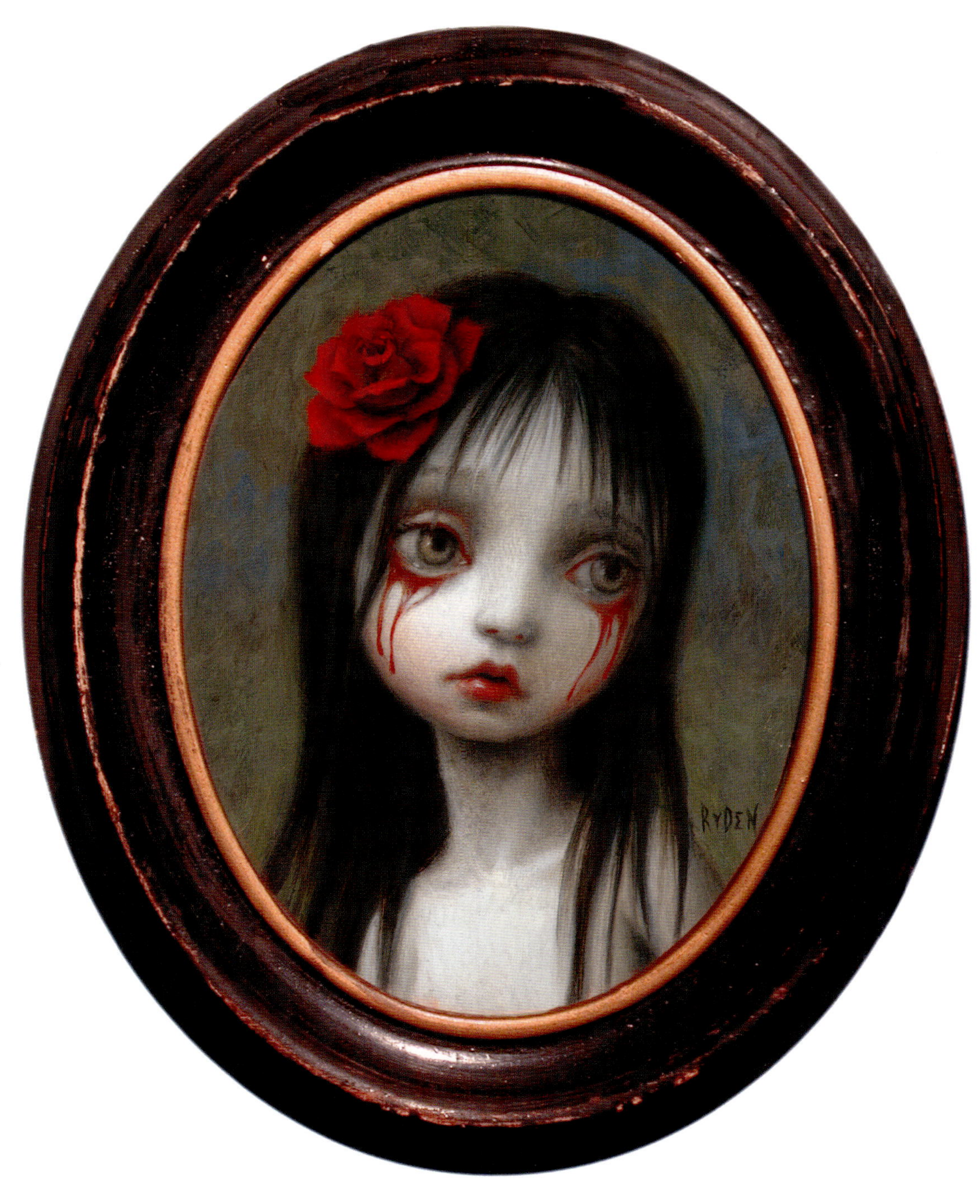


2003, oil on panel, 3.5" x 4.75"

ROSE

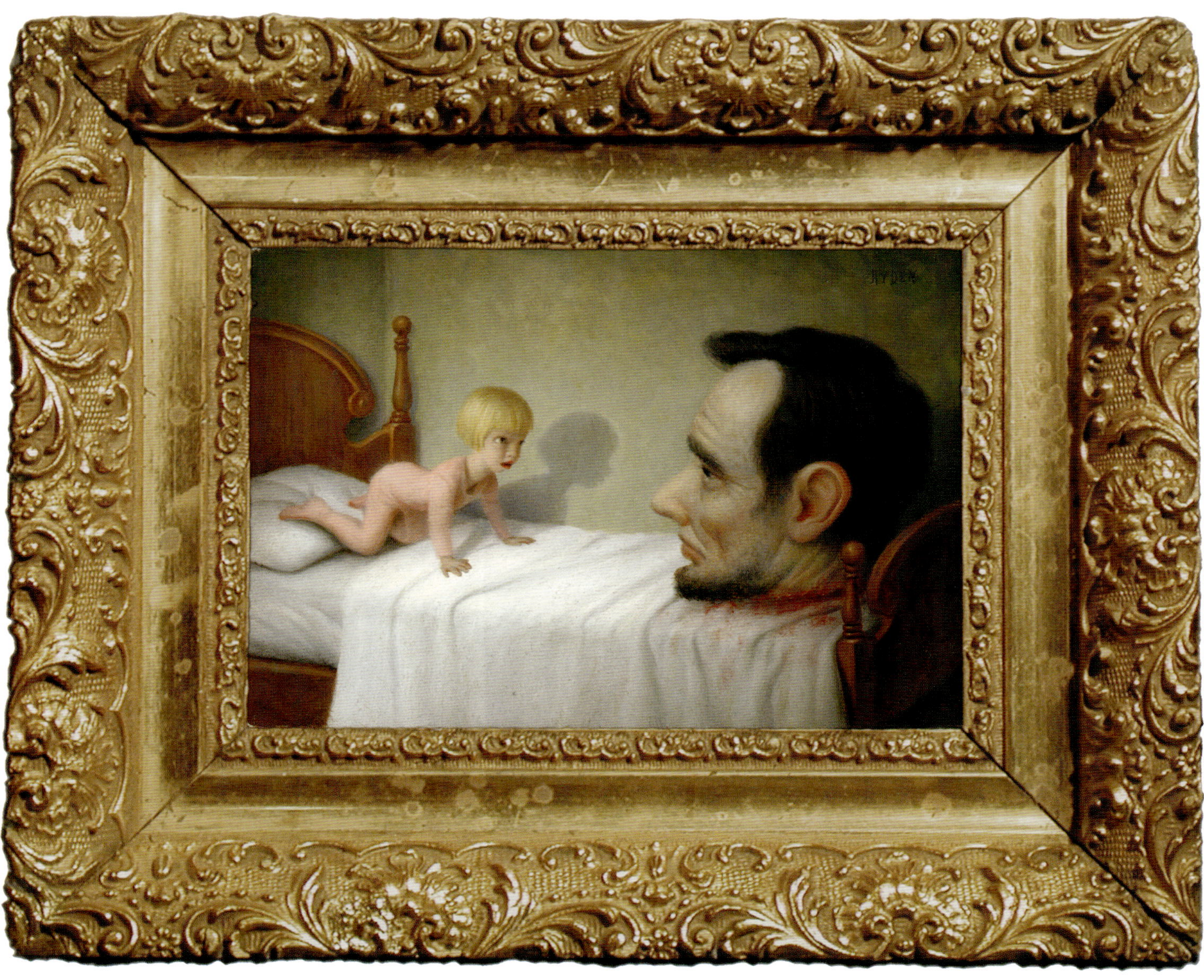

LINCOLN'S HEAD

2003, oil on panel, 4.5" x 6.5"

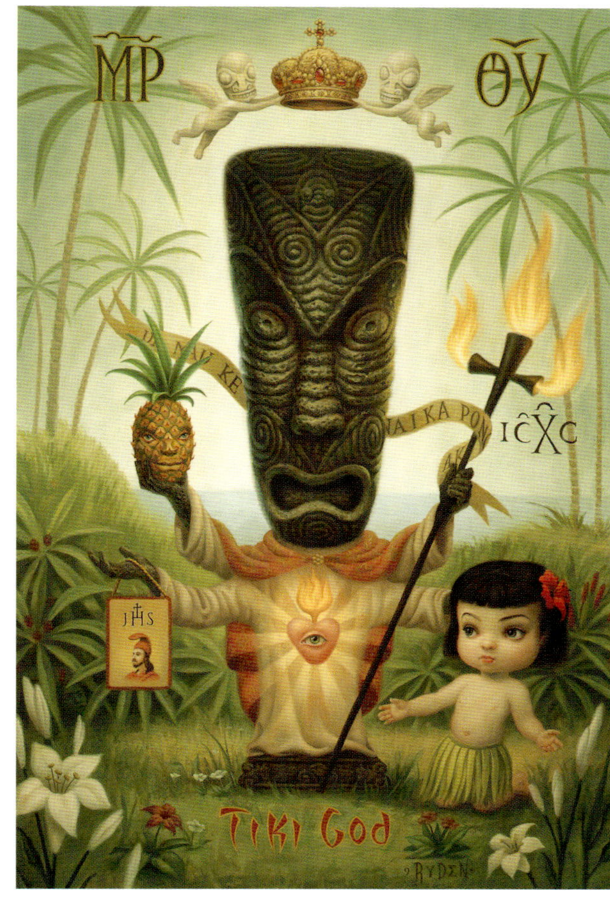


1996, oil on canvas, 45" x 30" Tiki God

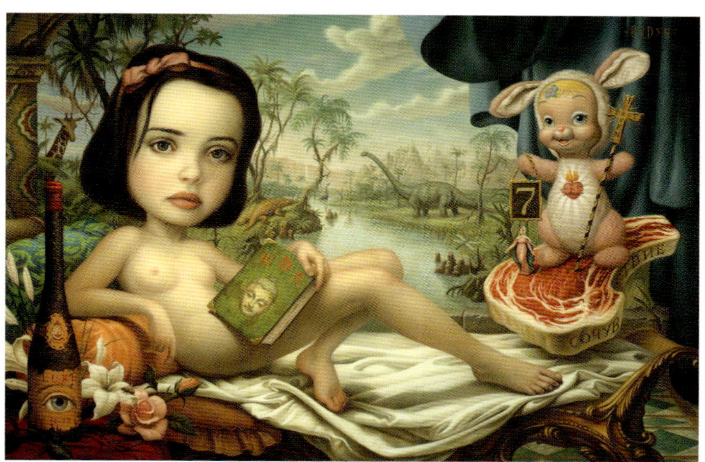

1997, oil on canvas, 48" x 72" Snow White

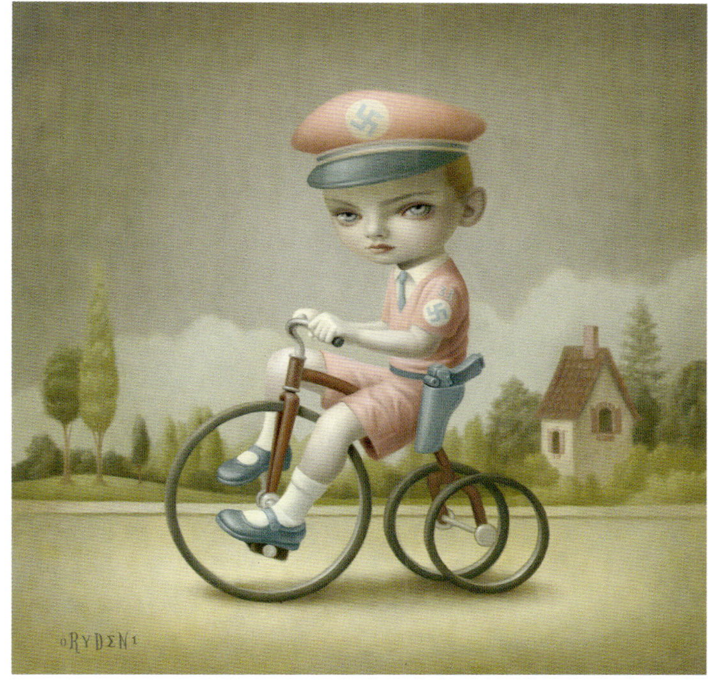


2001, oil on canvas, 20" x 20" Little Boy Blue

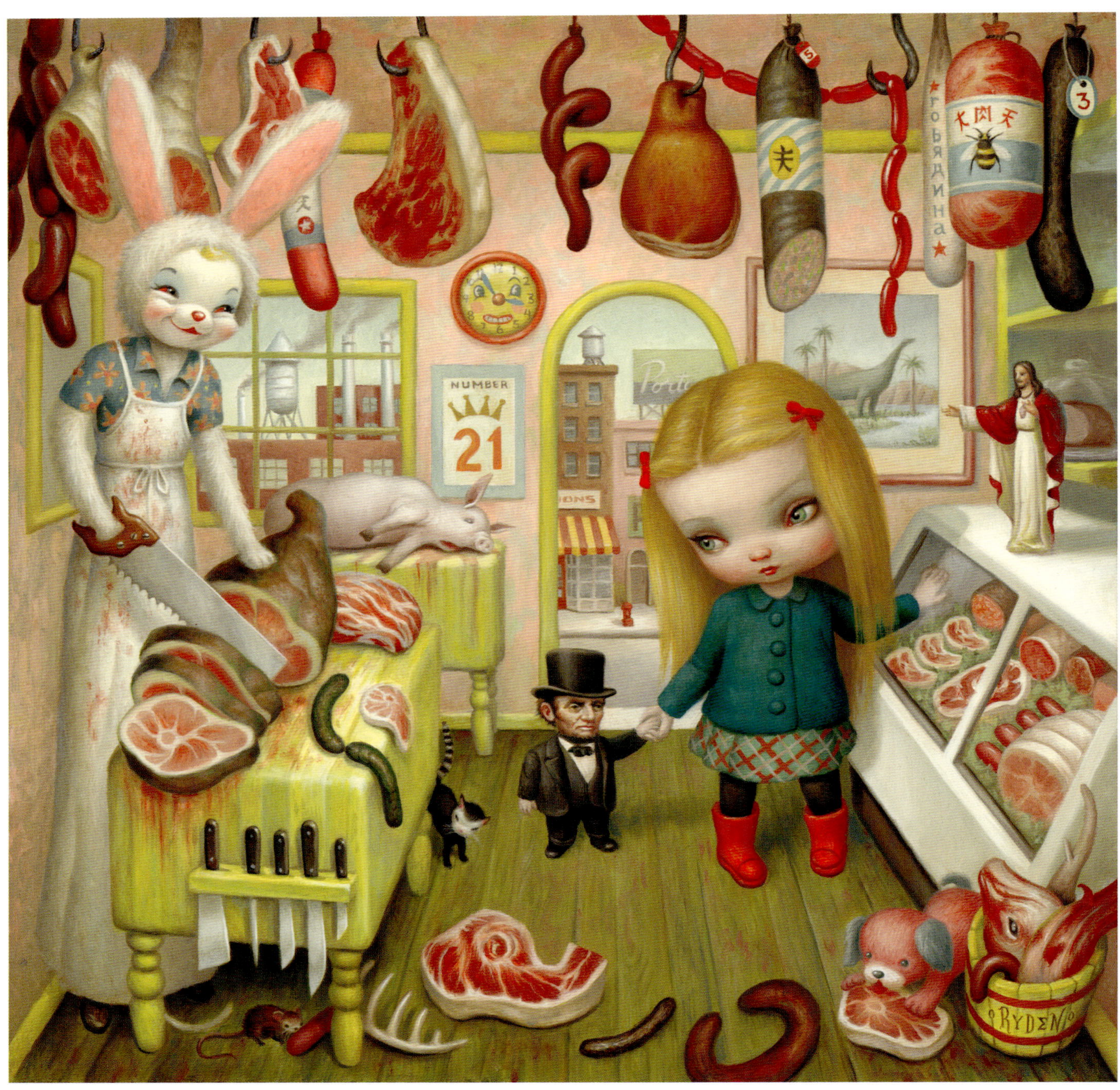


THE BUTCHER BUNNY

2000, oil on panel, 16" x 16"

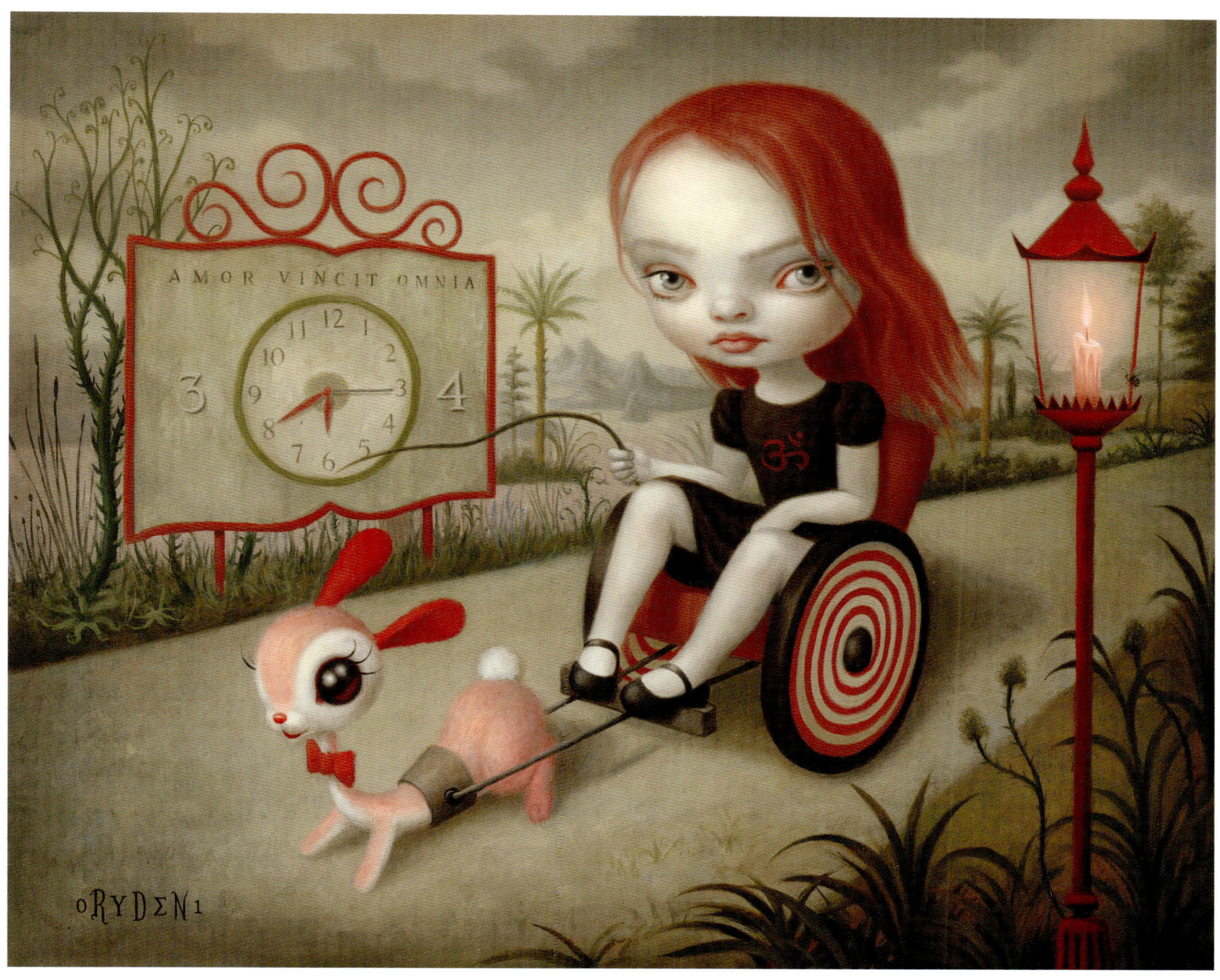




2001, oil on canvas, 12" x 14"

JESSICA'S HOPE

# Isabel SAMARAS

(San Francisco, California)

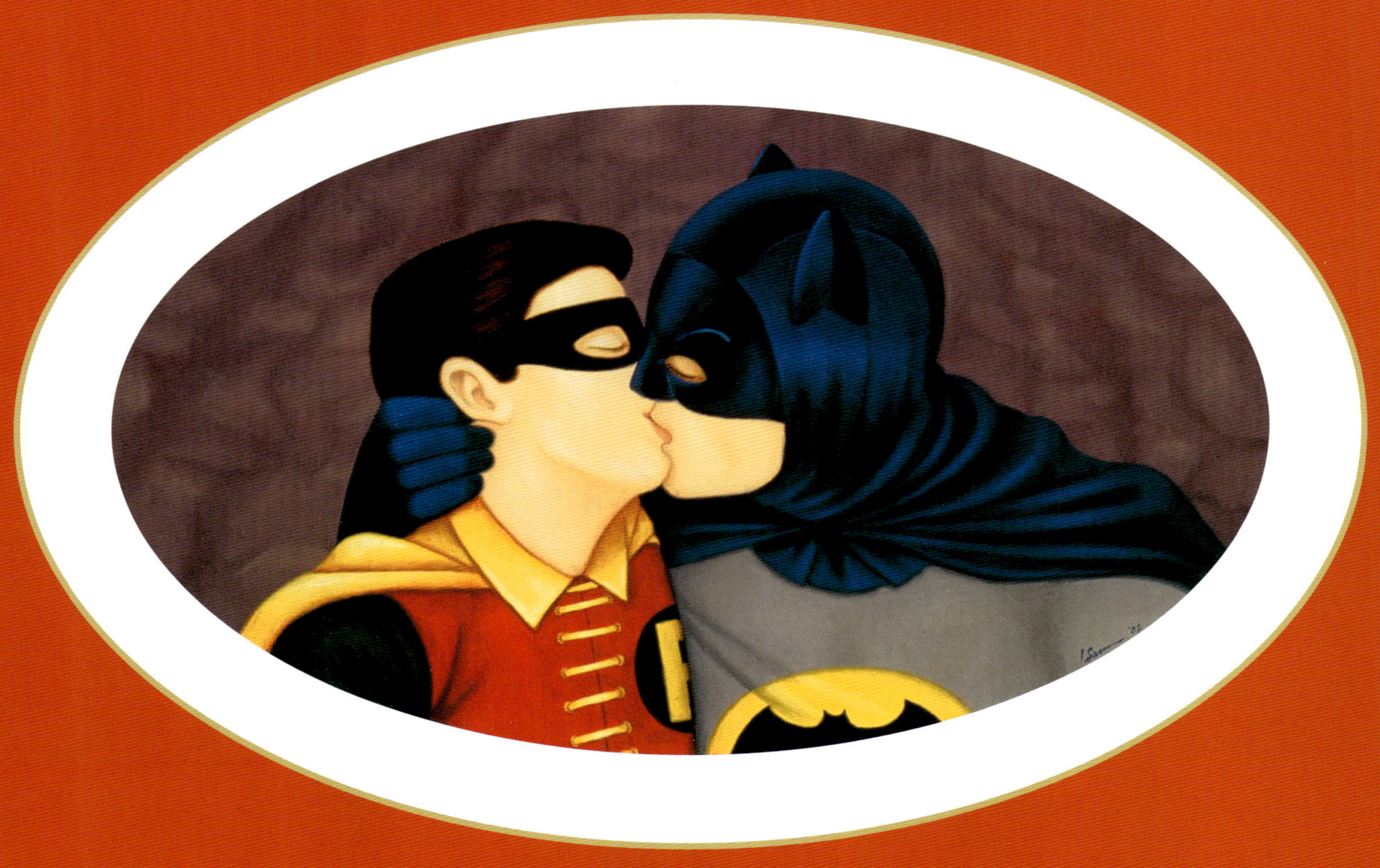

SECRETS OF THE BATCAVE PART 2

2002, oil on wood, 12" x 20"

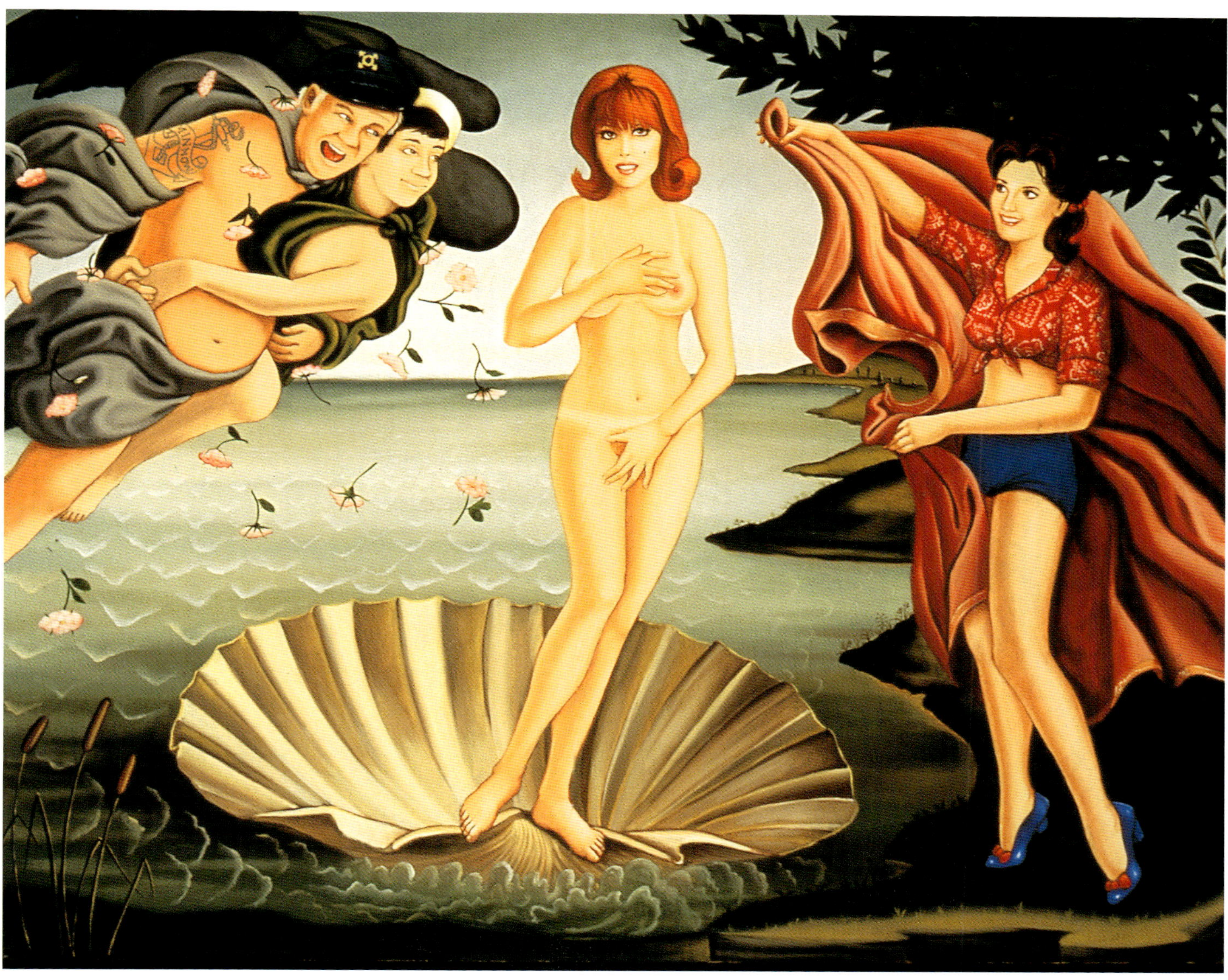

2002, oil on wood, 16" x 20"

Birth of Ginger

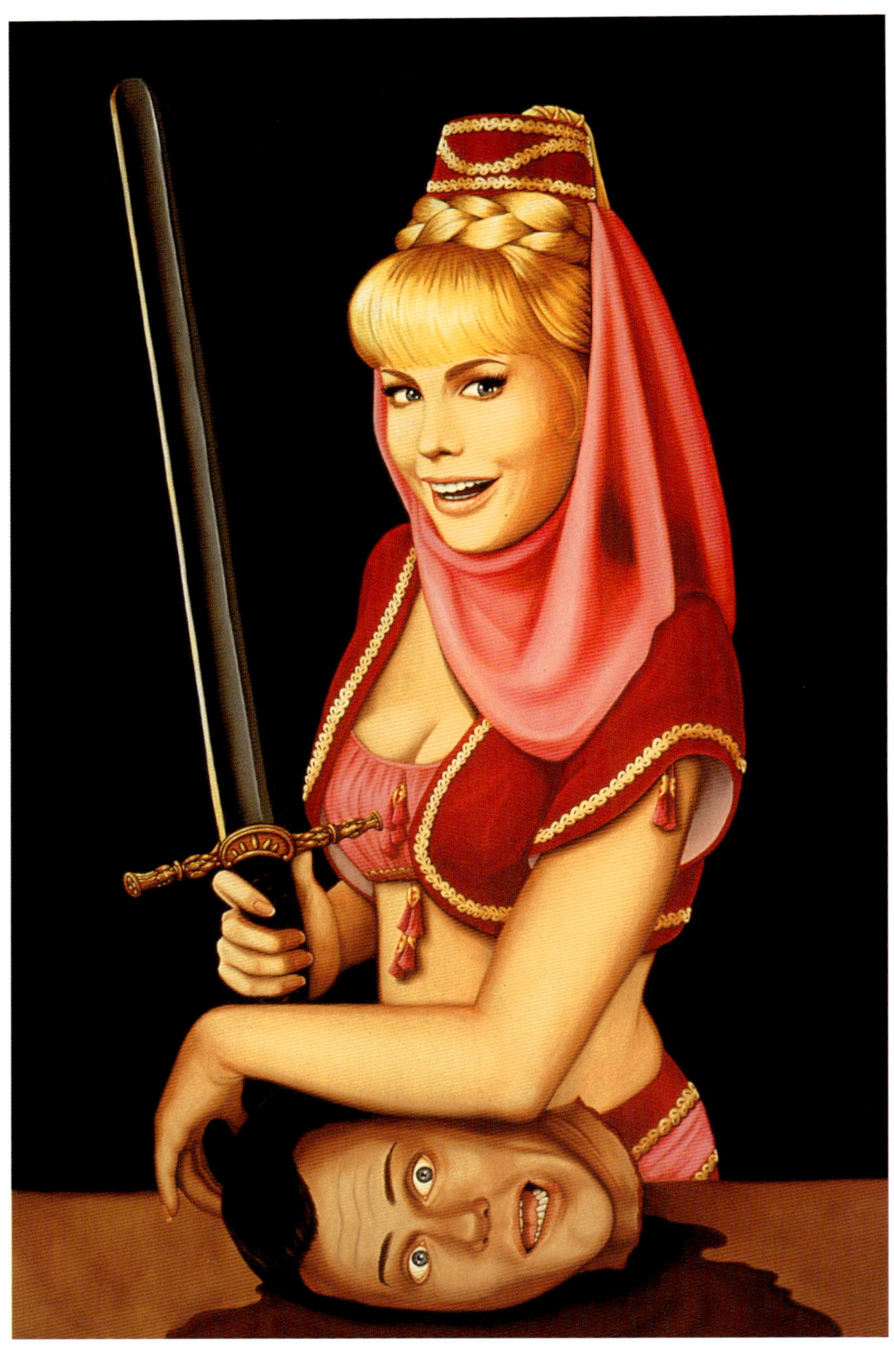

Golden Silence 2002, oil on wood, 36" x 12"

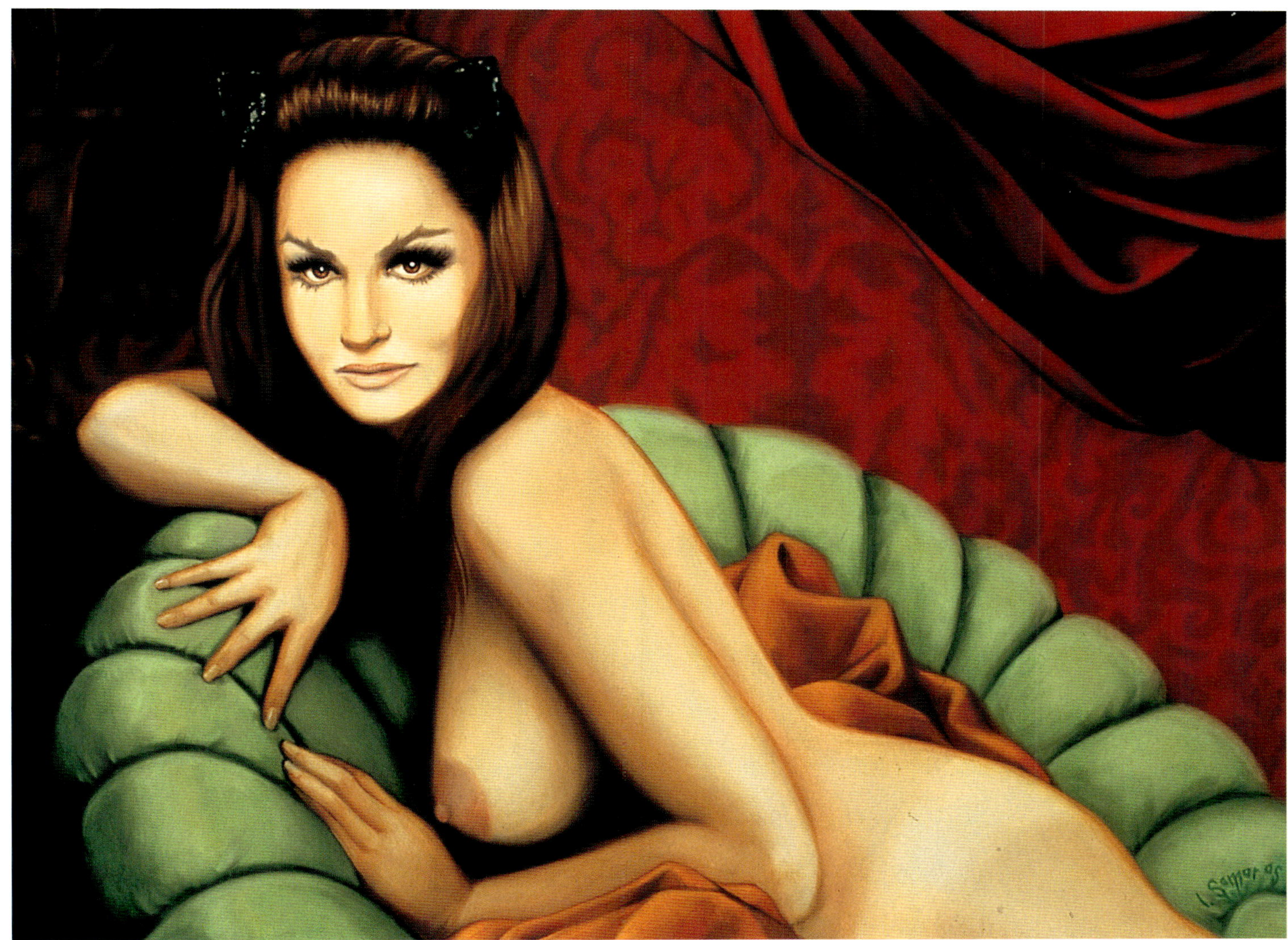

2003, oil on wood, 12" x 16"

Purrrfect

(opposite page) BEHOLD MY HEART 2003, oil on wood, 16" x 12"



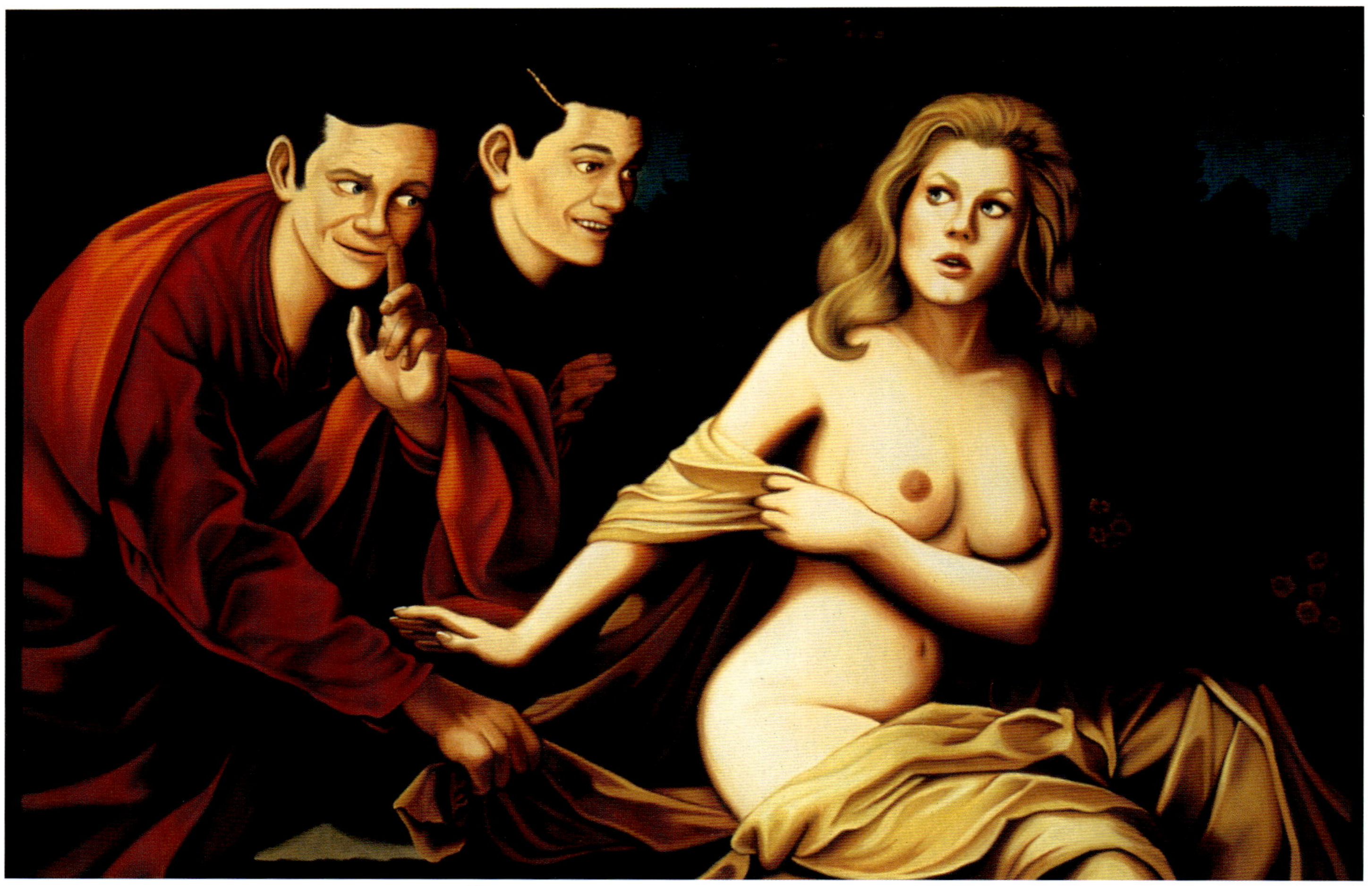

SAMANTHA AND THE DARRINS 2002, oil on wood, 24" x 36"

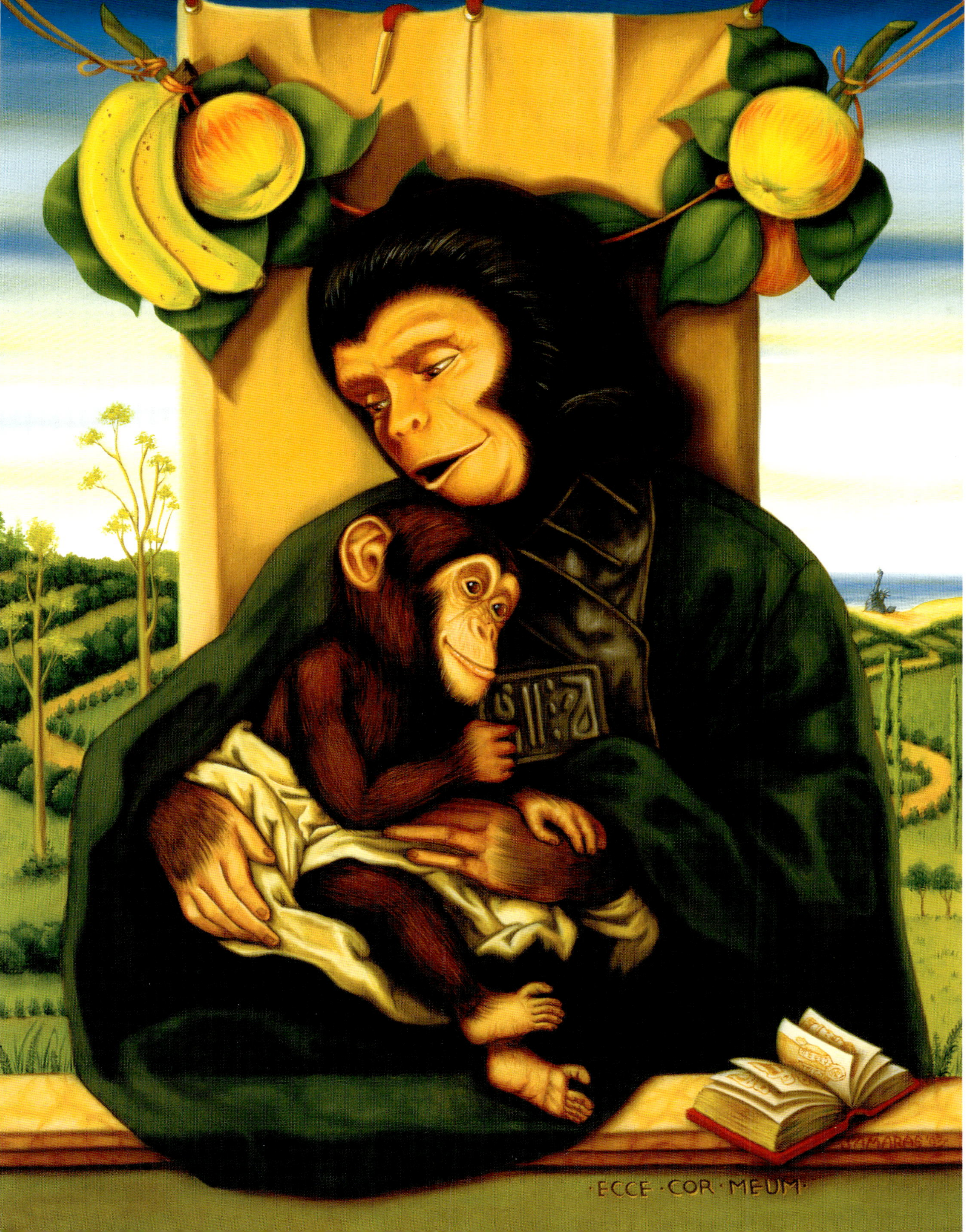
·ECCE·COR·MEUM·

# Todd SCHORR

(Los Angeles, California)

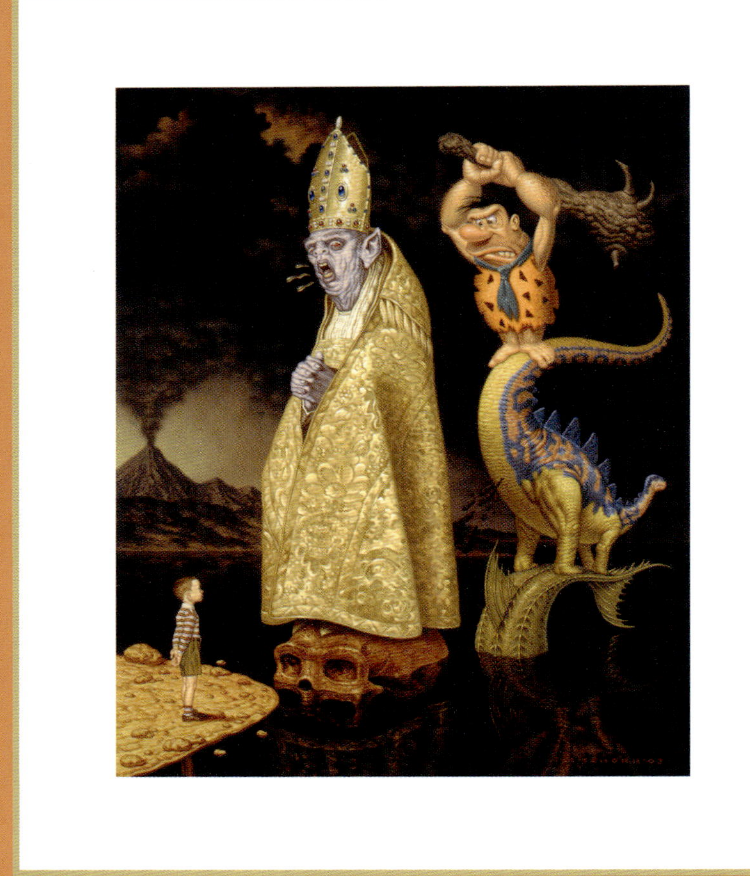

THE EVOLUTION OF SUPERSTITION    2003, acrylic on canvas, 30" x 24"

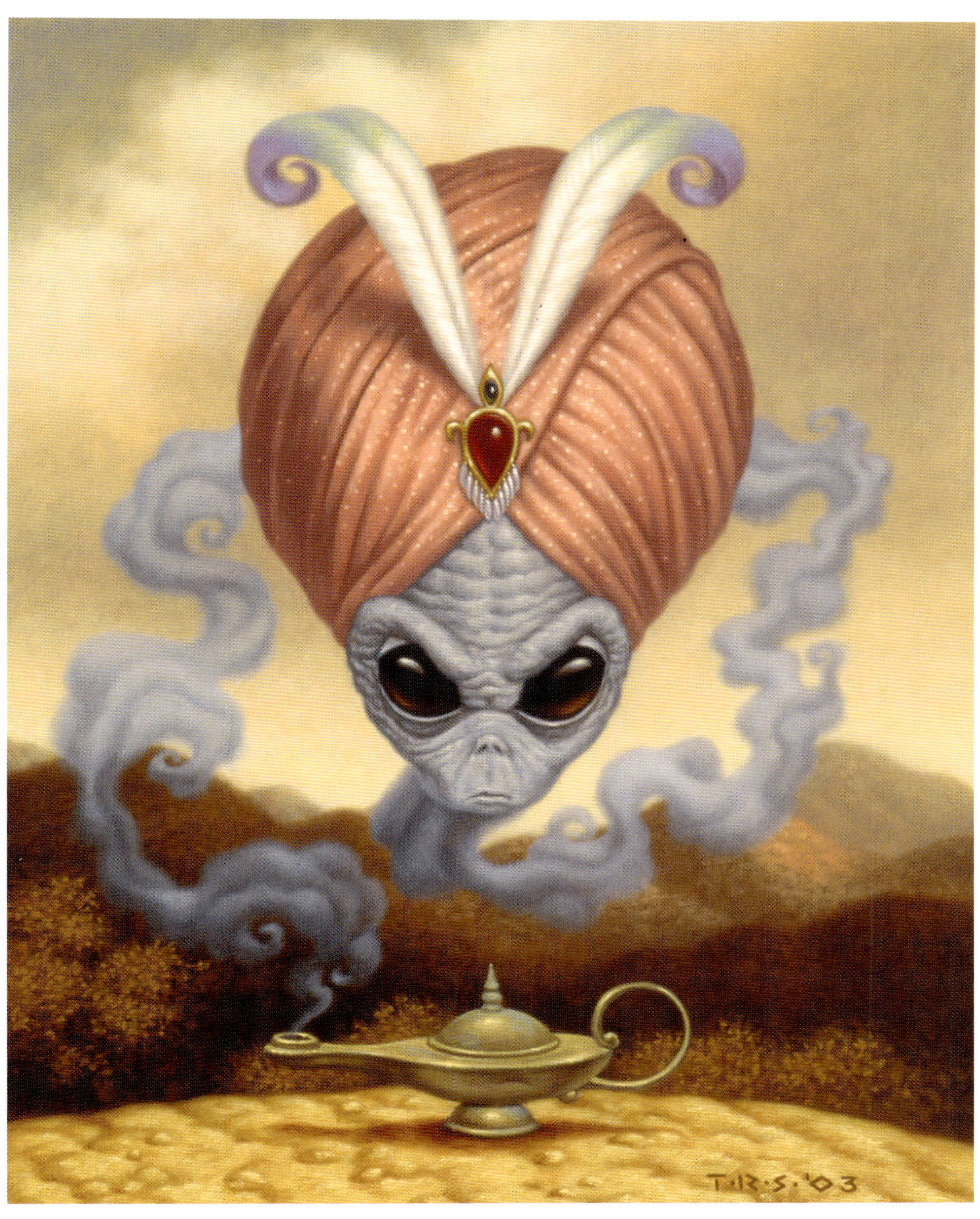


2003, acrylic on canvas, 14" x 11"

WISH FULFILLMENT FROM ANOTHER WORLD

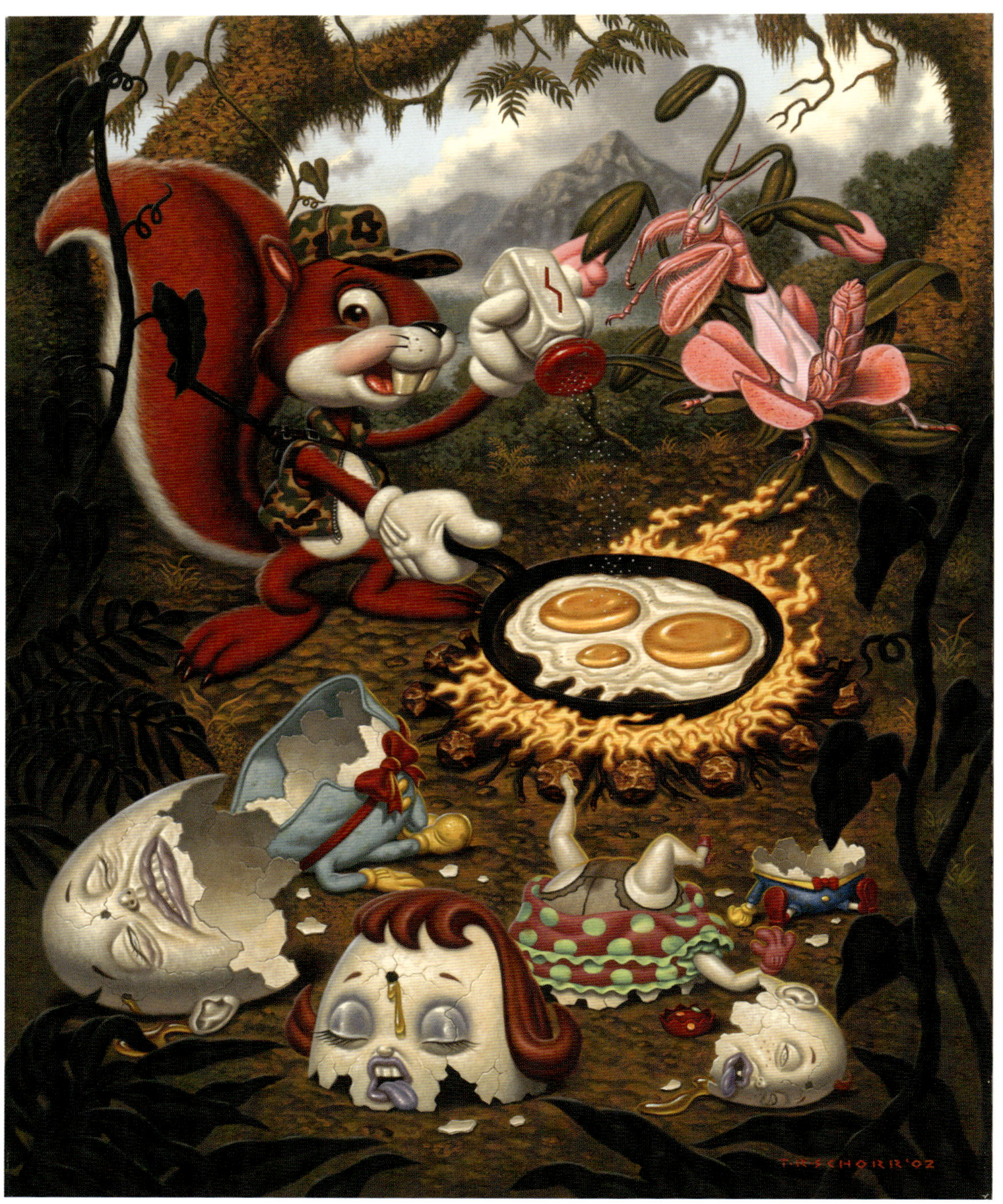

The Egg Hunt

2002, acrylic on canvas, 30" x 24"

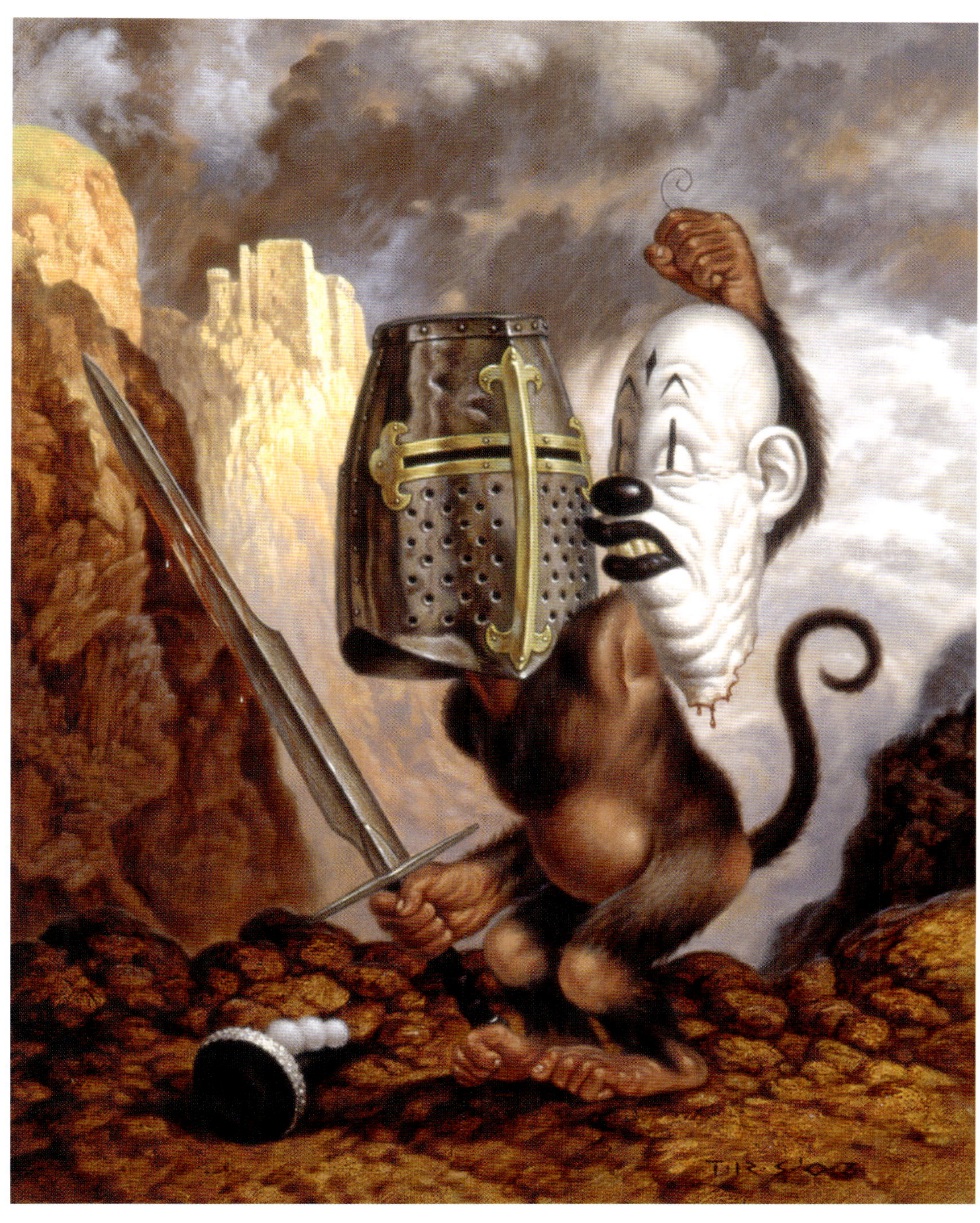

2003, acrylic on canvas, 14" x 11"

The Monkey's Trophy

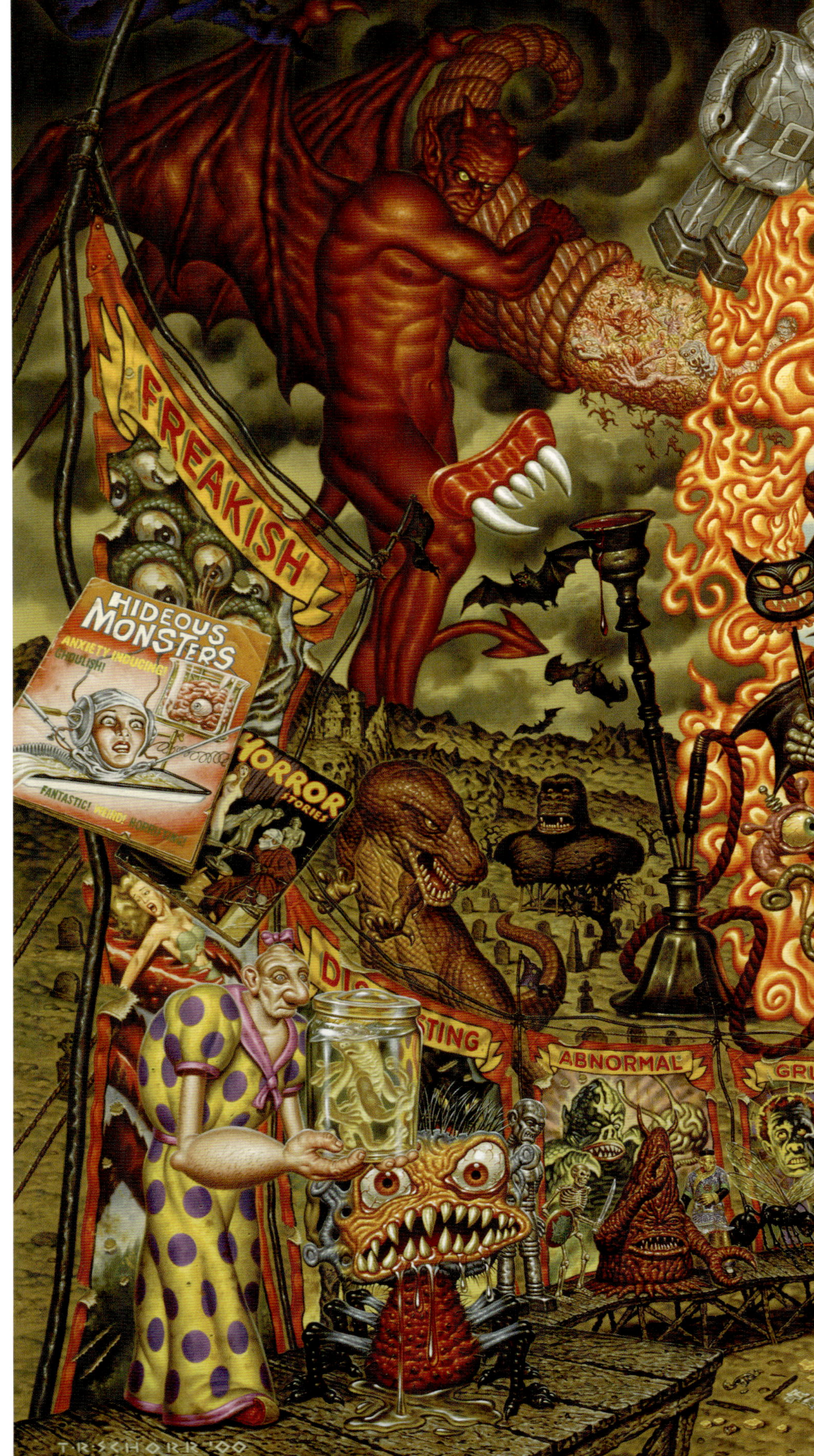


THE SPECTRE OF MONSTER APPEAL
2000, acrylic on canvas, 60" x 84"

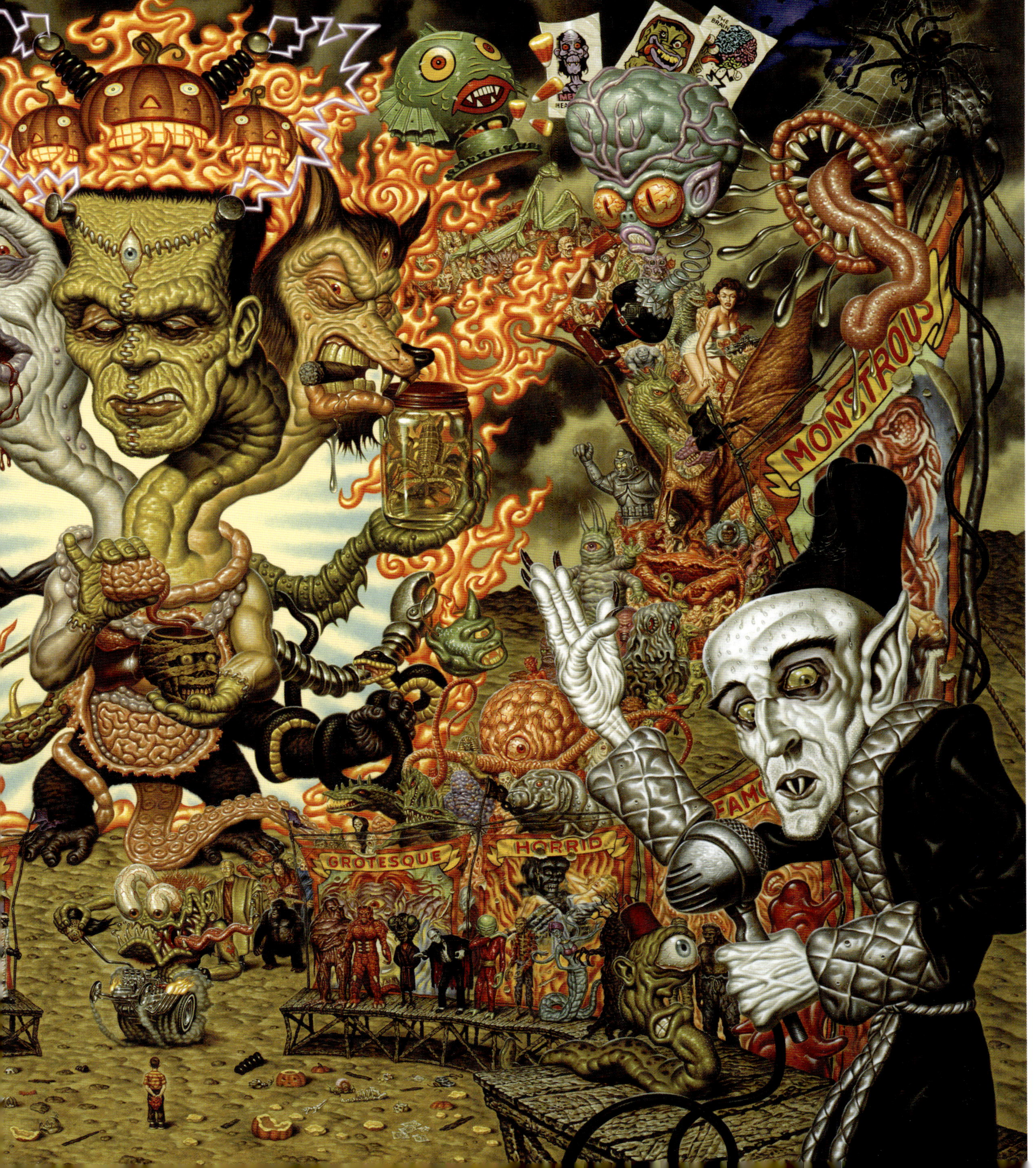
THE BRAIN
MONSTROUS
GROTESQUE
HORRID

# SHAG

(Los Angeles, California)

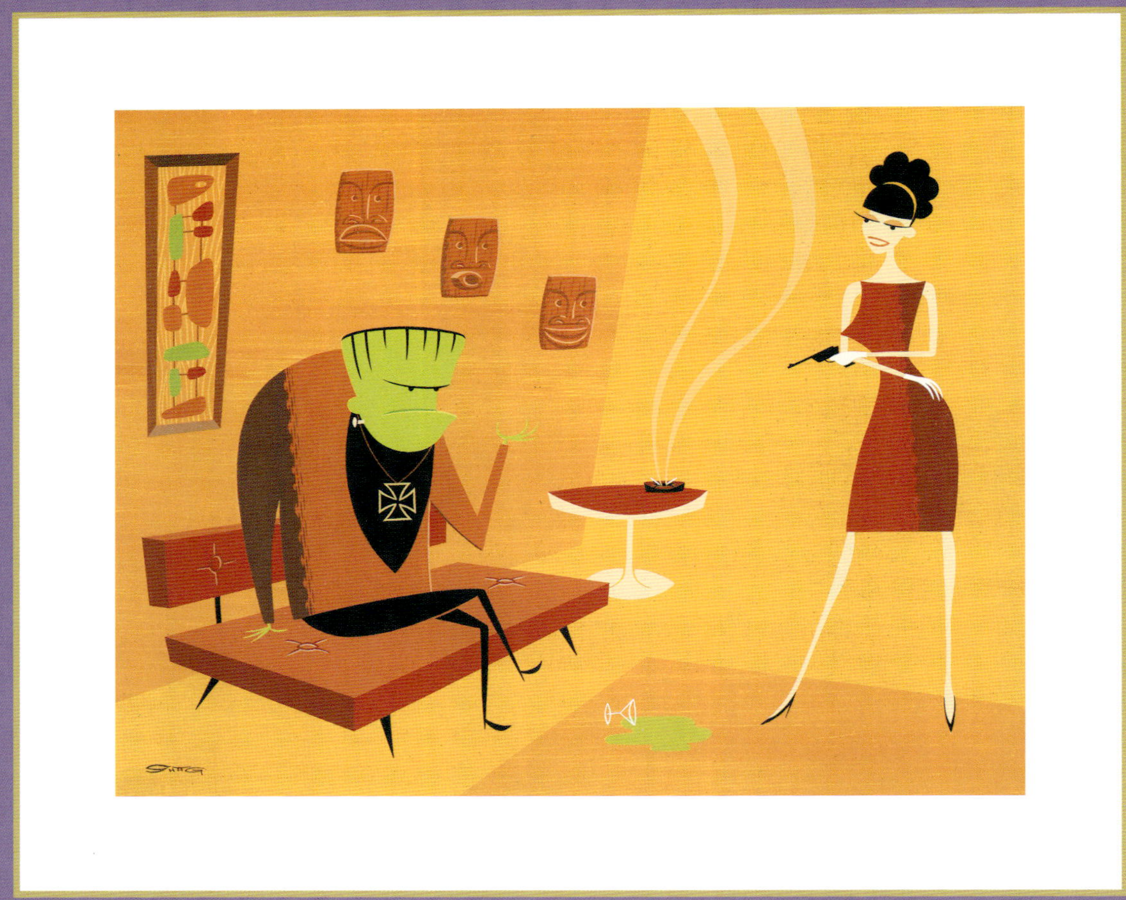

PRELUDE TO DOMESTIC STRIFE 2001, acrylic and vinyl paint on panel, 17" x 21"

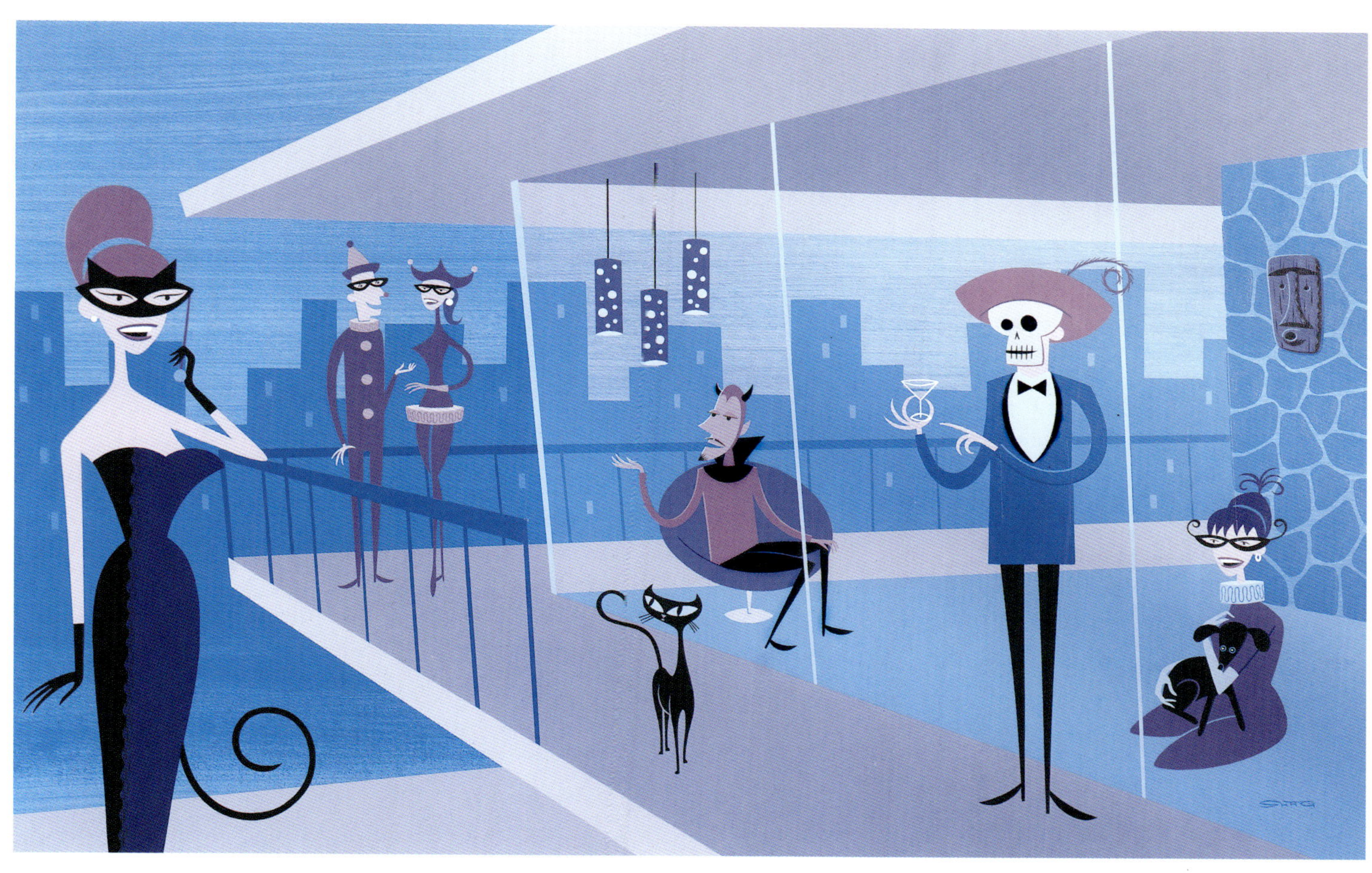

2003, acrylic and vinyl paint on panel, 24" x 38"

MASQUERADE

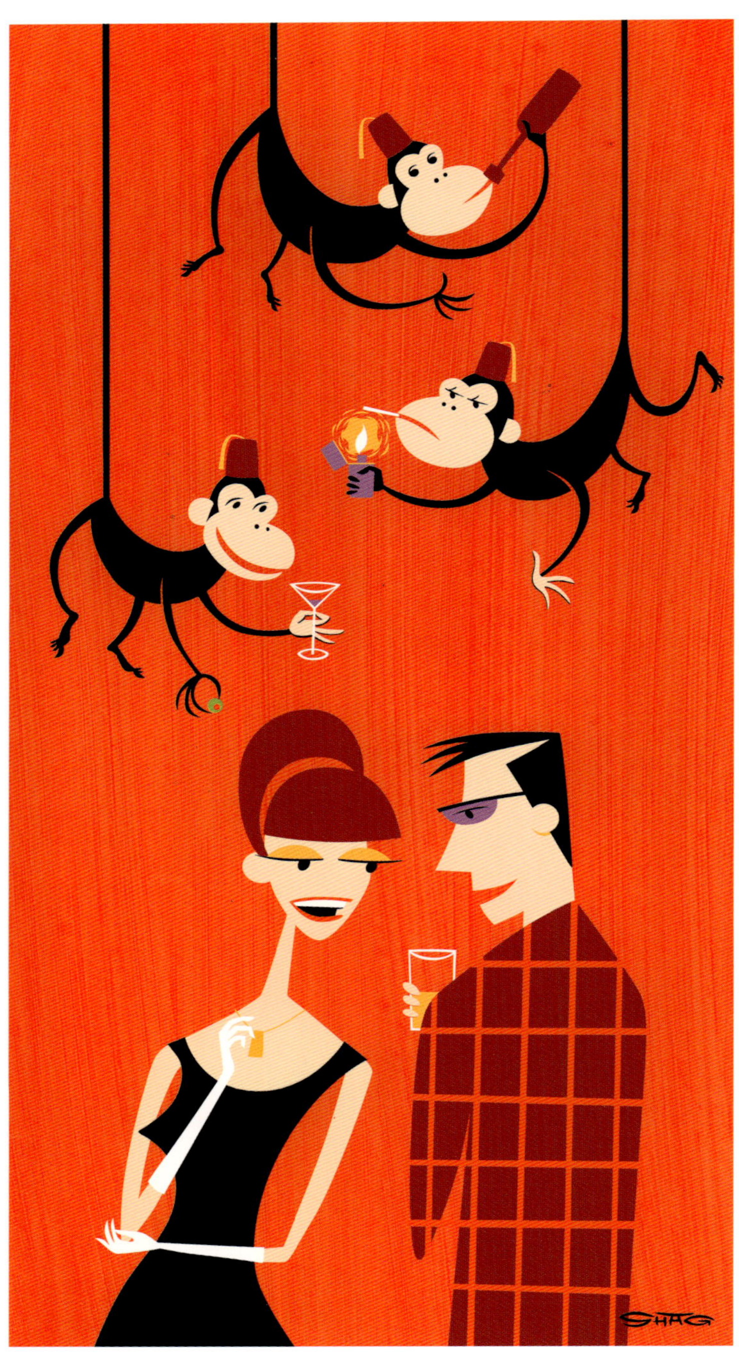


VICE MONKEYS 1999, acrylic on canvas, 20" x 30"

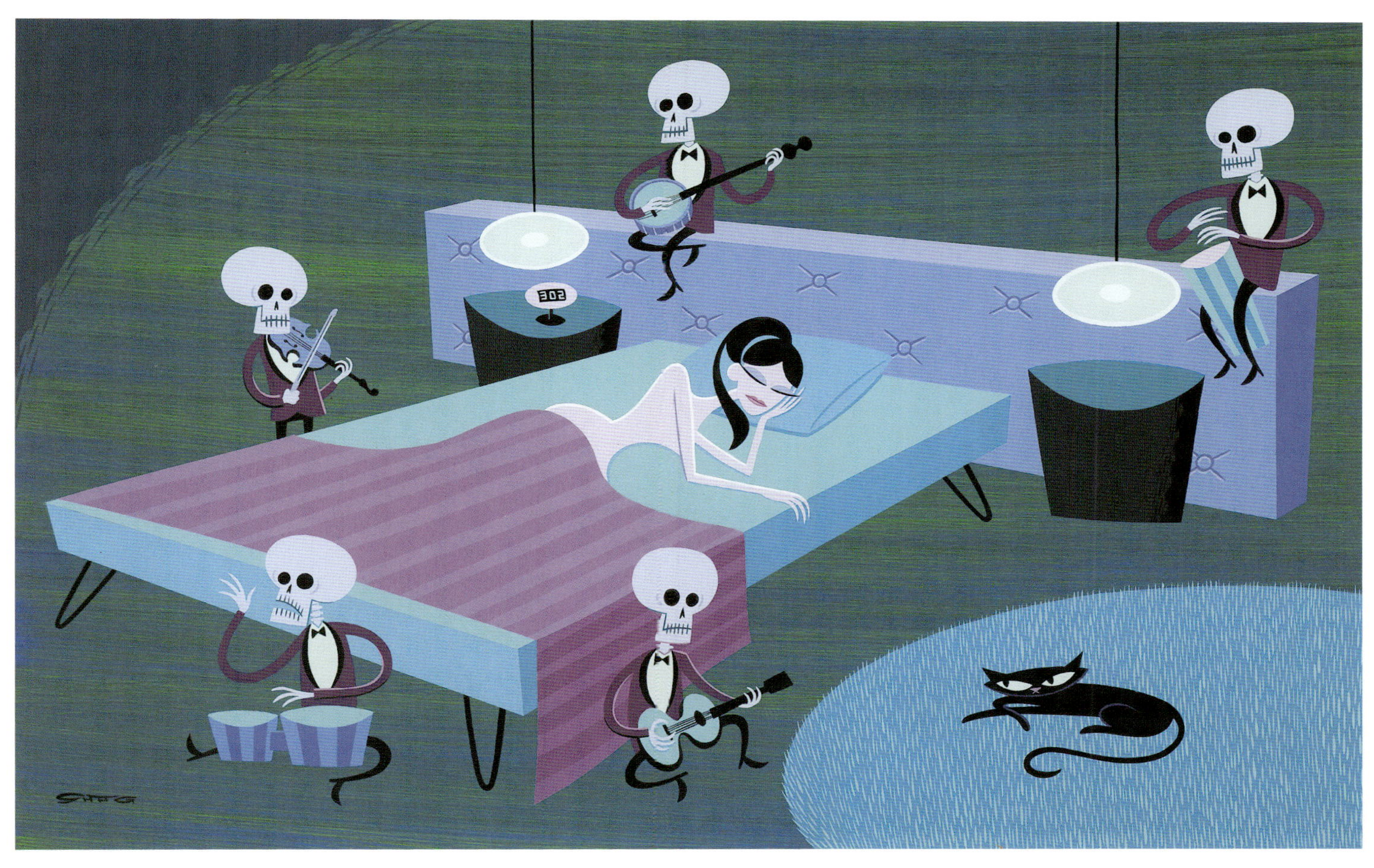


2003, acrylic and vinyl paint on panel, 15" x 24"

IN DREAMS

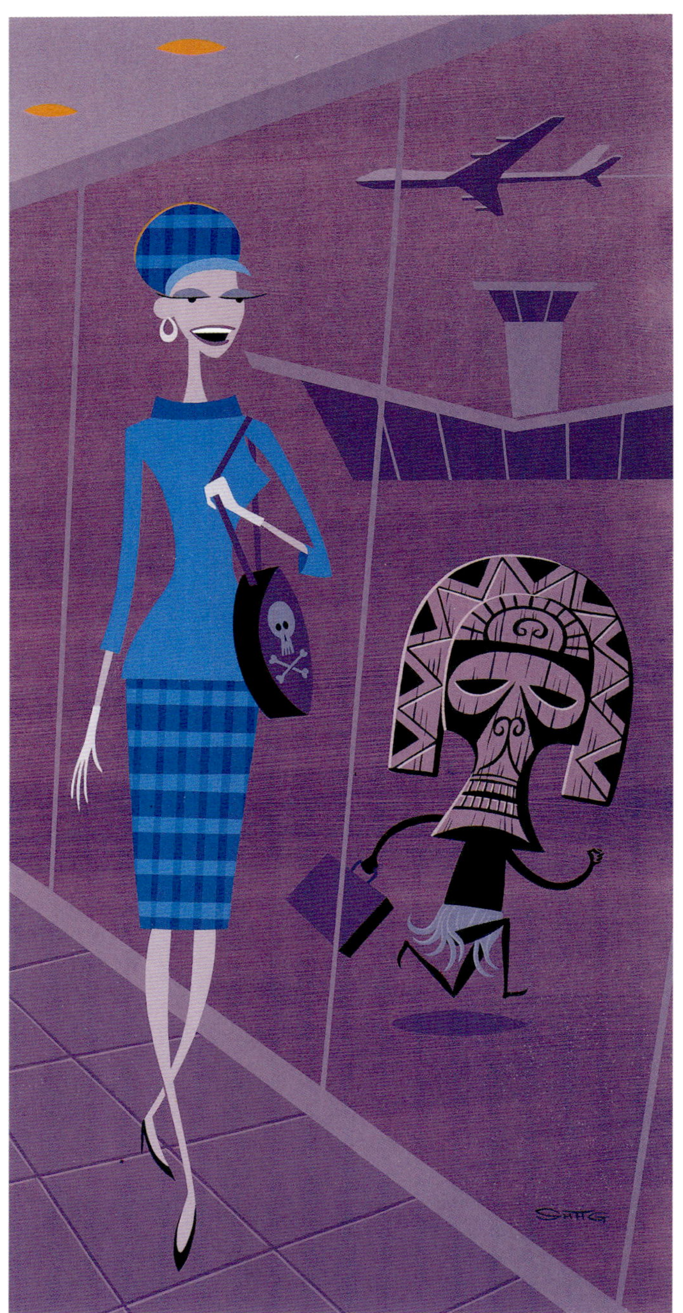

Fashionable Terrorist
2001, acrylic and vinyl paint on panel, 12" x 24"

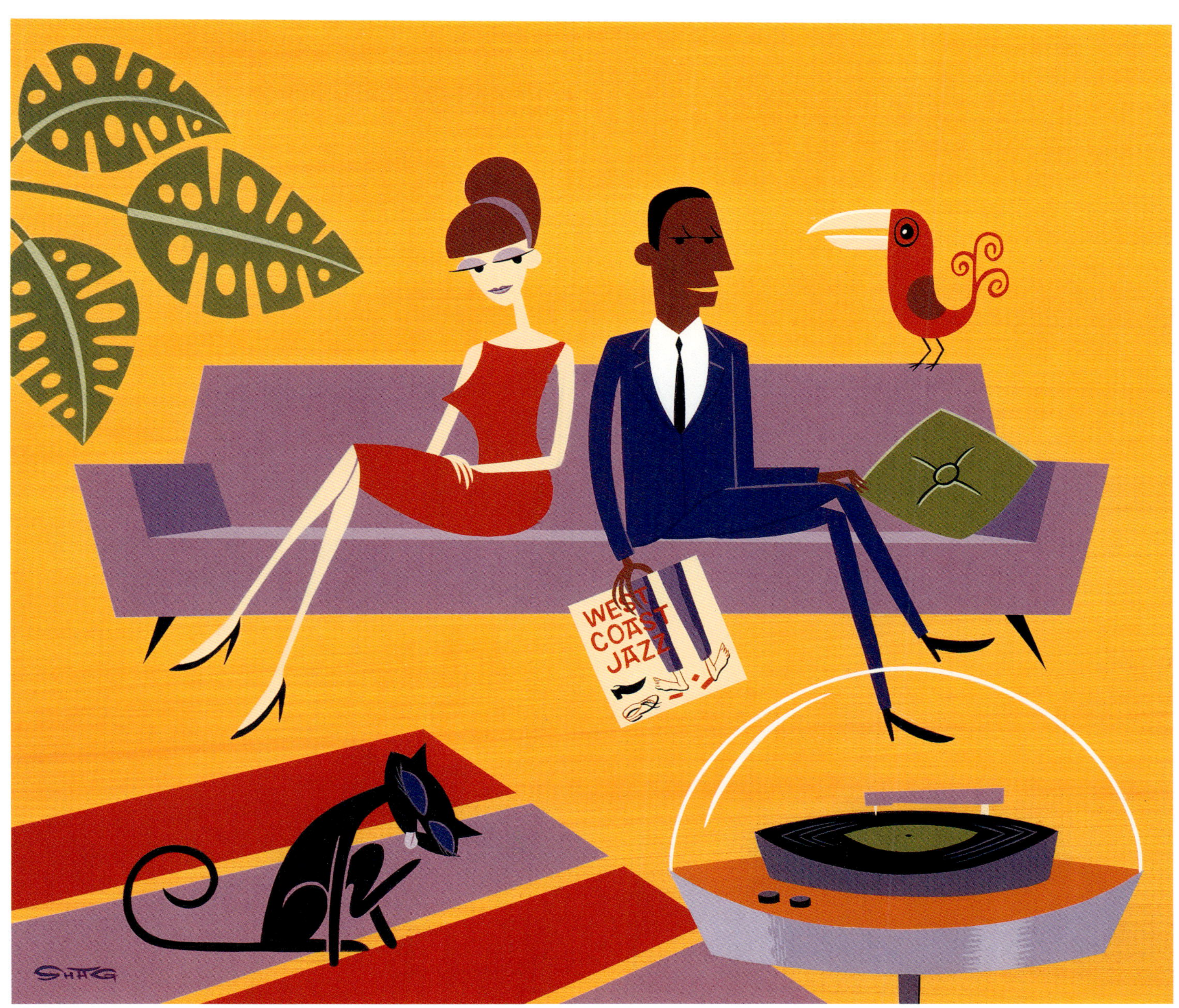


2003, acrylic and vinyl paint on panel, 16" x 18"

WEST COAST JAZZ

# Eric
# WHITE

(New York City, New York)

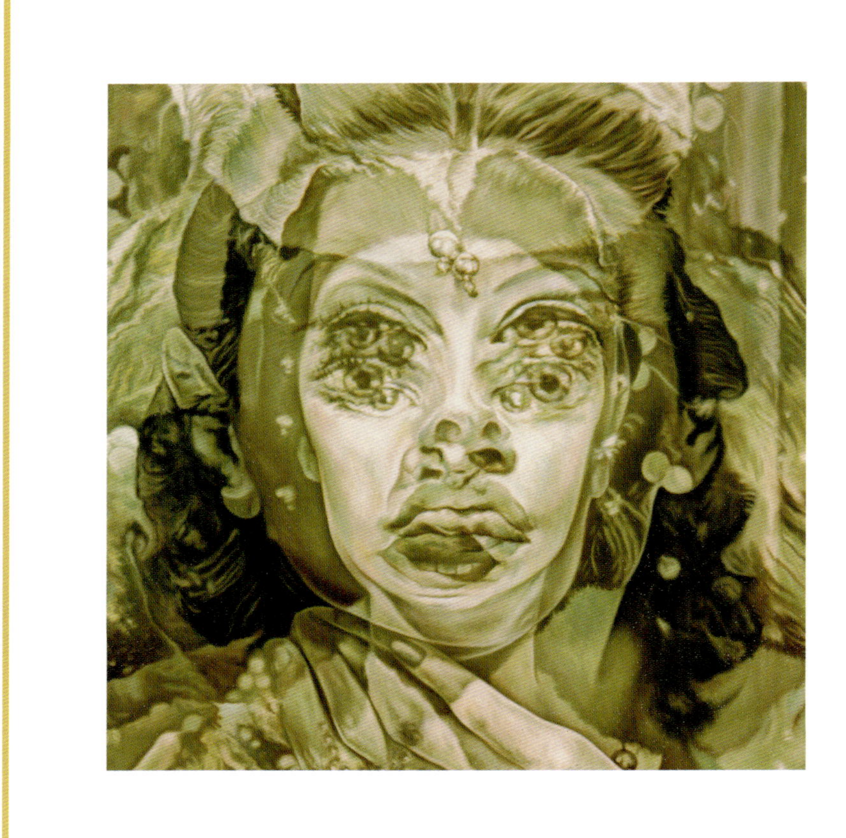

Divine Mother of Guilt 2002, oil on canvas, 36" x 36"

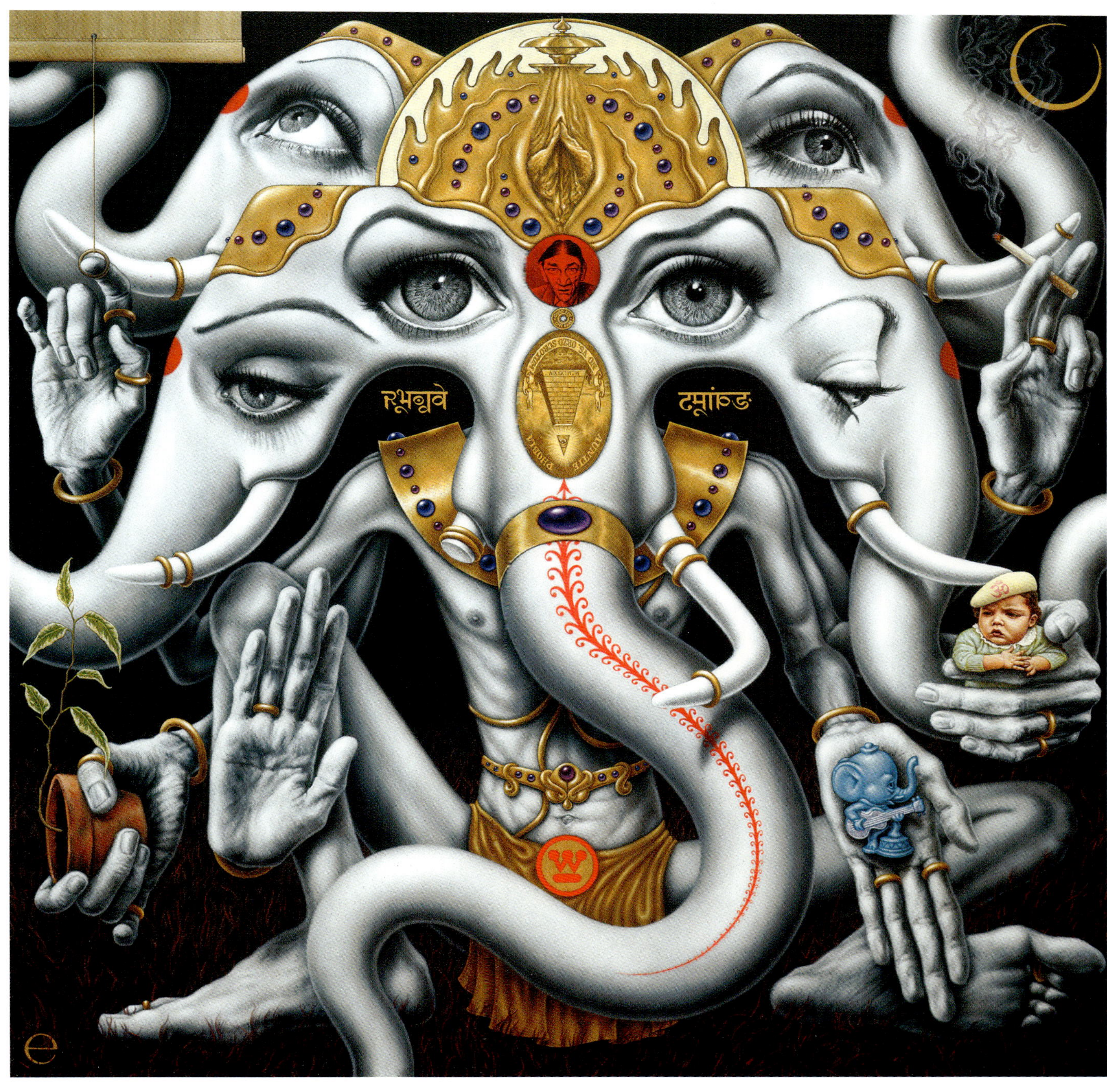



1998, acrylic on canvas, 36" x 36"

OUR BELOVED GANESA

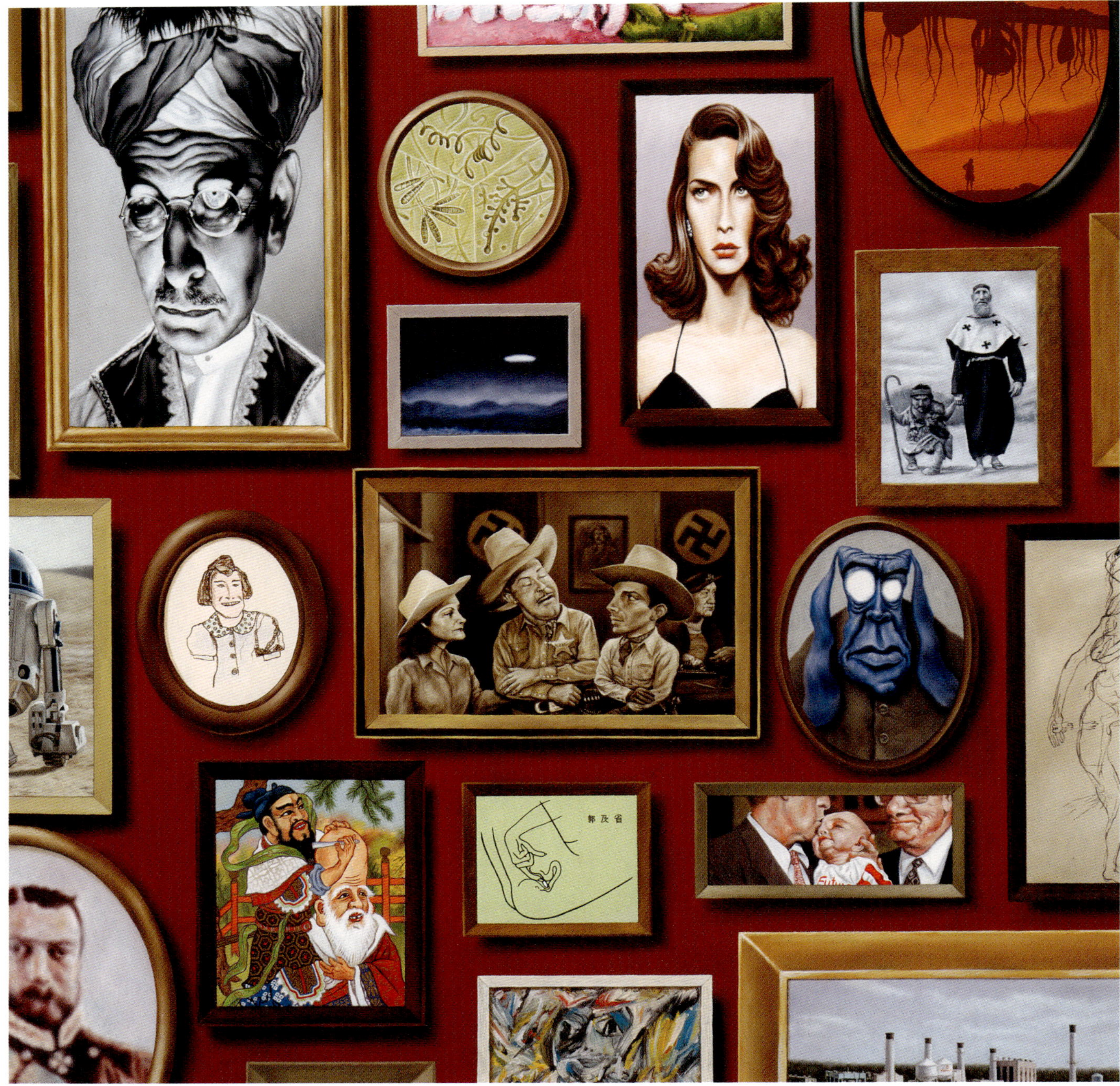

COLLUSION

2002, oil on canvas, 24" x 24"

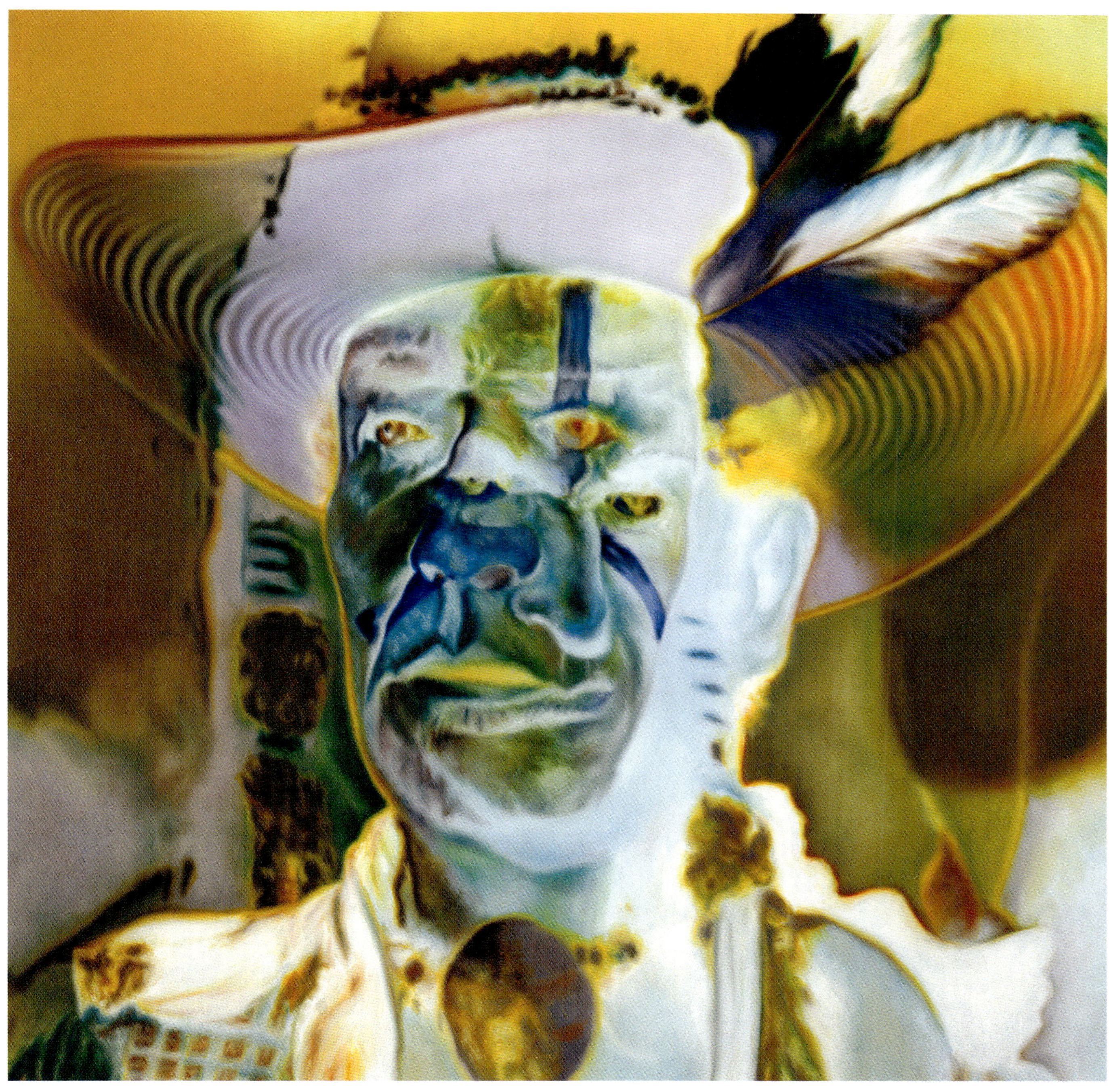

2003, oil on canvas, 18" x 18"

Them or Us

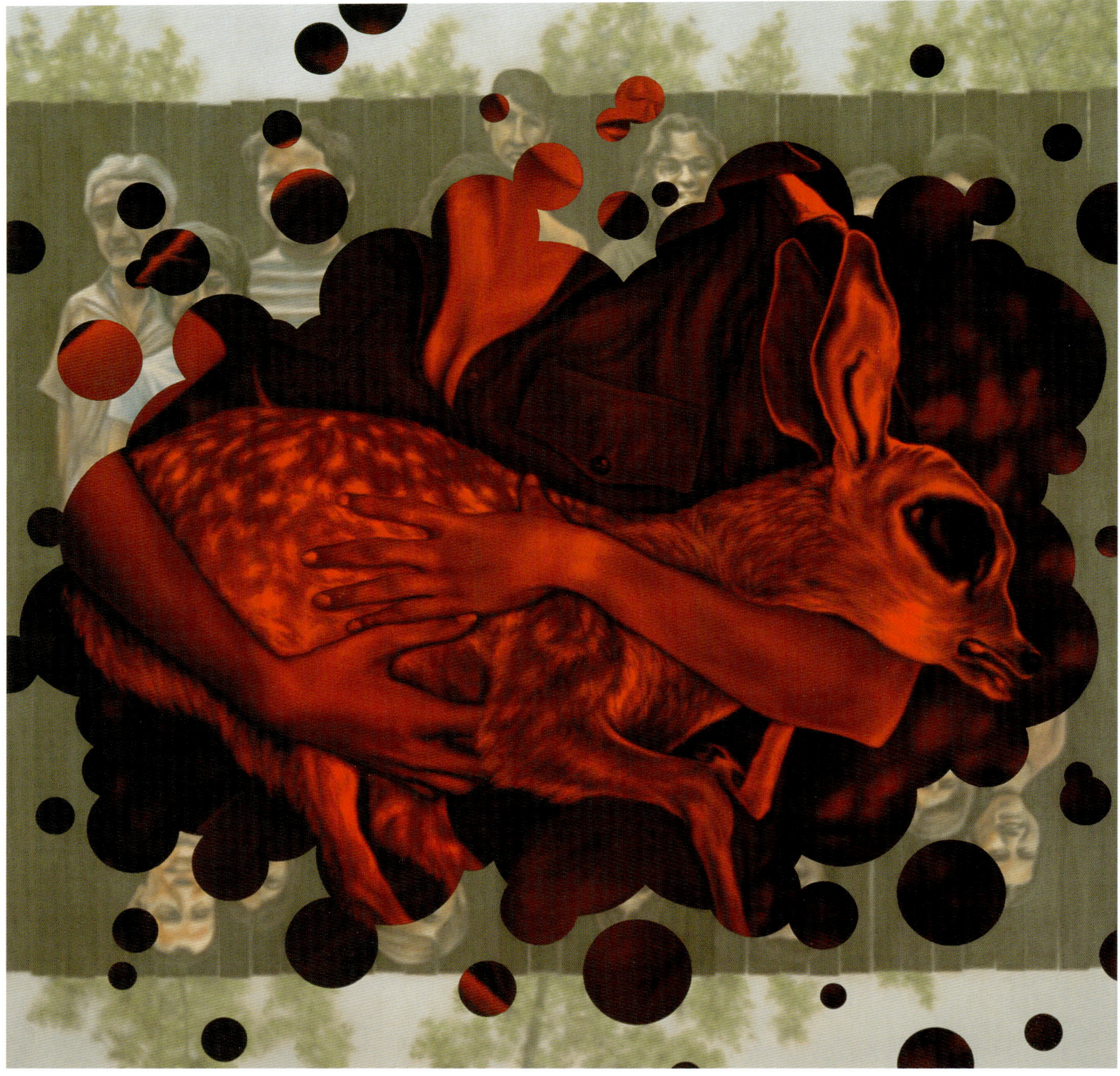

GOLDEN MOMENTS 2001, oil on canvas, 36" x 36"

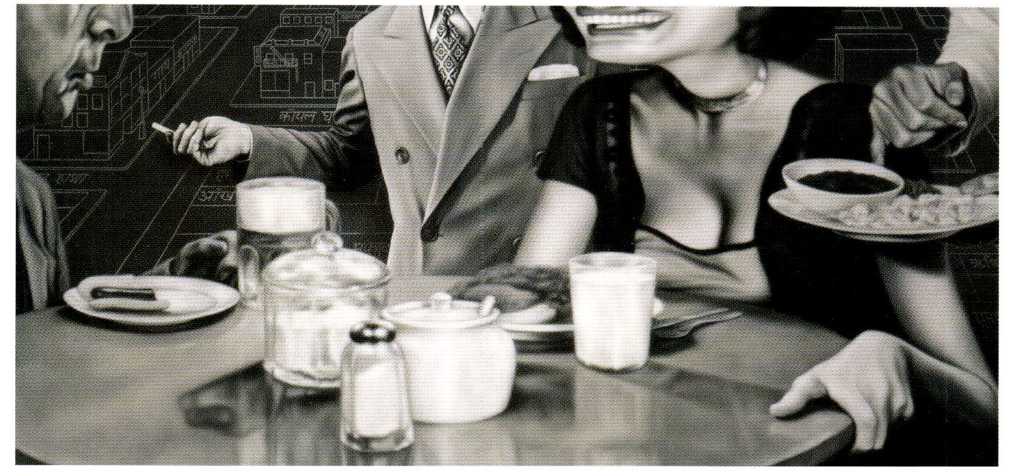

1999, oil on canvas, 36" x 72"

INTERMEZZO



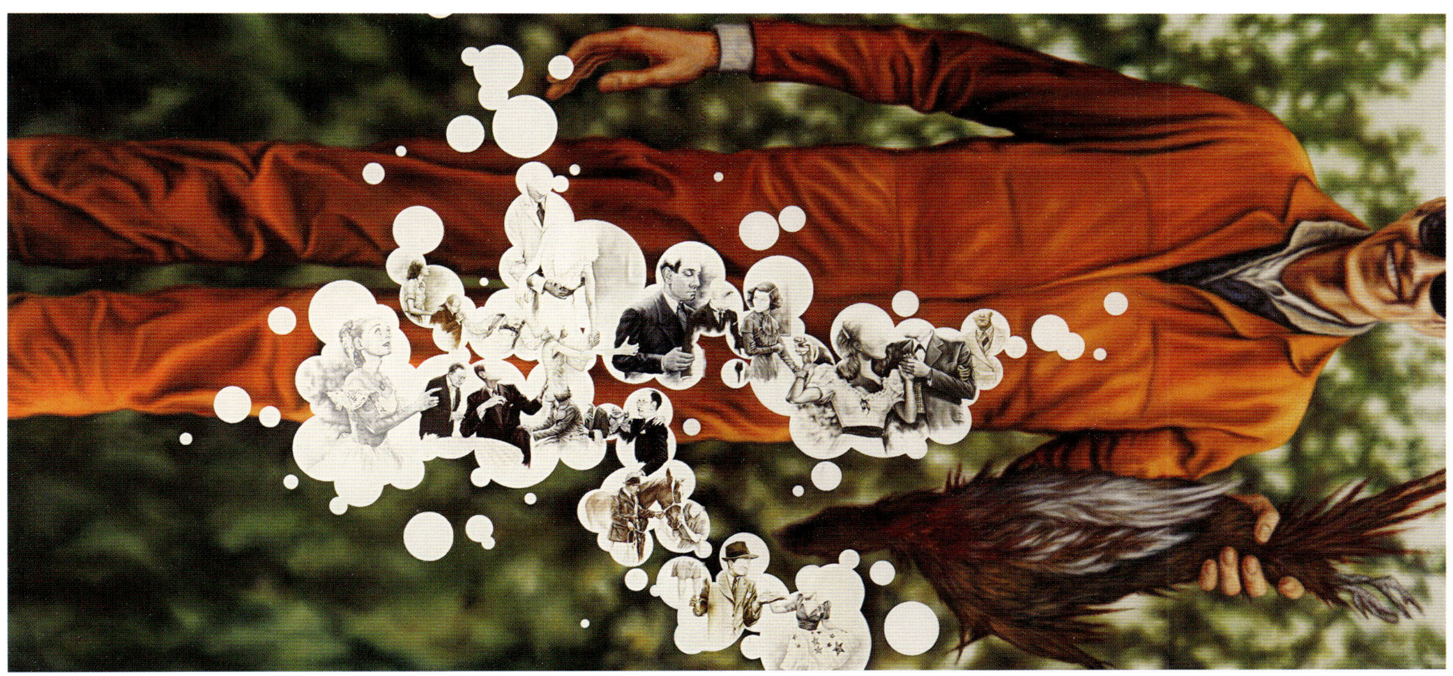

2000-2003, oil on canvas, 35" x 72"

SPORES OF TODAY (ANIMA RISING)

# Robert WILLIAMS

(Los Angeles, California)

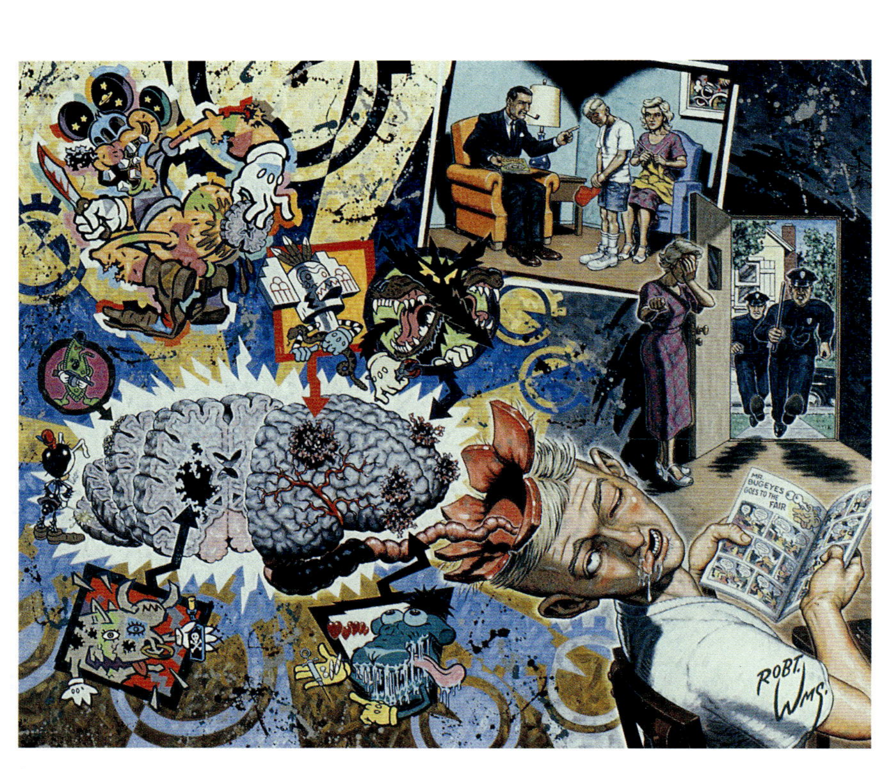


THE CARTOON DISEASE

1991, oil on canvas, 30" x 36"

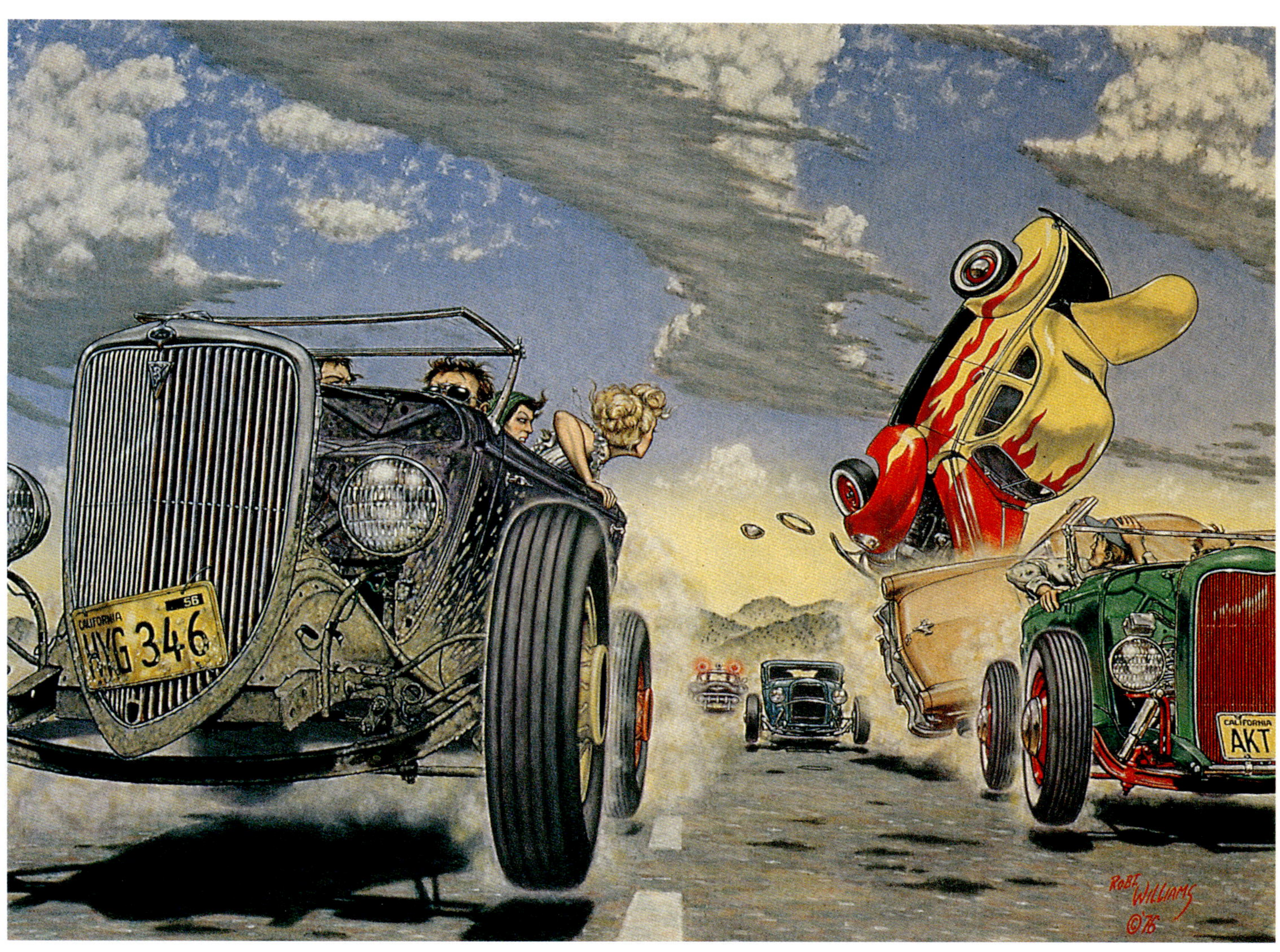


1976, acrylic on board, 16.25" x 12.75"

HOT ROD RACE

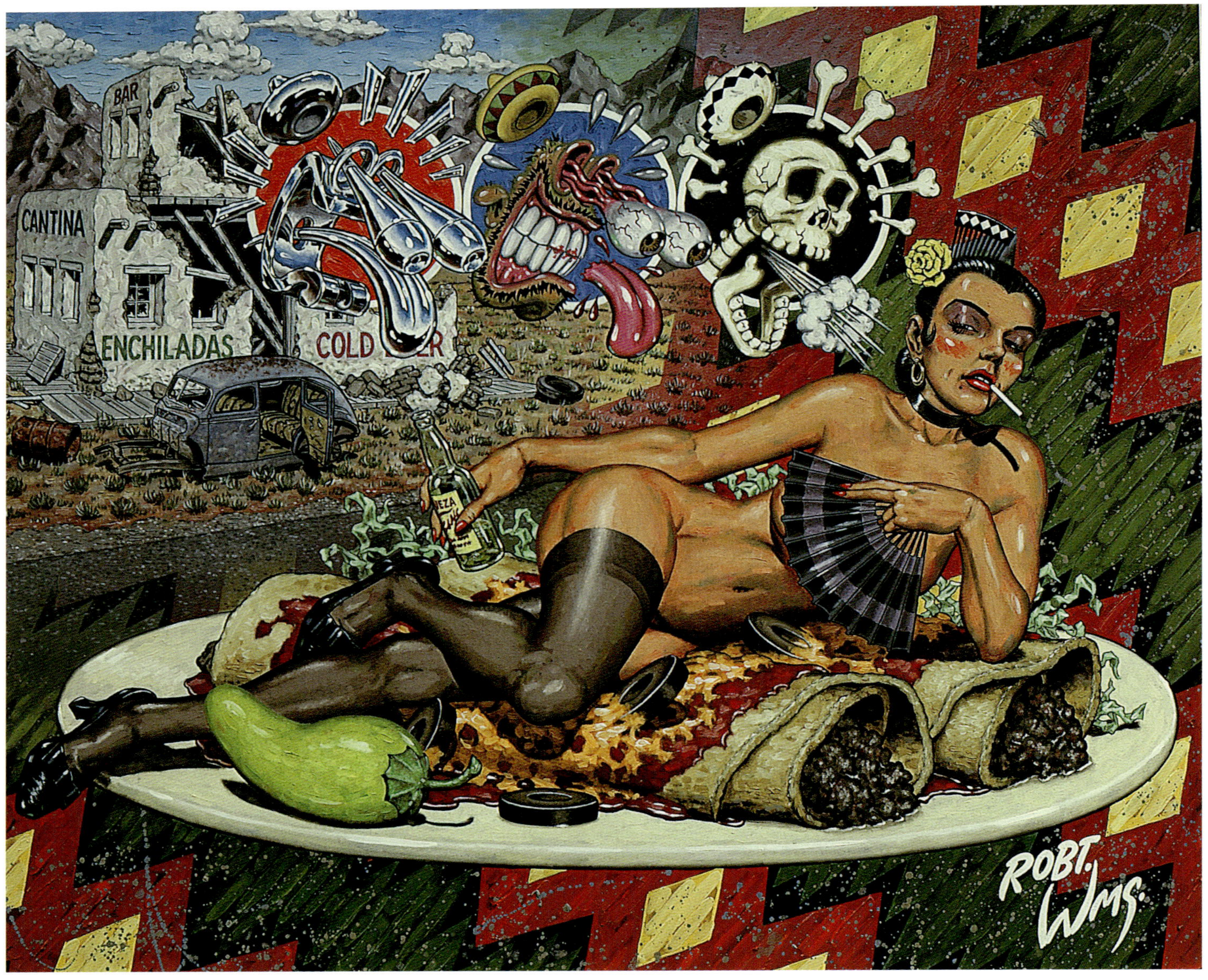


ENCHILADA DE AMORE

1988, oil on canvas, 30" x 36"

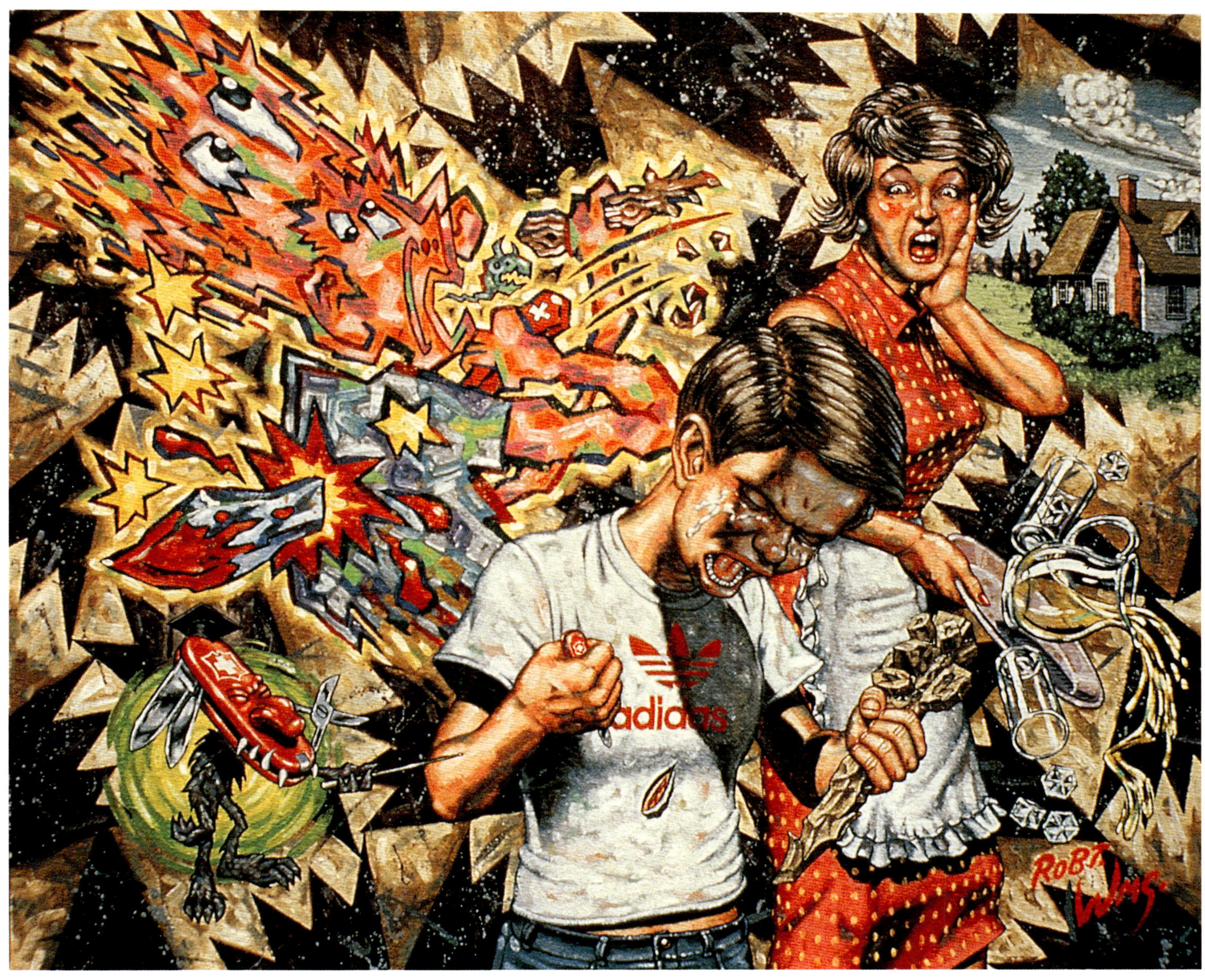


1987, oil on canvas, 30" x 36"

NEVER CUT TOWARDS YOURSELF

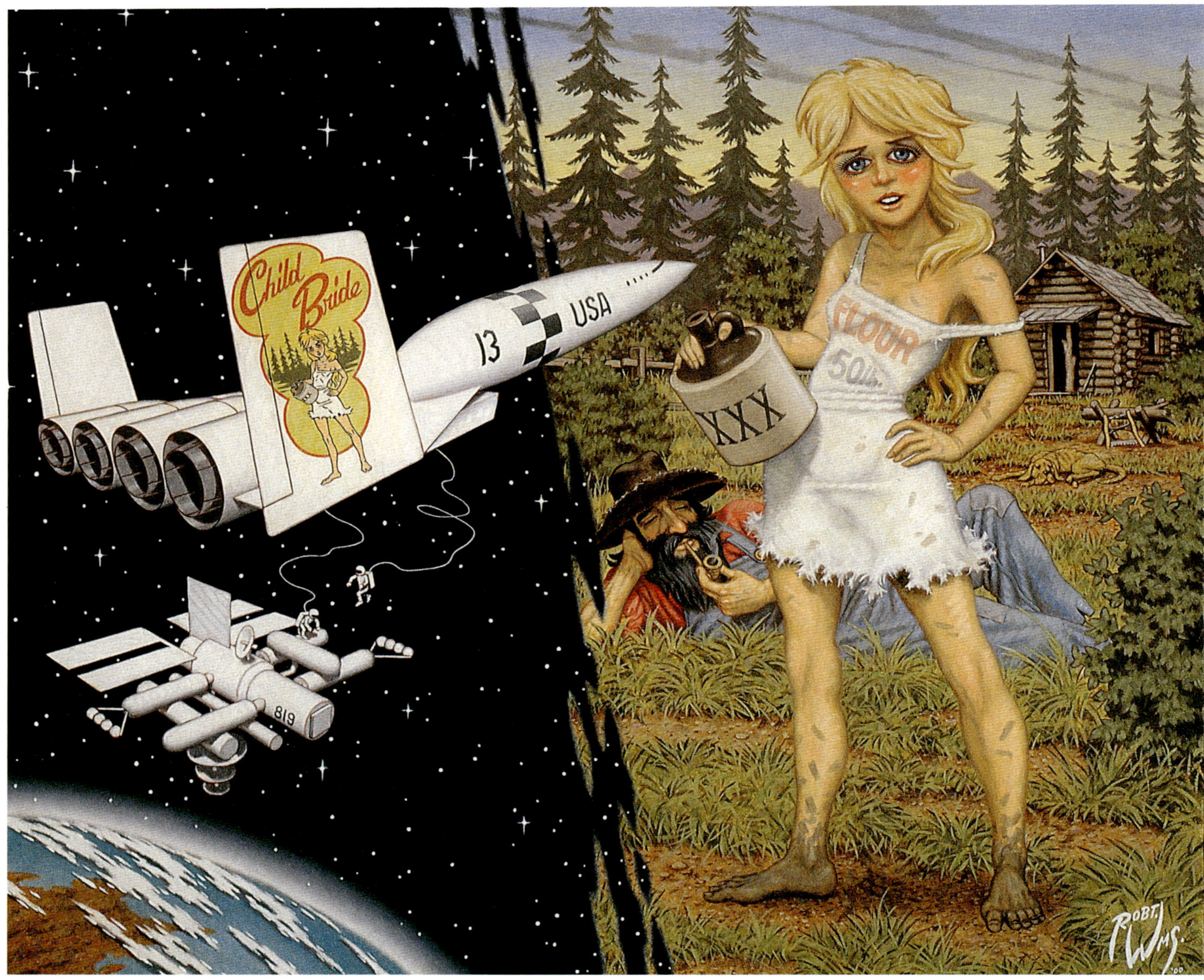


CHILD BRIDE

1999, oil on canvas, 30" x 36"

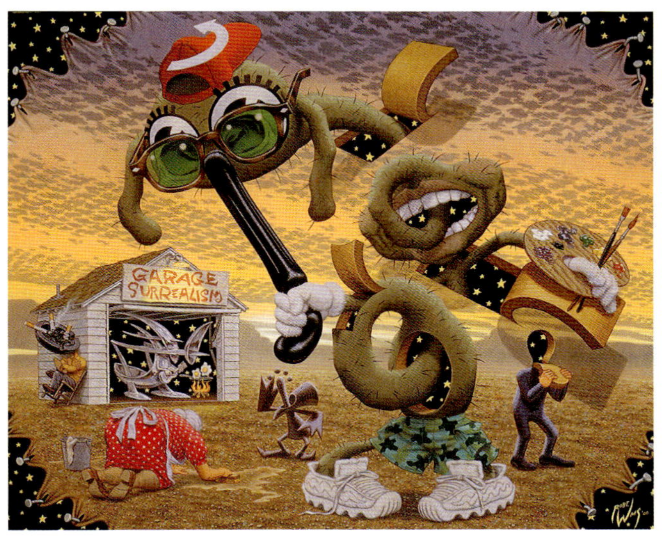


BASTARDIZING THE AUTONOMY OF PERSON, PLACE AND THING
2000, oil on canvas, 30" x 36"

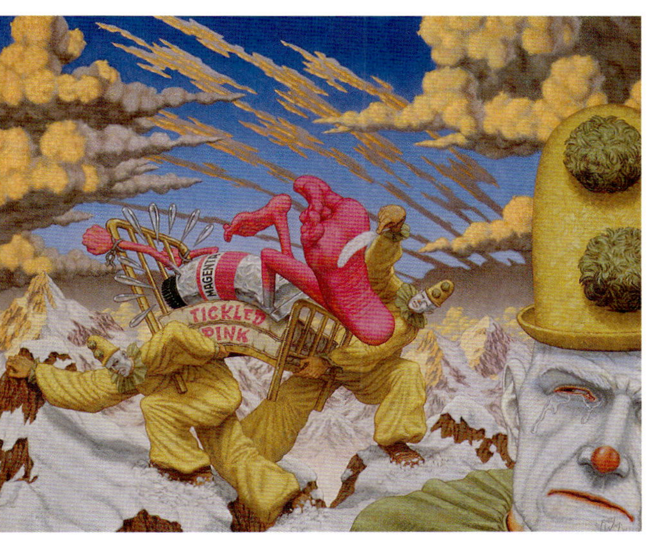


ART'S TRIUMPH OVER SUBSTANCE
2000, oil on canvas, 30" x 36"



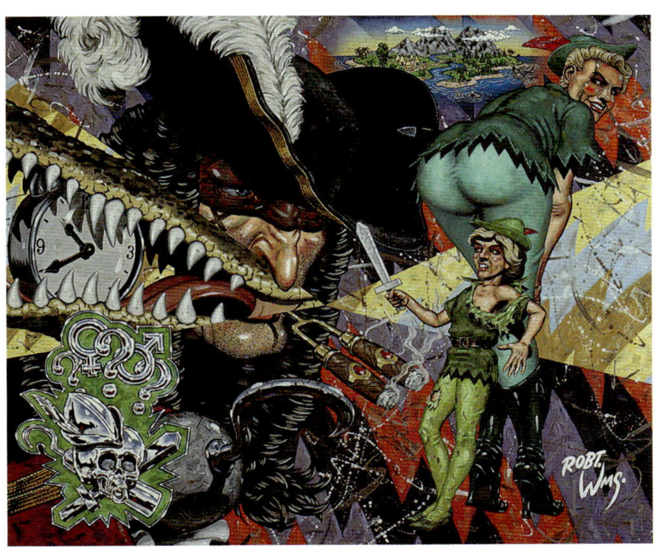


ALLEGATIONS OF FAIRY ABUSE ON CHICKEN HAWK ISLAND
1987, oil on canvas, 30" x 36"

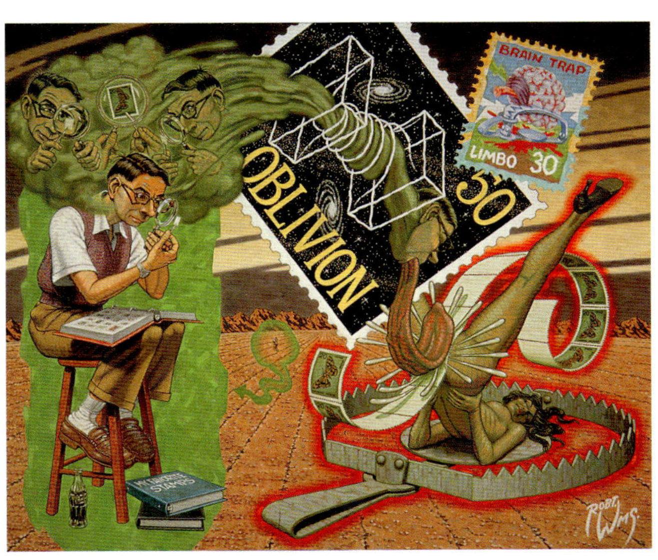


THE BRAIN TRAP
1997, oil on canvas, 30" x 36"

# XNO

(Melbourne, Arkansas)

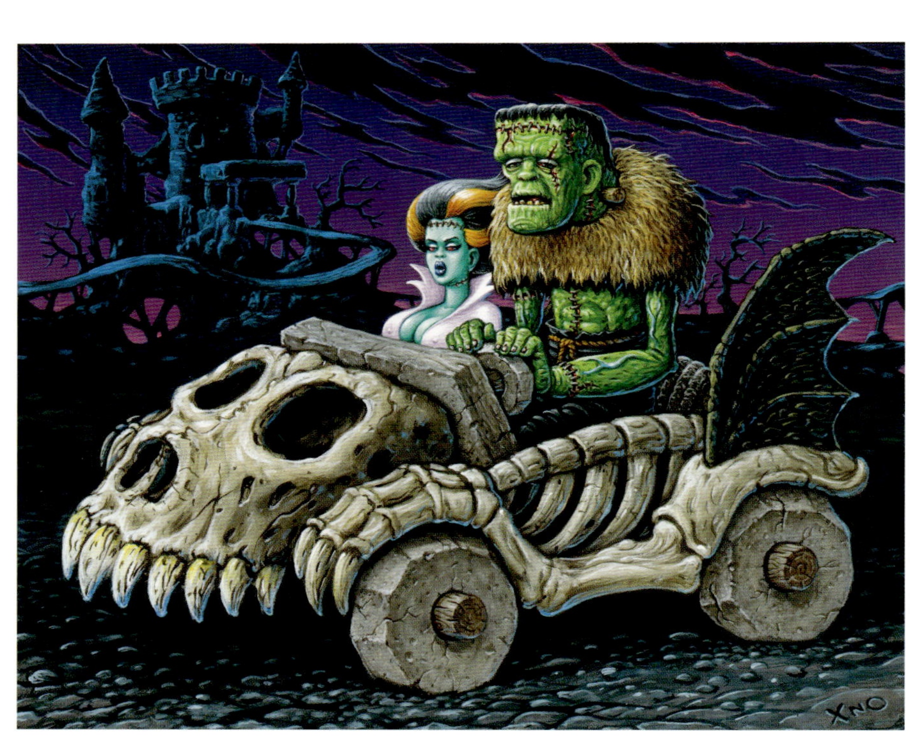


MIDNIGHT DRIVE 2000, acrylic on masonite, 16" x 20"

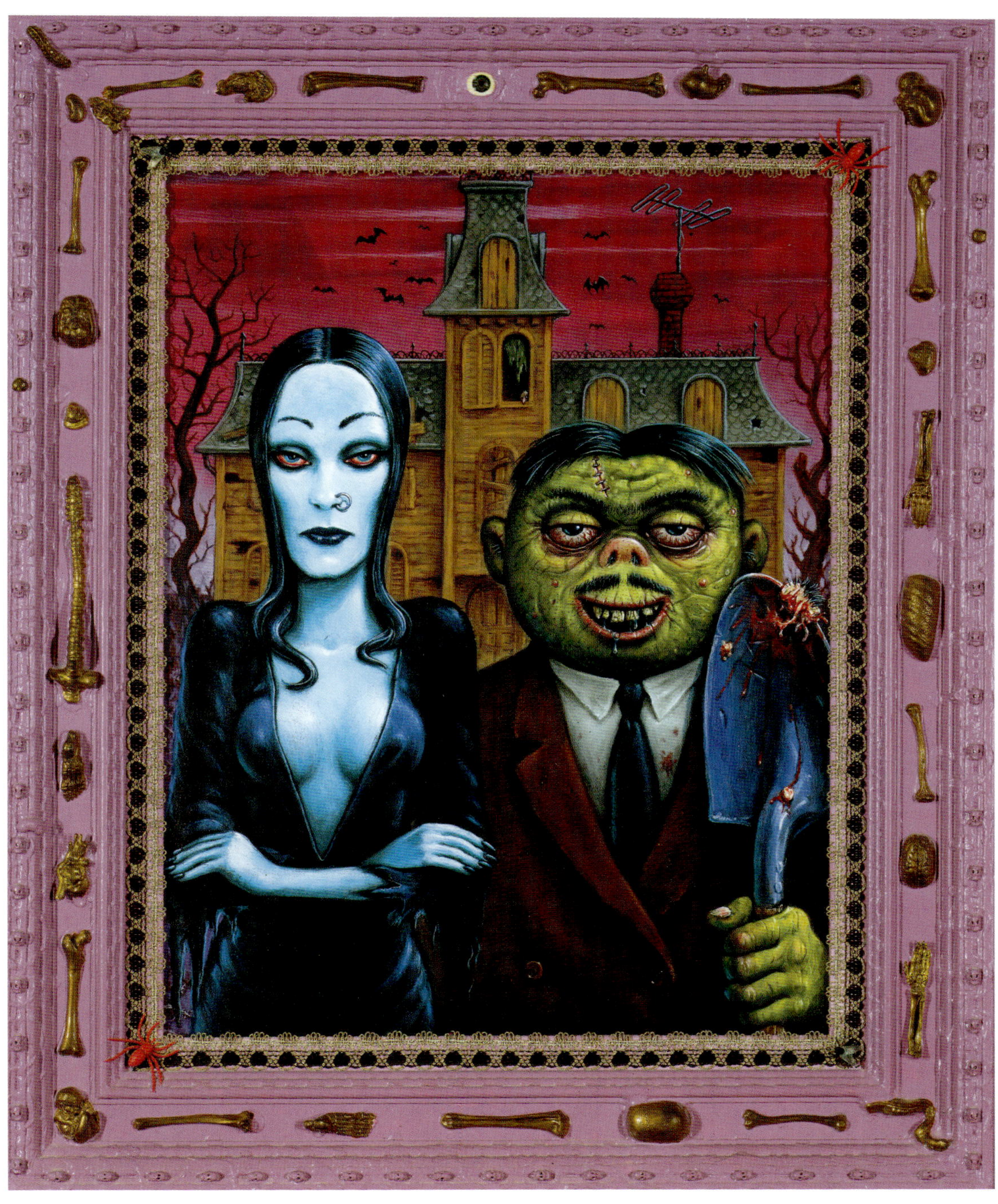

1994, acrylic on masonite, 18" x 24"

ADDAMS GOTHIC

(opposite page) BEATNIK 2001, acrylic on masonite, 9" x 12"



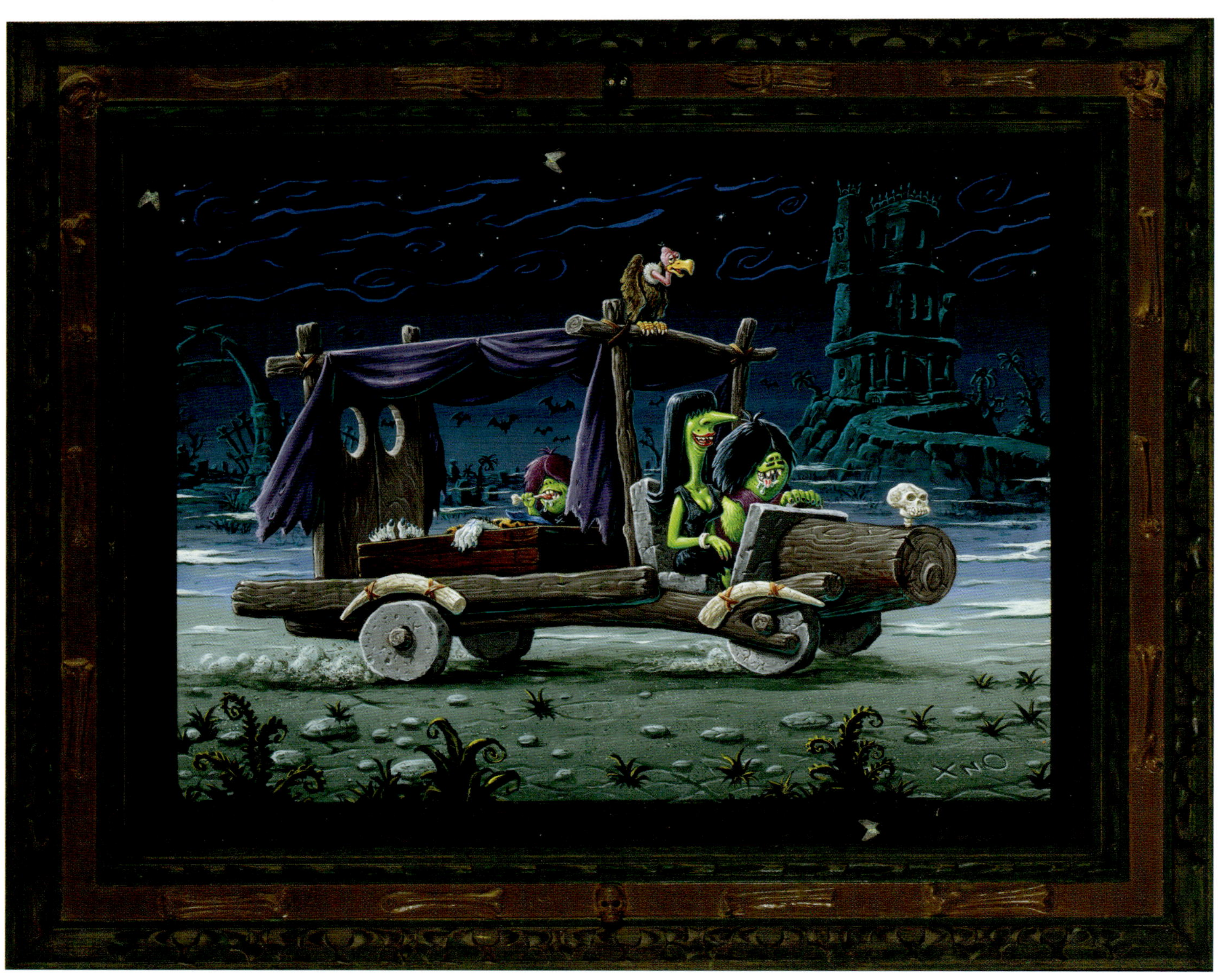

GRUESOMES 2001, acrylic on masonite, 18" x 24"

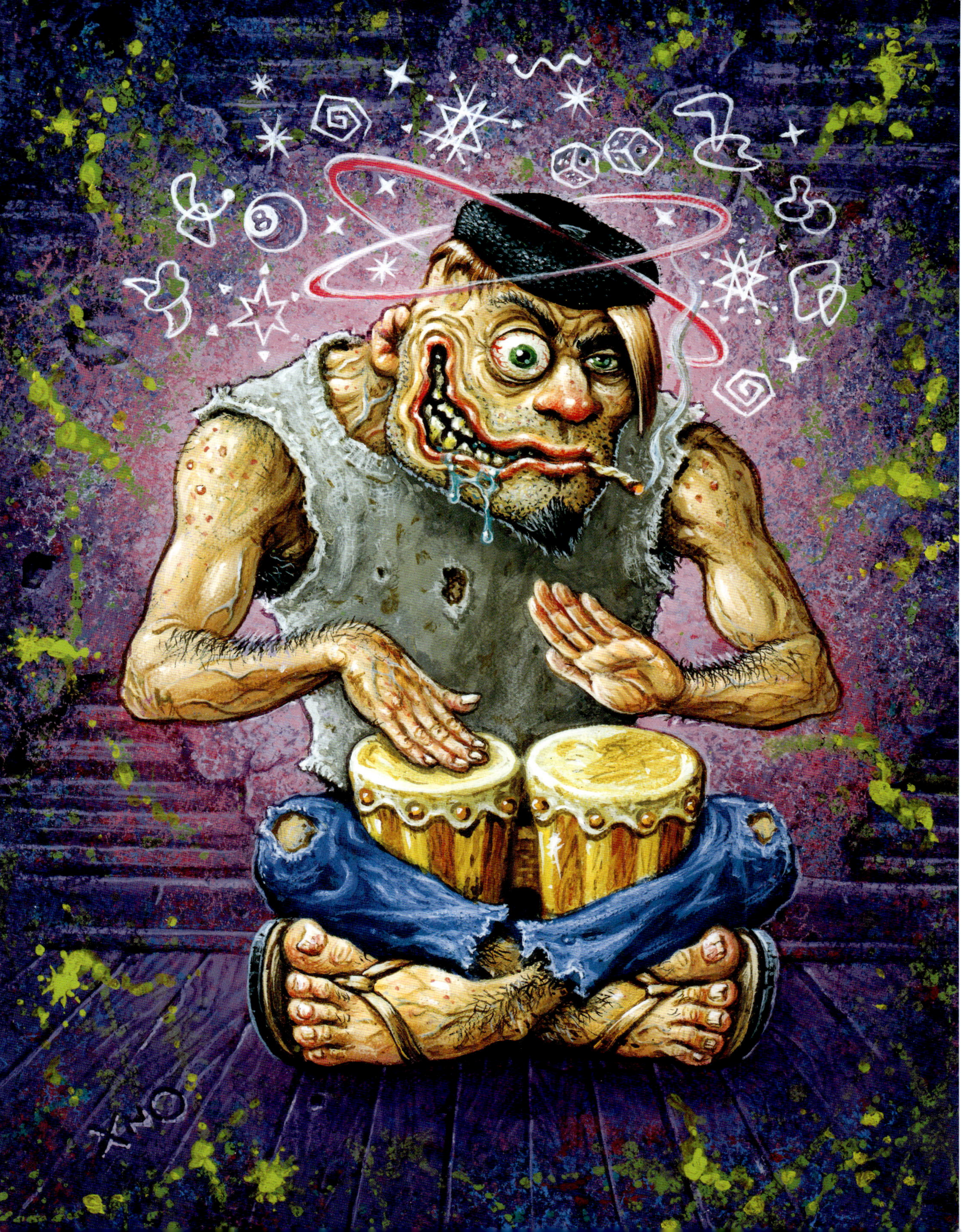

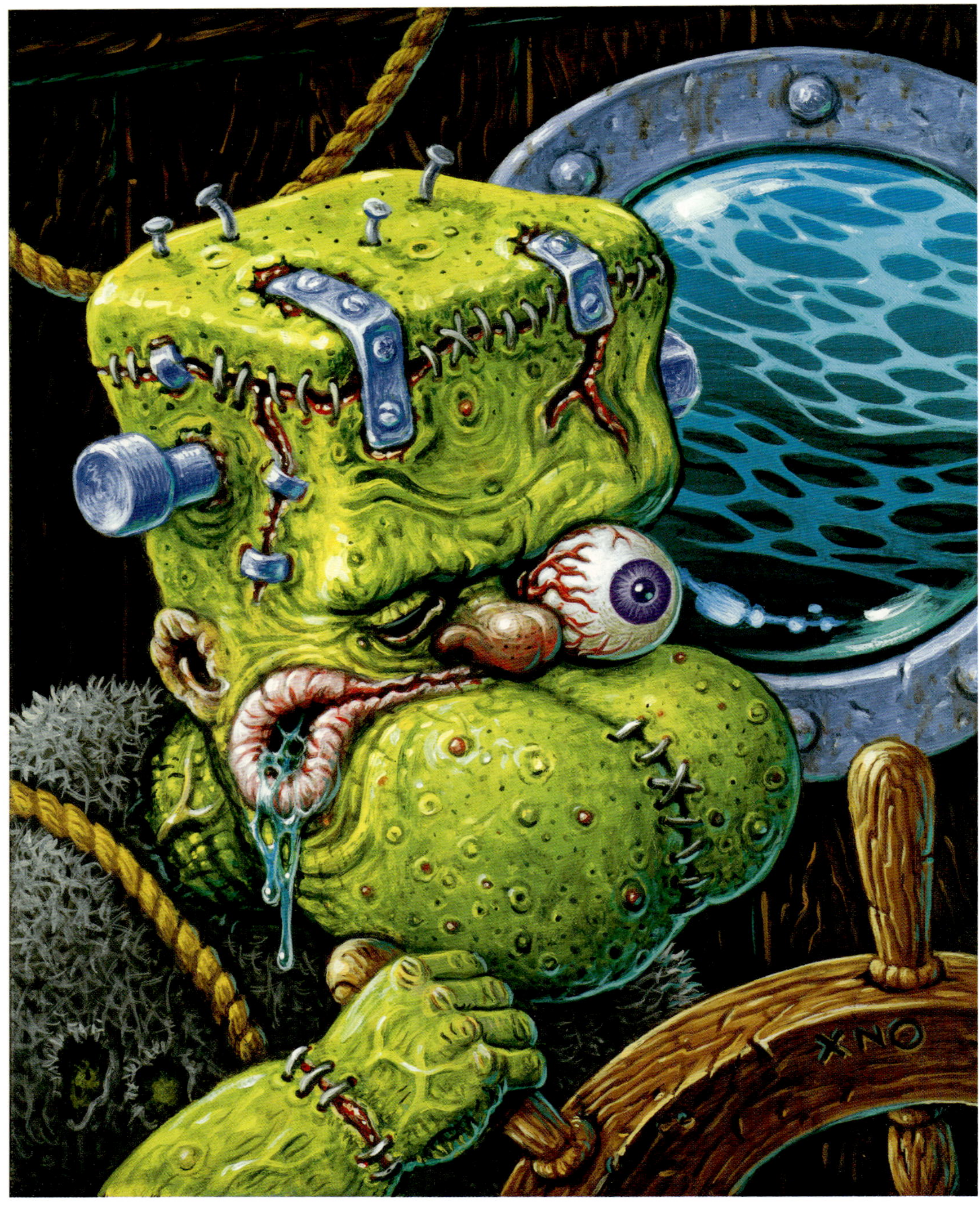

FRANKENPOP

2001, acrylic on masonite, 9" x 12"

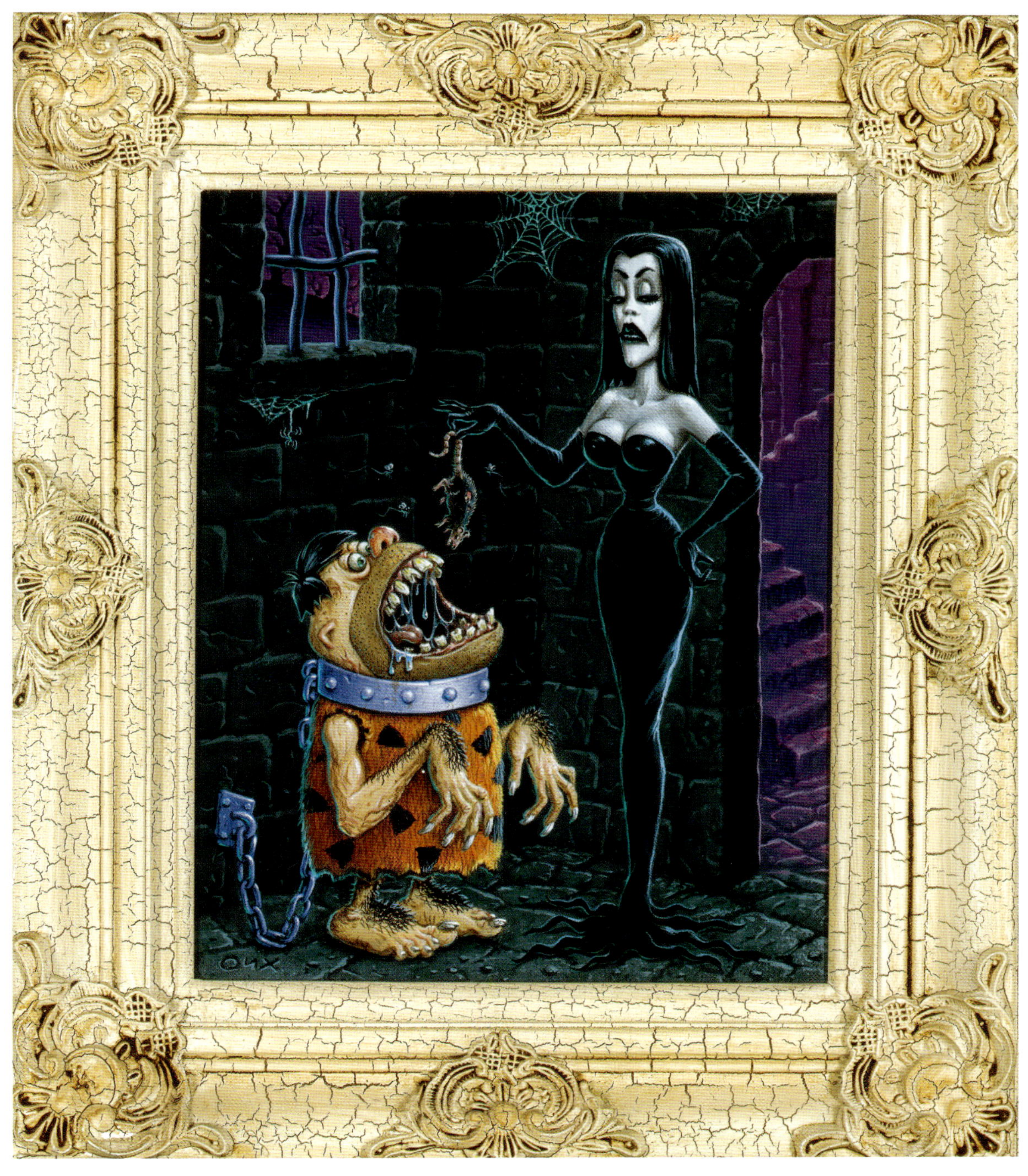



2001, acrylic on masonite, 9" x 12"

Slave Fred

# Artist Index

This index is not comprehensive — it is intended as a springboard for further artist research. The artists are organized in alphabetical order.

**Anthony Ausgang** lives in Los Angeles, California.

Among the places he has exhibited are: Zero One Gallery, The Laguna Art Museum's "Kustom Kulture" show, Kantor Gallery, Merry Karnowsky Gallery, and Roq La Rue Gallery.

He has been profiled in Art Alternatives magazine, Juxtapoz magazine, and the L.A. Times.

His website is *www.ausgangart.com.*

**Glenn Barr** lives in Detroit, Michigan.

Among the places he has exhibited are: Cpop Gallery, Roq La Rue Gallery, La Luz De Jesus Gallery, and Tin Man Alley Gallery.

Books about Barr's work are " Lowlife Paradise" (La Luz De Jesus Press/Last Gasp) and "Lowlife Companion" (Tin Man Alley Press).

His website is *www.glbarr.com.*

**Tim Biskup** lives in Los Angeles, California.

Among the places he has exhibited are: MModern Gallery, La Luz De Jesus Gallery, and Roq La Rue Gallery.

He has a book available entitled "100 Paintings" (Dark Horse).

His websites are *www.timbiskup.com* and *www.flopdoodle.com.*

**Kalynn Campbell** lives in Los Angeles, California.

Among the places he has exhibited are: Zero One Gallery, Bess Cutler Gallery, and Laguna Art Museum's "Kustom Kulture" show.

His website is *www.roulettestudios.com.*

**The Clayton Brothers** (Rob and Christian Clayton) live in Los Angeles, California.

They work and exhibit both separately and together.

Among the places they have exhibited are: La Luz De Jesus Gallery, Roq La Rue Gallery, Ann Nathan Gallery, and Varnish Gallery.

A book available about the Clayton Brothers is entitled "The Most Special Day Of My Life" (La Luz De Jesus Press/Last Gasp).

Their website is *www.claytonbrothers.com.*

**Joe Coleman** lives in Brooklyn, New York.

Among the numerous places he has exhibited are: Jim Corcoran Gallery, Wadsworth Athenaeum, Ann Nathan Gallery, The Horse Hospital (London, England), Psychedelic Solution, La Luz De Jesus Gallery.

Some of his many books include: " The Book Of Joe" (La Luz De Jesus Press/Last Gasp), " Original Sin: The Visionary Art Of Joe Coleman" (Heck Editions), "The Man Of Sorrows" (Gates Of Heck), "Cosmic Retribution: The Infernal Art Of Joe Coleman" (Fantagraphics/Feral House).

His website is *www.joecoleman.com.*

**Camille Rose Garcia** lives in Los Angeles.

Among the places she has exhibited are: Merry Karnowsky Gallery, La Luz De Jesus Gallery, and Roq La Rue Gallery.

She has been profiled in Paper Magazine and Blab Magazine.

Her website is *www.camillerosegarcia.com.*

**Alex Gross** lives in Los Angeles.

Among the places he has exhibited are: Earl McGrath Gallery, Merry Karnowsky Gallery, and La Luz De Jesus Gallery.

His website is *www.alexgross.com.*

**Don Ed Hardy** lives in San Francisco, California and Honolulu, Hawaii.

Among the numerous places he has exhibited are: Track 16 Gallery, Robyn Buntin's Oceania Gallery, Yerba Buena Center For The Arts, Spratt Gallery, Boulder Museum Of Contemporary Art, and La Luz De Jesus Gallery.

A few of the available books and catalogs about his artwork are " Tattooing The Invisible Man" (HardyMarks/Smart Art Press), "Permanent Curios" (Smart Art Press), and "2000 Dragons".

His website is *www.donedhardy.com.*

**Charles Krafft** lives in Seattle, Washington.

Among the places he has exhibited are: Seattle Art Museum, Defense Ministry (Ljubljana, Slovenia), Roq La Rue Gallery, Davidson Galleries, Grand Central Art Center, Copro Nason Gallery, and the Bess Cutler Gallery.

He has a book available entitled " Charles Krafft's Villa Delerium" (Last Gasp).

His website is *www.antiquesatoz.com/artatoz/krafft.*

**Liz McGrath** lives in Los Angeles, California.

Among the places she has exhibited are: La Luz De Jesus Gallery, Copro Nason Gallery, American Visionary Art Museum, 111 Minna Gallery, and Gallery Bink.

She is profiled in the book "Vicious, Delicious, And Ambitious" by Sherrie Cullison (Schiffer Books).

Her website is *www.elizabethmcgrath.com.*

**Scott Musgrove** lives in Seattle, Washington.

Among the places he has exhibited are: Tin Man Alley Gallery, La Luz De Jesus Gallery, and Roq La Rue Gallery.

He has a book available about his work entitled " The Accidental Taxidermist" (Tin Man Alley Press).

His website is *www.scottmusgrove.com.*

**Niagara** lives in Detroit, Michigan.

Among the places she has exhibited are: Cpop Gallery, Copro Nason Gallery,

Roq La Rue Gallery, Ox-Op Gallery, and Shooting Gallery.

She is profiled in the book "Vicious, Delicious, And Ambitious" by Sherrie Cullison (Schiffer Books).

Her website is *www.niagaradetroit.com.*

**Marion Peck** lives in Los Angeles and Seattle.

Among the places she has exhibited are: Roq La Rue Gallery, Davidson Galleries, La Luz de Jesus Gallery, and CoCA.

She has an available catalog/book entitled "Marion Peck - Paintings" (Porterhouse).

Her website is *www.marionpeck.com.*

**Lisa Petrucci** lives in Seattle, Washington.

Among the places she has exhibited are Roq La Rue Gallery, MModern Gallery, Copro Nason Gallery, Cpop Gallery, and Bess Cutler Gallery.

She is profiled in the book "Vicious, Delicious, And Ambitious" by Sherrie Cullison (Schiffer Books).

Her website is *www.lisapetrucci.com.*

**The Pizz** lives in Los Angeles, California.

He has exhibited in La Luz De Jesus Gallery and Roq La Rue Gallery.

He has a book available about his work entitled "Atavistic Avatar" (La Luz De Jesus/Last Gasp).

His website is *www.thepizz.com.*

**Mark Ryden** lives in Los Angeles, California.

Among the places he has exhibited are: Frye Art Museum, Earl McGrath Gallery, La Luz De Jesus Gallery, Roq La Rue Gallery, Tokyo's Press Pop Gallery, Grand Central Art Center, Outre Gallery, and Mendenhall Gallery

Books about Ryden's work are: "Anima Mundi" (Porterhouse/Last Gasp), "Bunnies And Bees" (Porterhouse), "The Meat Show" (Porterhouse), and "Blood" (Porterhouse).

His website is *www.markryden.com.*

**Isabel Samaras** lives in San Francisco, California.

Among the places she has exhibited are: Roq La Rue Gallery, Cpop Gallery, Tin Man Alley Gallery, Fuse Gallery, and the Detroit Contemporary Museum of Art.

She is profiled in the book "Vicious, Delicious, And Ambitious" by Sherrie Cullison (Schiffer Books).

Her website is *www.astrocat.com/samaras.*

**Todd Schorr** lives in Los Angeles.

Among the places he has exhibited are: Tamara Bane Gallery, Psychedelic Solution, Merry Karnowsky Gallery, La Luz De Jesus Gallery, La Foret Gallery Museum in Tokyo, and a retrospective at Florida's Art and Culture Center.

Books about Schorr's work include "Dreamland" (Last Gasp) and "Secret Mystic Rites" (Last Gasp).

His website is *www.toddschorr.com.*

**Shag** (aka Josh Agle) lives in Los Angeles, California.

Among the numerous places he has exhibited are: Outre Gallery, La Luz De Jesus Gallery, Roq La Rue Gallery, Copro Nason Gallery, and Fumiyart Gallery in Tokyo.

Books about Shag's work are: "Bottomless Cocktail" (Last Gasp/La Luz De Jesus Press), "Supersonic Swingers" (Outre Gallery Press), "Night Of The Tiki" (Last Gasp).

His website is *www.shag.com.*

**Robert Williams** lives in Los Angeles.

Among the numerous places he has exhibited are: Tony Shafrazi Gallery, Laguna Art Museum, Psychedelic Solution, Zero One Gallery, La Luz De Jesus Gallery and Tamara Bane Gallery.

Books about Williams' work are "The Lowbrow Art Of Robert Williams" (Last Gasp), "Zombie Mystery Paintings" (Last Gasp), "Views From A Tortured Libido" (Last Gasp), "Visual Addiction" (Last Gasp), "Malicious Resplendence" (Fantagraphics), and "Hysteria In Remission" (Fantagraphics).

He is also the founder of Juxtapoz Art Magazine.

His website is *www.robert-williams.com.*

**Eric White** lives in New York City.

Among the places he has exhibited are: Earl McGrath Gallery, Varnish Gallery, La Luz De Jesus Gallery, and Track 16 Gallery.

An available book about his art is "It Feeds Itself" (Last Gasp) and he is profiled in the book "Mutant Kiddies" (Mondo Bizarro Press).

His website is *www.ewhite.com.*

**XNO** lives in Melbourne, Arkansas.

Among the places he has exhibited are: Copro Nason Gallery, La Luz de Jesus Gallery, Tamara Bane Gallery, Psychedelic Solution, and the Laguna Art Museum's "Kustom Kulture" show.

He has been profiled in Art Alternatives Magazine and Juxtapoz Magazine.

His website is *www.lowbrowartworld.com.*

CONTRIBUTORS:

**Carlo McCormick** is the senior editor at Paper Magazine. Having worked in the "cultural trenches" for over 20 years, McCormick has also worked as a freelance arts writer for such publications as Artforum, Art In America, ArtNews, ArtNet, Juxtapoz, and Spin, in addition to writing hundreds of essays in books, monographs and exhibition catalogs, and has had his work translated into over a dozen languages. In addition to teaching and lecturing, McCormick is also a noted and respected independent curator.

**Larry Reid** is an independent curator and freelance critic living in Seattle, Washington. He is a regular contributor to national pop culture publications including Juxtapoz and The Comics Journal. Over the course of his 25 year career he has presented the work of internationally recognized artists including Mike Kelly, Robert Williams, Chuck Close, William S. Burroughs, Daniel Martinez, Kathy Acker, Robert Crumb, Karen Finley, and Nirvana.

**Robert Williams** sprang from the custom car culture of Southern California and the roots of the Underground Comix movement. He is known today as one of the world's most iconoclastic fine artists. He is the founder of Juxtapoz Art Magazine, and he also writes a column for each issue.

EDITOR/COMPILER:

**Kirsten Anderson** is founder and owner of Roq La Rue Gallery In Seattle, Washington, which has been promoting Lowbrow and Pop Surrealism since 1998. In addition to also acting as a freelance independent curator, she is the co-owner and editorial director of Ignition Publishing. More information can be found at *www.roqlarue.com* and *www.ignitionpublishing.com.*